D1103764

Praise for
10 Choices

"Just in case you're trying to make a decision about reading this book and aren't sure about James MacDonald . . . I'm happy to tell you that I know the heart of this man. He loves God and believes that the Bible is true and transformational. I know the choices he's made, and I trust his message. This is a wonderful book."

— Beth Moore
Best-Selling Author and *Speaker*

"When a man is acting, you're never sure if he really means what he's saying. Now you're going to meet a man—Dr. James MacDonald—who is not an actor. I know James, and he's as authentic as they come . . . and he speaks truth. You will love this powerful book."

— Kirk Cameron
Actor

"A strong building is constructed, stone upon stone. A strong life is built, precept upon precept . . . truth upon truth. This significant book is exactly what you need to make the right choices to build the life you've always wanted."

— Kay Arthur
Author

"No one can escape the endless cycle of sowing and reaping. If you want your life to get to a better place, you have to make better choices—God-honoring choices. Here's a book that if applied carefully, in the power of God's Spirit, will catapult you into a future filled with the blessings of God."

— Jim Cymbala
Senior Pastor, The Brooklyn
Tabernacle, Brooklyn, NY

"I would encourage anyone to listen to anything James MacDonald says or writes. James's boldness and directness stands out in a world of increasingly mild and fuzzy leadership on matters of biblical importance and Truth. Read *10 Choices* and make your own decision about his insight and counsel. Whatever it does, this book will not waste your time."

— Mark DeMoss
President, The DeMoss Group, and
Author, Little Red Book of Wisdom

"I have been with James in many personal and ministry contexts, and I know first-hand that he lives what he teaches and writes. That's why I encourage you to read this book. James lives the choices he writes about; they are profoundly biblical and will change your life!"

— Dr. Crawford W. Loritts, Jr.
Author, Speaker, and *Senior Pastor,*
Fellowship Bible Church, Roswell, GA

"Looking for meaning in life? This is a place to start. James MacDonald is a man who has been remarkably used by God. Anyone who has met him knows that he's something like a hurricane would be—if it were friendly and constructive! James says that 'this is a book to change your life.' That's its purpose. Do you need a change?"

— Mark Dever
Senior Pastor, Capitol Hill Baptist
Church, Washington, DC

"There is no escaping the power of personal choice. You are what you choose to be, and if you want your life to get to a better place, you need to start making better choices. Reading this book would be an excellent place to start. James is a good friend of mine, and I trust him to always speak God's truth."

— Bob Coy
Pastor, Calvary Chapel,
Fort Lauderdale, FL

"The expression *life-changing* is thrown around pretty carelessly. This book promises a plan that could do exactly that for you. This time I don't think it's an overstatement . . . *10 Choices* could change your life."

— Dr. Jack Graham
Author and *Pastor,* Prestonwood Baptist
Church, Dallas, TX

"James McDonald never fails to challenge my thinking about spiritual matters. He proclaims the Word of God with a spirit of fervency and earnestness that is greatly needed in our day. Making the choices he advocates in this book could change your life forever."

— Nancy Leigh DeMoss
Author and *Host,* Revive Our Hearts radio

10 CHOICES

10 CHOICES

A Proven Plan to Change Your Life Forever

Dr. James MacDonald

THOMAS NELSON
Since 1798

NASHVILLE   DALLAS   MEXICO CITY   RIO DE JANEIRO   BEIJING

Published in Nashville, Tennessee, by Thomas Nelson. Thomas Nelson is a registered trademark of Thomas Nelson, Inc.

Published in association with the literary agency of Wolgemuth & Associates, Inc.

Page design is by Walter Petrie.

Thomas Nelson, Inc. titles may be purchased in bulk for educational, business, fund-raising, or sales promotional use. For information, please e-mail SpecialMarkets@ThomasNelson.com.

Unless otherwise noted, all Scripture quotations are taken from the English Standard Version. © 2001 by Crossway Bibles, a division of Good News Publishers.

Scripture quotations marked CEV are from the Contemporary English Version. © 1991 by the American Bible Society. Used by permission.

Scripture quotations marked NASB are from the New American Standard Bible®, © The Lockman Foundation 1960, 1962, 1963, 1968, 1971, 1972, 1973, 1975, 1977, 1995. Used by permission.

Scripture quotations marked NKJV are from the New King James Version®. © 1982 by Thomas Nelson, Inc. Used by permission. All rights reserved.

Scripture quotations marked NLT are from the *Holy Bible*, New Living Translation. © 1996. Used by permission of Tyndale House Publishers, Inc., Wheaton, Illinois 60189. All rights reserved.

Scripture quotations marked KJV are from the King James Version.

Library of Congress Cataloging-in-Publication Data

MacDonald, James.
    10 choices : a proven plan to change your life forever / JamesMacDonald.
      p. cm.
    Includes bibliographical references.
    ISBN 978-0-7852-2820-2 (hardcover)
    1. Choice (Psychology)—Religious aspects—Christianity. 2. Will—Religious aspects—Christianity. 3. Decision making—Religious aspects—Christianity. I. Title. II. Title: Ten choices.
BV4509.5.M2535 2008
248.4—dc22   2008018275

Printed in the United States of America

08 09 10 11 12 QW 5 4 3 2 1

To Abby
Deuteronomy 30:19

[Contents]

Acknowledgments xi

Introduction: You Have a Choice xiii

Part I—My Identity Choices I

Choice I: I Choose God's Love 5

Choice 2: I Choose God's Forgiveness 25

Part II—My Authority Choices 53

Choice 3: I Choose Jesus Christ as Lord 57

Choice 4: I Choose the Bible as God's Word 81

Part III—My Capacity Choices 113

Choice 5: I Choose to Forgive 117

Choice 6: I Choose to Trust 145

Part IV—My Priority Choices 163

Choice 7: I Choose to Love My Family First 167

Choice 8: I Choose to Be Authentic 191

Part V—My Destiny Choices   **215**

Choice 9: I Choose to Serve   219

Choice 10: I Choose to Stand   243

Epilogue   265

Appendix A: That's My King   270

Appendix B: Scriptures to Pray   272

Notes   275

About the Author   278

[Acknowledgments]

Writing a book involves many important choices. Most of those choices are about people—people who quietly do their part to get so much good content to the people who need it most. More than ever I am humbled by the way these people do their jobs and fulfill the Lord's call upon their lives. I understand more than ever how ineffective my ministry would be apart from the choices they have made.

I am thrilled with the opportunity to publish with Thomas Nelson. Joey Paul, Tami Heim, and Mike Hyatt are the kind of partners authors dream about. Entering into relationship with them has been the most delightful part of this process.

Barb Peil from Walk in the Word has been exceptional in getting the project off to a great start and picking it up again to take across the finish line. Her faithfulness to God's call is inspiring to watch and a rich blessing to experience.

Neil Wilson has been fantastic in the role of smoothing and expanding the material into a clear, readable format. Without his help the book just could not have happened. A busy senior pastor is not much without a capable committed editor, and Neil is all that and more.

Kathy Elliott, my assistant of nearly twenty years, was again in the center of it all, administrating the process and passing my extensive edits back through the pipeline in every direction.

Janine Nelson, the executive director of Walk in the Word, will do much to get this message of life-change into the hands of people who can choose it for themselves. Without her partnership it's quite possible you would never have connected with this author or any of the teaching God has entrusted to me.

Robert Wolgemuth has become so much more than an agent or friend; he truly is an elder to my life and ministry for whom I continually thank the Lord. Seeing his life reproduced and his ministry expanded in his colleagues Andrew and Erik is a beautiful thing.

I thank God also for the people of Harvest Bible Chapel, before whom we live out the reality of personal choices and their life/death power.

My family has chosen to love me continually, warts and all, and I am greatly humbled by their presence and patience.

Most of all, I thank the Lord Jesus Christ for the grace He gives to keep on choosing—better and better all the time. PTL!

[Introduction]

You Have a Choice

I have set before you life and death, blessing and curse.
Therefore choose life.

—DEUTERONOMY 30:19

Are you ready—I mean *really* ready? Chomping at the bit? Beating down the door? Pacing back and forth on the front porch of life transformation, ringing the bell every ten seconds waiting for the door to open to you? Are you anxious to be done with excuses and finger-pointing and rationalizations that have kept you so trapped and tragically racing your engine in neutral for so long?

If the answer is *yes*, you are in the right place. It's time to shed the self-deception of the blame game and take total responsibility for your life. All of your hopes and dreams; all of your deepest heart longings; and all of the things about which you seldom speak but silently ponder and anguish—those things are right in front of you. The key is believing with all your heart that the choices are yours and then making the right choices that can alter the course of your life. You can do it. I believe with all my heart that you can and that you will. This is your time! I'm gonna lay out the choices, you're gonna make them, and things will never be the same. And there is a reason I believe this . . .

I want you to know that I was thinking about you as I wrote this book. Dreaming of a better future for you. Perhaps I don't know your name, but I have imagined you in great detail. I have thought about who you are and where you have come from. I have conceived of your exact circumstance and the fears that crowd your mind this moment, prompting you to procrastinate and postpone using the power that is at your fingertips. I've been thinking about the direction your life is headed and the varied outcomes of the particular options you are currently considering. Most importantly, I have been praying to the God who knows and loves you more than you know yourself. I have been asking Him to give you an unusual focus and clarity as you read these pages. I have been praying for you to be freed from burdens and distractions, to rightly estimate and execute the power of personal choice. I have been asking God to give you the hope that a better future for you is 100 percent tied up in your personal decisions. It really is all about what you choose. You *chose* to sit where you are sitting or stand in the place you are standing right now. Oh, you're lying down? You chose that too! You chose to open this book and where. You chose what you are wearing, and you chose to love whom you love. You choose to think how you think, and every day you choose a thousand other realities. You really do; you choose it all! We lie to ourselves and say that others made the choices, but we let them choose for us, and that was our choice too! Yes, it's true; you chose the choices that led to every reality in your life, and you will choose the way forward from here. Just you; nobody else. Yes, yes, yes! Everything that blesses and burdens our lives is tied up in the choices we make.

Someone argues: *But I didn't choose to have cancer or for my company to go bankrupt. I didn't want my spouse to leave me or my child to rebel.* Well, first of all, there is probably more personal responsibility in each of those situations than any of us readily admits. Secondly, your choices may not have entirely determined those outcomes, but there are many people who are doing better than you are in a similar circumstance, and their improved outcomes from such terrible conditions *are* 100 percent related to how they have chosen to deal with them. It's not *what* happens to us, but how we choose to respond makes the difference. There is just no escaping the power of personal choice.

So why even try? Why not embrace the reality that your future, for good or bad, is tied up in the choices you make from here going forward? Does that sound too good to be true? If the answer is *yes*, it's because you believe the lie that a good life is a lucky thing some people stumble into rather than a wonderful thing responsible people choose!

OK, enough. I am getting ahead of myself. Suffice it to say, this book could be the total turning point for you. This is the book not just to convince you of the power of personal choices but also to lay out for you what the top ten choices actually are and how to make them—starting now. You're right on the edge, so fasten your seat belt and get ready to select specific thoughts and actions so your life can improve immeasurably, immediately!

What to Expect

Choose now to make the best use of your time by understanding the various chapter elements and how they work together. I don't want to waste a minute of your day, so stick with me here for a couple more paragraphs and you will be a much more productive reader and choice maker.

Five Major Choice Categories

This book details ten specific life-changing choices that come to us in significant pairs. Each pair forms one of five major categories in life. Before each category—or part—is an explanation of the category itself and why it is so transforming to make deliberate, informed decisions in that area.

Four and Six

Four of the choices are foundational, and six of them are relational. The first four choices deal with who you are in connection with God; the remaining six deal with who you are in connection with others. These six choices are more easily applied to specific life situations you may be facing today.

I understand that urgency always trumps logical progression, so even though the ten choices are organized logically, you may want to review the contents page, then turn to the choices that address immediate needs before circling back to the beginning to cover the material in a more chronological way. In other words, you get to choose how to read this book. Just remember, you can visit the six rooms in the house before you look at the four rooms in the basement, but if you ignore the foundations, you'll never really appreciate the house they hold up.

A Choice per Chapter

Each chapter covers a specific choice. Many choices could have made the top ten. I am blessed to pastor a church of more than ten thousand weekly worshippers and teach God's Word every weekday by radio to several million people around the country and the world. I have invested the past twenty-five years of my life studying how people change and have carefully selected the choices I believe will have the greatest effect on you. There will be other choices to make down the road, but these ten choices are the highest impact choices a person can make. Start with these, and I believe a lot of things will quickly begin to fall in place for you. I may write about other choices sometime in the future, but I will never write about ones that are more important or life-transforming for you *now*.

A Biblical Proof

Regardless of what you may or may not believe about the Bible, it is a book that is unparalleled in its impact upon mankind. The truths of Scripture have satisfied some of the greatest minds in human history. As the all-time best-selling book, it is worthy of our respect and attention. Each chapter will review what the Bible has to say about the choice we are considering. If you have never done so before, a good choice to make right now would be to give the Bible a chance to speak to you.

A Choice to Make

If you have read anything I have written before, you know I am not writing to fill pages. I am writing in an effort to affect your life in profound and lasting ways. This cannot happen without your full participation. This is a book to change your life, not to pass an evening by the fireplace. For that reason, you will need to take action at the end of each chapter. Specific action points are laid out to help you go *beyond* agreeing with the importance of each choice to actually *making it!* Without the actual choosing, none of this really matters. You will find these action points in the following three categories at the end of each chapter:

Acknowledge the Choice

Several questions will help you clarify and recognize the choice.

Consider the Choice

Several questions will help you think through the implications of the choice.

Make the Choice

Several statements and questions will help you make and implement the choice.

A Closing Prayer

Nothing we do as human beings is quite so powerful as prayer. I have always believed that we pray more often and more intelligently when we have some words to help us express ourselves to the God who made us. I believe so strongly that God is working in your life right now. And I know that you will get further along sooner if you pray the prayers at the end of each chapter and invite the Lord to help you with your choice.

Think of this book as a relationship. If you give it your time and attention, it will become a wonderful friend to you, guiding you to the life you have always dreamed of having. If you give it only a moment and then turn away through discouragement or distraction, it will become yet another ditch of disappointment where dreams were discarded by a lack of discipline. Choose now to exert some focused attention, followed by deliberate action, and you will quickly reap the benefit of better choices.

PART I

MY IDENTITY CHOICES

Choice 1: I Choose God's Love

Choice 2: I Choose God's Forgiveness

Who am I? Why am I here? These are the questions that have plagued the minds of thinking people throughout the ages. The second question is, in fact, a subset of the first. Everything flows from the answer to the *who am I* question. When you know who you are, you will understand why you are here, and what you are supposed to accomplish.

At the center of the identity question is the issue of God Himself. If there is a God, if He made the universe and me, if He knows me and loves me and, incredibly, forgives me . . . well, that changes everything. But you have to choose that for yourself. Deep in the heart of every person is a longing for the God who made him. There is a big part of who you are that will always be restless until it finds identity in the God who loves you and made you for Himself.

What follows here is the furthest thing from a theology class or a Sunday school lesson. It's a presentation about the reality of who you are being tied up in the God of the universe. It's time to embrace your connection to God with your whole heart, as your identity. Choosing that reality will truly change your life forever. The first identity choice involves choosing God's love. The second identity choice is about choosing the forgiveness we all need and that He so generously offers to each of us. But you have to choose it. Let's get to work on these two identity choices.

Beginning Prayer

God, shine a searchlight upon me that I might see myself clearly and that I might find in You the love and forgiveness that my heart so desperately needs. Help me to see and embrace the identity that is available and mine in Christ through my choosing.

May all that You are to me become life in me, that I would draw it to myself and make it all that it can be in my life by Your grace. I ask for Your help in making these choices. Be at work in me. I invite Your presence. I welcome You. Change my life as You would want to.

In the name of Your Son, Jesus Christ. Amen.

For God so loved the world,
that he gave his only Son,
that whoever believes in him
should not perish but have eternal life.

—John 3:16

I Choose God's Love

*I choose to believe there is a God who knows me perfectly
and yet loves me unconditionally.*

I'm kinda feeling the pressure now! I mean, what a title—*10 Choices: A Proven Plan to Change Your Life Forever.* That's really promising a lot, isn't it? And if you're like most readers, I get about ten minutes to start delivering on that promise; so let's start at the top. Let's go for the mondo, massive, monumental choice right now. Let's go for the summa cum laude of choices, the absolute mind-bending, life-altering choice . . . (drum roll, please).

Choose God

The most important choice you will ever make in your life is to choose God. To choose to connect with the God who made you and me and everything in this twisted universe. Not that He made it twisted; He did not. He made it perfect, and we snarled it up with bad choices. But we can still regain most of what we have lost just by choosing God again, on His terms.

Now I know for many who are reading this, God is just some vague, foggy notion. You may even feel that you really can't choose God because He's not the kind of thing you'd choose, right? Have you bought into the notion that either you believe in God or you don't, and that nothing can alter your current condition? Maybe you have said, like so many people,

"You know, I have never had faith, not genuine faith, not like my sister/ friend/mother/other. Sometimes I get a bit of the vertical in a crisis, something like, '*Oh God*, save me from that truck that just swerved into my lane!' but when He does, the feeling passes, and faith fades into, I don't know, numbness or something." Is that you—crisis faith for a moment and then nothing?

Possibly you have thought that the faith-in-God thing is a trait you're born with (or without), like blue eyes, brown hair, or a dad with a membership at the country club. Have you concluded that believing is a characteristic you may or may not have but one you most definitely cannot obtain simply by choosing? Well, let me promise you that God is not like that. God is most assuredly someone you choose, and choosing Him does make a huge difference. He is less like the options on a new car and more like the person you decide to marry. Faith is for people who want it and are willing to go for it with passion. In fact, God only shows up for people who are looking, and He chooses to reveal Himself exclusively to people who *really* want to know Him. In the Bible, God asserts, **"You will seek me and find me, when you seek me with *all your heart*. I will be found by you declares the Lord"** (Jeremiah 29:13–

> **THE MOST IMPORTANT CHOICE YOU WILL EVER MAKE IN YOUR LIFE IS TO CHOOSE GOD.**

14*a*, emphasis mine). Listen, God advertises! What else could the Psalm mean when it says, **"The heavens declare the glory of God, and the sky above proclaims his handiwork. Day to day pours out speech, and night to night reveals knowledge. There is no speech, nor are there words, whose voice is not heard. Their voice goes out through all the earth, and their words to the end of the world. In them he has set a tent for the sun"** (Psalm 19:1–4). God's Word and God's world are full of advertisements about Him, but as with even the best-marketed products, you still have to choose what God is offering.

Yep, no question about it, you can choose God. Don't let some stale seminarian talk you out of it. We've all heard the well-worn declaration that we don't choose God, but He chooses us. You've heard that, right? The fact is, both are true; God chooses us, and we choose God! The other way is like arguing that I didn't choose my wife; my wife chose me. At the human level, we may kid each other over who chose whom first, but to try to describe a relationship in which only one party gets to choose doesn't make sense. Do you see? Since we're talking about the God who created us, there's not much point in arguing over who chose whom first. I suggest we get over the distracting discussions of who chooses who and go at this from the only angle we actually experience—our own. We choose God. That's the way it feels, and that's the way it functions. And until you get out of your armchair or ivory tower and choose God for your life, you will always be missing the main ingredient for human happiness.

I'm not trying to say God's not in charge, but the fact about God's choice of you being the *original* choice can cause apathy in humans. We must not lose our sense of responsibility in the ocean of God's sovereignty. One of the first decisions God made when He planted our ancestors in the garden of Eden was to give them the capacity to make significant choices. Adam and Eve got to choose names for the animals and which of a wild assortment of fruit to eat. But there was only one fruit they were told not to choose. The rest, as they say, is history. Constant choices.

When Joshua stood before the nation of Israel and challenged them to make a decision, he was not snickering up his sleeve that it was actually God who would be making all the choices. He didn't say, *You really don't have any options in this, just sit tight, and we'll see what God does. If you're the "faith" type of person, something will work out.* No, Joshua faced the nation and raised his voice with an incredible offer . . . *What's it gonna be, boys, the idols your fathers worshipped or the one true God?* **Choose this day whom you will serve"** (Joshua 24:15). Faith is a volitional thing. You flat-out choose to believe, and there is incredible factual evidence for faith in God upon which to base your decision. Trust me when I tell you, you can choose God. Want some of that evidence?

Factual Evidence for Faith in God

Hang on to something tightly! We're going to move quickly through some staggering landscape. I want to give you a bird's-eye view of three rational reasons to choose faith in God. Yes, you'll be making a choice. I'll explain the arguments and then invite you to choose whether you believe them or not.

First, the Cosmological Argument

A commonly accepted rational argument for the existence of God is the idea that for every effect there has to be a cause. I would never do this, but just imagine if I slapped you. The cause—my slap—would create an effect: a red, stinging handprint on your face (and maybe a further cause—your strong reaction—would produce another effect: me flat on my back).

Do you get the idea of cause and effect? Scientists agree that for each and every observable effect there has to have been a cause. For instance, a science professor was out walking in the forest with one of his students. Along the way, the student said, "Hey, look, there's a little glass sphere on the ground." And so they picked it up and examined it.

The professor said, "I wonder where that came from?" They looked around but didn't see anybody.

The student said, "Yeah, I wonder." Then, with a little twinkle in his eye, he said to his science professor, "I wonder, if it were ten times bigger, would we know where it came from then?"

And the professor said, "Well, it had to come from somewhere; I don't think it just showed up."

The student responded, "Yeah, I agree with that. But what if it were, like, a hundred times bigger than it is?"

"Well," said the professor after a moment, "all the more reason to know it had to come from somewhere."

The student asked, "So let me ask you this. What if it were, like, a million times bigger?"

The professor finally picked up the student's drift and said with a chuckle, "Well, then it would have gotten here on its own."

How foolish! But is that not exactly what people do? They look at the universe that God created, which is so incredibly immense that the numbers are mind-boggling, and quickly reach the conclusion that nothing is bigger or greater than the universe! Light from the closest star in our galaxy takes more than four years to reach us. Our galaxy, the Milky Way, one of countless other galaxies in the universe, would take 150,000 years to cross if we could travel at the speed of light. People are more impressed by the size of creation than by the thought of what miraculous cause would be able to create such an effect! The human mind cannot even comprehend the universe that God made, yet so many people arrogantly say, "No. That is the one time that there was an effect without a cause. Yes, that one time we got this whole thing from nothing."

The Bible calls that **"suppress[ing] the truth in unrighteousness"** (Romans 1:18 NKJV). The fact is, when people accept the universe as the ultimate and deny that it had a cause, they are often doing so because they don't *want* it to be true. Admitting that the universe has an intelligent cause has far more implications than admitting that something found in a forest had to have been placed there. Admitting the cause of the universe is perilously close to admitting an ultimate accountability for my choices. Because most people are not ready to answer for the choices they make, they don't want to believe what is painfully obvious: there must be a God who made all of this. All that we see couldn't possibly have emerged from nothing. Choosing to believe in a God who made the universe is far easier and more logical than delaying the inevitable moment of accounting to Him. It takes pride to choose to ignore what is obvious in every sincere reflection. There is a God—or there wouldn't be anything else! That is the cosmological argument for God's existence. Its details are extremely compelling and can fill several books, but that's the gist of it. What do you think?

Second, the Evidential Argument

Creation itself has design, not just size and scope, but actual, obvious features of design. There are consistent patterns everywhere. The intricacy and the design of creation and the order in the universe insist that it came from an intelligent source. Hugh Ross, a well-known astrophysicist, has calculated fifty-nine things that are "just right" about our earth's place in the solar system, things that are needed for life to exist. If one of those circumstances were off, life would be impossible on this planet. For example, here are two of the Earth's characteristics that Ross details in his article, "Fine-Tuning for Life on Earth":

1. *The Earth's proximity to the sun.* If we were closer even by a few degrees, we would be incinerated. If we were farther away, we would freeze to death. Most of our planets have elliptical orbits with a broad variance of proximity to the sun as the seasons come and go, but we have an almost circular orbit, so there is a constancy to our climate that other planets do not enjoy.

2. *The Earth's speed of orbit.* We're going around the sun at 68,000 miles per hour. If it were any slower or faster, there'd be no life. Again, the precise alignment of our place in the solar system in a way that allows our existence seems to be far more than coincidental.[1]

Let me ask you, if you went down in your basement and saw a thousand dominos standing up on their ends in perfectly ordered succession, would you say to yourself, *I wonder what blew up down here?* Of course you wouldn't, and the logic of that needs to extend beyond dominos in your basement to the way you view the universe and the solar system and the planet you live on—and especially the way you choose to view the God who put it all in place.

We have already mentioned the words of Psalm 19, **"The heavens declare the glory of God."** Creation itself is shouting, *There is a God! There is a God!* Some choose to listen while others choose to ignore the demanding sound of God's created order. In the cosmological argument, we acknowledge God as the source of the universe itself. In the evidential argument, we choose to admit that design is proof of a designer. To do otherwise would put us right in the sights of Psalm 14:1, which says, **"The fool says in his heart, 'There is no God.'"** What do you think?

Third, the Moral Argument

More than six billion people in this world have the same moral DNA. God Himself engraved a moral code on the human heart. It's one of His fingerprints. You don't have to teach a kid that it's wrong to lie or steal. We have that moral code within us—I know I sure did!

When I was three or four years old, all the kids in my neighborhood played with marbles. We'd make a hole in the dirt with our heels in the middle of a large circle. Then we would try to roll our marbles from outside the circle so they would land in the hole (maybe that was what set me up to love golf!). If the marble went in the hole, it was safe, but if it stayed outside the hole, it was game to be taken by another player. We could aim for the hole as well as the "sitting duck" marbles. Every time one of your marbles hit another one, you got them both. It was a brutal game that left a lot of kids crying when they literally lost their marbles. All of the big kids walked around with sacks full of marbles. One of my earliest memories is of going over to a friend's house to play marbles. He had this amazing silver sphere, which was a large ball bearing about the size of a child's fist. In my young imagination, I pictured all the marbles I could take out with this giant one. So I stole it. My sinful heart wanted it, and before I could stop myself, it was in my pocket and I was out the door. What now? Well, when I left my friend's house, the little ball weighed a few ounces. But, of course, by the time I walked the two blocks home, that sphere in my sweaty palm weighed a thousand pounds.

I dragged myself into the front door and looked up through drooping eyes to my mother behind her apron, with her hands on her hips. She knew right away something was very wrong.

"What's the matter?" she asked.

I produced the contents of my pocket and became pathetically unglued. "I stole the marble!" I cried as I collapsed into a bundle of tears and regret.

How could that be? How could that little four-year-old boy be so gripped by the wrongness of what he had done? Surely you could tell a similar story. It's God's moral law, written on our hearts. Every one of us has it, even if we deny or ignore it, stuff it down or sin against it. Animals don't have that. Only people created in the image of God have a moral compass that points in the same direction no matter what corner of the globe they were birthed onto. It's God's fingerprint upon you. It points directly to your moral center and shouts the reality that you are more than an animal and the product of chance. You were made by God and for God, and your heart will always be restless until you choose that identity as your center.

I have given these arguments for God's existence in a superficial way on purpose. Most people don't require more. According to recent polls in the United States, over 90 percent of the population still believes God exists. However, if you are one of the few whose intellect calls out for a deeper consideration of these and other proofs, please don't believe that I have come remotely close to exhausting the subject. Volumes by Lee Strobel (*The Case for Faith*) and Ravi Zacharias (*Jesus Among Other Gods*), as well as numerous other books, discuss these issues in greater detail. My prediction is that the further you honestly dig, the more it will bolster your faith. The bottom line is that there are plenty of good, rational reasons to believe in God, and if you don't believe, it's because you choose not to.

Hugh Ross's Reasons to Believe Web site is a trove of helpful information. All in all, Ross and his team have listed dozens of these highly improbable features of our earth's design. Among the fascinating statistics on that site, I found this statement: "Much less than one chance in a hundred thousand trillion, trillion, trillion, trillion, trillion, trillion exists that even one such planet would occur anywhere in the universe."[2] We live in a universe that demands an explanation outside what is observable or provable by traditional means.

Some people stand off at a distance with phony intellectualism and say, "Well, I don't see the proof for God." Why don't you go out on a starlit night and look up at the skies. Now what's your answer? "What's your proof," you ask? I'll tell you—the heavens are declaring the glory of God. The scientific world has no substantive, satisfying explanations for the existence of the universe. They just have speculations.

I'm going to go with the fact there is a God. I don't understand Him or how He made it all. But it doesn't take a genius to see that you can't throw a stick of dynamite into a printing factory and get the Declaration of Independence. A design shouts a designer. I'm convinced by these arguments; therefore, I choose. I choose God.

But listen, I do not choose just any God.

You've Got to Choose the Right God

When someone tells you he believes in God, ask him to clarify which God he believes in. Ephesians 4:6 reminds us there is **"one God and Father of all, who is over all and through all and in all."** You see, some people are going around these days inventing their own god according to their damaged moral compass. Others, grudgingly admitting there must be a god, turn to a caricature of God they have picked up along the way. These gods are about as divinely ineffective as no God at all! In that sense, God has something in common with Elvis—many imposters but only one *real thing*. In fact, there may be a few Elvis impersonators who come close to the original, but all the imitation gods miss the genuine by a mile. Have you seen or heard of any of these?

Fake God #1: The Gruff God

A lot of people think of God as a cranky deity. He's always in a sort of bad mood and is easily irritated. Remember the little story we read as kids called *Three Billy Goats Gruff*? Some people think God is like the awful one-eyed troll who lives under the bridge and gets all sideways whenever someone wants to get across. Now maybe your dad or some other authority figure in your life is or was a bit like that, but God is not cranky in the least. Let's separate truth from fiction. God doesn't get gruff, and He is never in a bad mood. In fact, God loves you deeply! But more on that later.

Fake God #2: The Game God

Some people think God sneaks around playing games such as hide-and-seek. *Where are You now, God? I can't find You.* To which God answers, *You're getting warmer. Oh, now you're getting colder.* Some erroneously think God leads us like a Simon Says game: *Simon says do this; Simon says do that; do this. Hah! I tricked you!*

But God is not like that. He does not change; He is ever the same. And while His actions are sometimes hard to understand, His ways will always ultimately prove to be for your good because He loves you deeply! But that's for later.

Fake God #3: The Guessing God

Some people follow a Guessing God, as in *I think He's happy with me today. At least I hope He is. He might not be, though. I never know. I'd better not go to church since I didn't do so good this week.* They imagine God is capricious and unpredictable in the extreme as though He intentionally keeps us off balance by continuously changing the rules so we really never can know how it all works. But God is not like that. He's laid out perfectly all the regulations for human happiness in His Word, the Bible. He wants us to know what choices to make so we can live with confidence. God is extremely predictable. He cannot lie because that would be sin, and He will not lie because He loves you deeply! More on that later.

Fake God #4: The Genie God

North Americans know all about this fake God. People pull out their lamps and rub them. *Oh, give me favor today, Genie God. Grant me three wishes.* This fake god is the one we bring out when we feel an urgent need. Once the difficulty is past, we put Him back in the lamp for later. *OK, now go away, God. I'll call you when I need you.* Sadly, there are preachers on every corner selling this god we have made to suit our own whims. Sorry if you didn't know, but the North American Genie God is not the real God.

God

But there is a real God who created the universe, who placed Adam and Eve in the garden, and who came in love to correct the consequences of their sinful choices.

The Bible says that God *is* love—not only that God does loving things but also that His very nature is love. We may do loving things, but we're not love. When 1 John 4:8 says **"God is love,"** it's making an incredible statement about how very loving and selfless God really is.

I Choose God's Love

I've been working with people long enough to know that when I say God is love, some people pull back and look at me sideways. Often, they can hardly hide the anger in their tone as they say, "Really? God is *love*? Well, if that's true, then how could He have allowed . . ."—and out comes a painful story. Are you like that?

Something happened to you. A wrong was done to you. A selfish person took what wasn't his. Maybe one of your children broke your heart, or you don't have children, or you can't do anything about the starving children in Africa. My point is that many people point to God when pain comes because they cannot reconcile what they see with the message that *God loves them.*

I'm so sorry for your hurt—I truly am.

Please hear me now. The way out of that corner of confusion is not to deny or run from God's heart for you. Instead, you must turn and look squarely into the reality of who He actually is. Too often we self-define God's love: "This is my concept of love, and God must conform to this view, or I can't believe He is loving." Many have made this mistake without realizing or calculating the fallout from such a belief-banishing choice.

God has never represented His love for you or me as that pampering "here, Billy, have another cupcake; take the one with the extra icing," permissive-mother kind of love. But I do understand why people sometimes struggle to see God as loving.

For example, most people would agree that when you love someone, you protect that person, right? God's love *is* a *protecting* love, but it's not always a *preventing* love. God doesn't always keep hard things from happening. Here's why. He has higher purposes for our pain:

- *God may allow pain to humble us.*
  When we are brought low by pain, we see how much we need Him. One of C. S. Lewis's best-known comments describes pleasure as God's whispers and pain as God's megaphone!

- *God sometimes allows pain to restore us.*
  Some of you were so far from God, off on your own, running away from God, going who knows where with your future. God allowed some hard thing in your life so that the pain of it brought you back to Him. If you would have never turned to Him without that heartache, isn't it true that in some sense that pain was a very loving thing for God to allow? Wasn't it that hurt that brought you to the wonderful place of asking for His help?

  A hundred years from today, as awful as that pain was, you'll thank God for it if you choose to let its purpose be fulfilled in you. God's love is revealed in the ultimate purpose for which He allows our momentary affliction. God does not have to prove He loves us at the end of every hour or every day. He does invite us to trust what He is doing and choose to embrace by faith that time will reveal the reality of His love. Friend, choose to believe He loves you!

- *Sometimes God allows pain to refine us.*
  This refining fire allows us to be more like Him. I've said to my wife, Kathy, many times, "I hate to think of the person that I would be, apart from God in my life." I shudder to imagine where I would be without God's refining influence. Without God allowing difficult things into my life, what kind of husband and father would I be today? What kind of pastor or friend would I be? What kind of man would I be without the excruciating hurts that have driven me to my knees before the God who loves to refine me?

Looking back, it's His love and mercy I see, even when His protection does not always prevent pain in my life.

Yes, God loves you with a perfecting love. You are under construction, my friend. God is working on you. There will be difficult times, but you can trust Him. No pain is allowed into your life but that which He chooses to use for your good. Your loving, protecting Father measures out the trial and carefully watches over you every moment. His eyes are upon you (Job 34:21). You are never far from His thoughts (Psalm

> **GOD IS WORKING ON YOU. THERE WILL BE DIFFICULT TIMES, BUT YOU CAN TRUST HIM.**

139:17). He counts the hairs on your head (Matthew 10:30). He saves your tears in a bottle (Psalm 56:8). He loves you with an everlasting love (Jeremiah 31:3). But let His love be what it really is—a perfecting love.

I choose God's love. What do you choose?

Don't Miss Heaven by Eighteen Inches

"For God so loved the world, that he gave his only Son, that whoever believes in him should not perish but have eternal life." John 3:16 has been considered by people of faith through the centuries as the most important verse in all of God's Word. One of the greatest authors of our day, Max Lucado, called John 3:16 the Hope Diamond of the Bible. It's the centerpiece. Everything starts and flows from John 3:16. Nothing in life will truly make sense until John 3:16 makes total sense to you. By *total* I mean in your head-sense and in your heart-sense. The message of that single verse has to permeate your thoughts and your feelings. Just eighteen inches separate those two locations in you, but responding to God with both is eternal and essential.

Did Rollen Stewart understand John 3:16? You probably don't know the name, but you would certainly recognize his screen character. He was the guy in the rainbow wig seen in the background at sporting events during the late 1970s and 1980s ducking in and out of the crowds with a sign that read JOHN 3:16. For a while he was almost a fixture on the screen during field goal attempts in football, visible between the goalposts. By the 1990s the only place he showed up was in the news. *Whatever happened to him?*

Now he's in prison for three consecutive life terms. He took a woman hostage. He fired off guns at airplanes. He attempted to set off some bombs in a church. You're thinking, *What? But I thought he was, like, the John 3:16 guy? You know, "God so loved the world"?* Yeah, I thought so too. I don't know his story in detail, but maybe back when he was bobbing in and out of television coverage, trying to get others to embrace John 3:16, he was not fully there himself. I don't want to be hard on him; I hope he now embraces the reality of the message more than he did back then. Sadly, he stands as an illustration not of the power and life-change that verse can bring, but of the real danger of choosing to only partially embrace it. Yes, you can choose to read and understand something without choosing to make it fully your own. You can carry a sign and not live by what it says!

You've got to choose to believe with your whole heart not just that God loves, but that He truly loves *you*, as you are, with full knowledge of your shortcomings. You've got to put your whole weight down on God's love as your identity. Beyond an intellectual piece of information, you must choose to embrace God's love for you as a life-altering identity to rest upon.

The key word that unlocks the door to John 3:16 is *believe*. And *believe* always includes *choice*.

A Father's Love

I want to tell you a story.

Imagine for a moment you have a son. Your son was a great kid. You loved him with a love you didn't know was in you. He was such a blessing to your family and brought you incredible joy, but something happened to him in high school. He changed and became awful, arrogant, and insolent. To your surprise and deep disappointment—in a matter of months, it seems—your son became someone you couldn't talk to or tell anything. There were many sleepless nights of tossing and turning, weeping, and wondering, *Where did my sweet son go?*

One day he showed up and demanded, "Mom and Dad, I want my inheritance."

You replied, "Well, generally the first thing that happens before you can have an inheritance is the people who have the money have to die. And, as you can see, we are very much alive here."

To which he answered, "I don't really care what you say. I know I'm in the will. I just want my money, and I want it now."

When a son says about his inheritance, "I just want my money, and I want it now," what he's really saying is, "I wish you were dead." Imagine how that would break your heart and trash everything you had previously treasured.

Your son's attitude and request created a tough choice for you. How does unconditional love respond in the face of rejection? For some reason you felt it best for your son to exhaust his ego and energy—to self-destruct if necessary. So you said, "Fine, son. If you really think that will make you happy, and you've decided having this now is better than us, just take your inheritance."

And he did. He packed his stuff and left. You didn't hear from him for a long time. But you did hear through the grapevine that he'd gotten himself into an awful, shameful lifestyle. It grieved you deeply to think of the filthy things he was choosing—the drinking and carousing, the women, the addictions, the mess.

In the meantime, your son thought everything was going just fine. He had all the money and the friends he wanted. He was living it up, spending his inheritance, partying with his piggish pals, and living like the selfish animal he had chosen to be until . . . his money ran out. His credit cards were rejected. The symbols of the good life—the big screen TV, the sports car, the entertainment center—were all repossessed.

It was an amazing coincidence, but around the same time he reached into his pocket to pay and came up empty, he also noticed that he suddenly had no more friends. Apparently his friends were figments of his imagination. And he found himself *very* much alone!

A short while later he had this most radical of ideas: *I'm going to have to get a job.* News flash! But in the real world, if you don't finish high school, it's kind of tough to get a job. Finally, he found a job on a farm—feeding pigs.

Well, he soon figured out that if you get a job that only takes seven minutes to learn, you don't get paid very much for it either. So even though he was working, he hardly had enough money to put a roof over his head. He had nothing, and no one was to blame but himself. His arrogance and pride began to fade under the bright lights of personal poverty and slave labor.

In fact, he got so hungry that as he was throwing out the pig slop, he started to imagine what it tasted like. In that moment he thought to himself, *Man, my dad treated the farm hands better than this.*

In the pain of the pigsty, his heart began to change. He felt ashamed for how he had treated his parents and how he had been living. Home was not looking so bad anymore. In his head, he began dreaming of a speech he would give his dad. *I'll tell it like it is. I'm not the person I used to be. I'm going to say, "Dad, I don't deserve to be your son . . . but I'll be one of your slaves."*

So he started for home. On the road he kept wondering, *What's Dad going to say when he sees me?* All the while he remembered how he left his parents. Now what would they say? *"Oh, you do look a little like our son, but he died to us a long time ago." Will Dad be like that?*

I think you realize by now that this is a story Jesus told when He wanted to describe His Father's love. The son was blocks from home—Luke 15:20 says, **"But while he was still a long way off"**—but close enough that his father recognized him. I think that father went down that road every day looking for his son. Every day. Amazingly, he couldn't wait for the son to come back. He waited and watched—always on pins and needles in hopes that maybe today would be the day his son returned. And so **"his father saw him and felt compassion."** The father wasn't angry; he wasn't going to unload on his boy. He didn't hold a hateful grudge. The father felt a gut wrench when he saw his son. As a human dad, maybe he thought, *I was young and stupid once too.*

When the father felt compassion, he instantly connected with his son's feelings. *He must feel so low; he must be so devastated. He must be so disappointed with the choices that he's made.* "**But while he was still a long way off, his father saw him and felt compassion,**" . . . (this is my favorite part) "**and ran**" (Luke 15:20).

You don't see God running a lot in the Bible. He mostly is just there. But Jesus pictured God the Father running. He ran to His son. What message does that send? Can you picture it? The son looks like he just came out of a pigsty. The father runs to him, embraces him, and begins kissing him on the neck.

But the son needs to get his speech out. "**Father, I have sinned against heaven and before you. I am no longer worthy to be called your son**" (Luke 15:21).

That's as far as he got. "**But the father said to his servants 'Bring quickly the best robe, and put it on him, and put a ring on his hand, and shoes on his feet. And bring the fattened calf and kill it, and let us eat and celebrate. For this my son was dead, and is alive again; he was lost, and is found'**" (Luke 15:22–24). The father in the story is so fired up. Can you picture the tears of joy streaming down his face and the smile that doesn't go away? Can you put yourself in the place of that father?

This is how God feels about you. Jesus' story about His Father's love is also a story about you. No matter where you have been or what you've done, or the poor choices you have made—God loves you like this. Life will never make sense

> NO MATTER WHERE YOU HAVE BEEN OR WHAT YOU'VE DONE, OR THE POOR CHOICES YOU HAVE MADE—GOD LOVES YOU LIKE THIS.

until you get your arms around this reality. He loves you with an everlasting love. Words cannot describe the love that God has for you.

But you have to choose it. You have to believe it. You've got to get up out of the pigsty and come home. He is waiting for you. He is watching for you. He is longing for you. You will only be able to imagine it when you are in His embrace. No one can make this choice for you. You have to choose it yourself.

I choose to believe God loves me. What's your choice?

What will you do with a love like this? You didn't earn it. You don't deserve it. You can't maintain it. Best of all, you don't need to. This love comes from God Himself.

Drink it deeply; breathe it in until your lungs are full. Dive into the bottomless sea of God's love, stay under until you can't hold it in anymore, then burst from the surface and shout to the world, "There is a God who loves me—and I choose to believe it!"

It doesn't matter what people say or think. Choose to believe that God loves you! That choice will change your life.

A Choice to Make

Acknowledge the Choice

- Where do you find yourself at this moment? Choose one:

  ___ Clueless about God

  ___ Wondering about God

  ___ Wanting to know God

- Can you think of any reason you wouldn't choose God's love?

Consider the Choice

- How is putting off this choice a choice for you?
- What immediate effect do you think this choice would have in your life if you made it?

Make the Choice

- The choice to respond to God and accept His love can't be made for you. You have to make it on your own. You can make that choice in a simple prayer: "Creator God, I accept Your love for me." Say it out loud and let it settle into your soul.

A Choice Prayer

Father, thank You for Your love. Thank You that You love me with an everlasting love. Thank You that the God of the universe, who doesn't need me, who is not diminished by my absence or increased by my presence, who is complete in Himself—somehow beyond what I can think or imagine—has chosen to set His love upon me. I respond to Your choice with a choice of my own.

God, I pray for any person thinking now about the manner of his life in regard to this. Perhaps he has never made the choice to accept Your love for him. Might he say from his heart in this moment, "I'm going to step toward that. I choose to believe there is a God who loves me."

Because of Your great love. Amen.

Who is a God like you, pardoning iniquity and passing over transgression for the remnant of his inheritance? He does not retain his anger forever, because he delights in steadfast love.

—MICAH 7:18

As far as the east is from the west, so far does he remove our transgressions from us.

—PSALM 103:12

And getting into a boat he crossed over and came to his own city. And behold, some people brought to him a paralytic, lying on a bed. And when Jesus saw their faith, he said to the paralytic, "Take heart, my son; your sins are forgiven." And behold, some of the scribes said to themselves, "This man is blaspheming." But Jesus, knowing their thoughts, said, "Why do you think evil in your hearts? For which is easier, to say, 'Your sins are forgiven,' or to say, 'Rise and walk'? But that you may know that the Son of Man has the authority on earth to forgive sins"—he then said to the paralytic—"Rise, pick up your bed and go home." And he rose and went home. When the crowds saw it, they were afraid, and they glorified God, who had given such authority to men.

—MATTHEW 9:1–8

[Choice 2]

I Choose God's Forgiveness

Only the choice to receive God's forgiveness can set us free once and for all from the dark clouds of guilt and regret that linger over bad choices from our past.

My dad had heart trouble last summer. The doctor told him he needed angioplasty to remove some serious plaque that was restricting blood flow to his heart by almost 95 percent. After that sobering diagnosis, Dad sat still all summer waiting for Canada's socialized medicine system to schedule the scouring of his artery and relieve his scary condition. I'm glad he took the doctor's word to heart and that he's OK. It was a close call.

If you are like many people—even most people—you may have a major blockage too. Not a physical restriction in your arteries but a spiritual blockage that keeps the message of God's love from getting to your heart. You can choose God's love and cherish it. You may rejoice and even revel in God's love at a conceptual level yet not be deeply affected by God's disposition toward you. The fact is, you may be holding God's love for you at arm's length because you still can't reconcile such a love with who you know yourself to be. Is that you?

You want to choose God's love, but you can't because you think, *He can't love me as I am, can't love me knowing what I've done.* God wants to remove that blockage. He doesn't want to ignore it or explain it away. He wants to remove it completely. And He will if you get your arms around your true condition and choose to embrace what He offers.

First, the bad news . . . then some good and great news! We have to be strong enough to open our heart to the bad news so the good news can be that much more glorious. No one gets excited about a solution to a problem he doesn't see. But no one is more relieved than the person who has recognized a catastrophic problem and then is offered the solution. It's like realizing you're about to drown and then feeling the grip of a lifeguard pulling you to safety.

This chapter is good news about forgiveness. I promise to get to the good news but not before we spend a reasonable amount of time on the bad news. Acknowledging how bad the bad news is will put you in a position to choose the good news with the urgency it deserves and demands.

A Case Study: The Power to Forgive Sin

In Matthew 9 we get an up-close and personal view of Jesus at work. He had just finished teaching the Sermon on the Mount and was traveling back and forth across the north end of the Sea of Galilee, healing people. He showed by His power and His words that He was God's Son. Not only was He a good, moral person and a capable teacher, but He also demonstrated He was God, the very God who had become flesh. He had the power to heal. Here is one of those healing episodes:

"**And getting into a boat he crossed over and came to his own city. And behold, some people brought to him a paralytic, lying on a bed. And when Jesus saw their faith, he said to the paralytic, 'Take heart, my son; your sins are forgiven.' And behold, some of the scribes said to themselves, 'This man is blaspheming'**" (Matthew 9:1–3).

I understand what the paralyzed man's friends were thinking. They carried him in on a cot and asked, *We heard you heal people—can you heal our friend?* But Jesus said instead, *Cheer up, son! Your sins are forgiven.* The friends probably thought, *No disrespect, but were you listening? We're not talking about a sin problem; we're talking about a walking problem. His problem isn't in his soul, it's in his body. You're in the ballpark but not on base—will You help him walk?* They were a little confused.

But the religious leaders standing around thought they understood Jesus' point right away, becoming offended and irate. How dare this moral teacher claim He could forgive sin? Only God could do that. He was claiming to *be* God—as in, blasphemy!

Back to Matthew's report: **"And behold, some of the scribes said to themselves, 'This man is blaspheming.' But Jesus, knowing their thoughts, said, 'Why do you think evil in your hearts? For which is easier, to say, "Your sins are forgiven," or to say, "Rise and walk"? But that you may know that the Son of Man has authority on earth to forgive sins' . . ."** (Matthew 9:3–6a).

Notice that Jesus was not going to heal the young man's body without healing his soul. What benefit would there be to getting him up on his feet for the next ten minutes only to let him fall into hell for eternity? So Jesus put first things first. He said, *Let me deal with your sin problem, and then we'll work on your walking problem.* He put spiritual matters at the top of the list and said, "Your sins are forgiven."

Then notice Jesus' strong assertion: "I have the authority to forgive sins." That's what provoked the scribes' meltdown. They understood what Jesus was saying. He was claiming to be God. No one else in the universe can make the claim to forgive sin except God Himself. *Who do you think you are . . . God?* And Jesus nodded, *Exactly.*

There were two things the scribes couldn't do: heal *or* forgive. They knew they couldn't help the paralyzed man walk away or walk away forgiven. In their minds, *your sins are forgiven* were just offensive words, nothing more. Jesus said to them, *I'm going to show you that my words of forgiveness have the power to speak physical healing into this man.* Jesus talked the talk, and the man walked!

This was not an accidental claim by Jesus. On another occasion, Jesus told the religious leaders quite clearly, **"You are from below; I am from above. You are of this world; I am not of this world. I told you that you would die in your sins, for unless you believe that I am he you will die in your sins"** (John 8:23–24). Another time He calmly declared, **"I and the Father are one"** (John 10:30). He also said, **"Whoever has seen me has seen the Father"** (John 14:9b).

The scribes shouldn't have been surprised. Jesus didn't have a problem with His own identity. The same story of the paralytic's healing is told in two other Gospels. In Mark 2:7 and Luke 5:21 the scribes thought, **"Who can forgive sins but God alone?"** Jesus heard their rhetorical thoughts and saw their raised eyebrows. To which Jesus could have easily replied, *Correct! Now you're getting it!*

Jesus didn't hedge at all. *I am God in the flesh. I am the only One given the authority by God the Father to forgive sins.* He told it like it was. He started with the real problem, not just the obvious one.

The Problem Is Sin

In God's eyes, the healing of the body and the healing of the soul are not that far apart. Both problems have the same cause. In fact, I would suggest to you that sin is the ultimate cause of *every* human problem. Sin is behind everything wrong in our world. Sin is behind every problem of substance in the universe. We call the world *fallen* because it is polluted by sin. Following are some examples:

- *Sin is the cause of every planet problem.*
  Volcanoes, tsunamis, earthquakes, famine, and flooding in my basement—are all because of sin. Special news reports tell us that our weather systems are more whacked than ever before. It's warmer at the poles and colder in the tropics. A flip-flop in weather conditions drenches Phoenix while Seattle dries up. Storms have become more frequent and intense but less predictable.

  The universe itself is broken. The sun is burning out. Scientists tell us that the earth is turning slower every year. The solar system is winding down and getting worse because of sin. All the amazing evidence for God's design that we saw in the last chapter is now tainted. Everywhere we look we see examples of the insidious damage caused by sin. The Bible tells us, **"For the creation was subjected to futility"** (Romans 8:20*a*) and that it is in **"bondage**

to corruption" (Romans 8:21*b*). The universe doesn't work as well as it used to.

And it's getting worse. In the last fifteen years, we've experienced more earthquakes than in the last fifty years—and more in the last fifty years than in the last five hundred years. The universe is wearing out under the weight of sin (Hebrews 1:10–12).

When Adam and Eve chose to sin and sent the human race into a death spiral, God stepped forward in the early chapters of Genesis and cursed the planet. He had said, *Here's a choice between right and wrong—choose.* One tree in the middle of the garden was the monument to that choice. When Adam and Eve decided, *We're going to choose* not to do *what God asked,* God followed up with the consequences. God cursed creation, subjecting it to futility. It hasn't worked right since, and God's not trying to fix it. Some day He'll completely wipe it out and create it anew, but not now (Revelation 21:1).

- *Sin is the cause of every sickness problem in our bodies.*

Every physical problem that you and I have is because of sin. Every cancer, every heart failure, every debilitating disease finds its origin in the garden of Eden. God made man perfect, but Adam and Eve's rebellion tore at the fabric of what God made them to be. God judged them with the same twisted brokenness that He proclaimed upon creation. We're part of that same curse. Our bodies break down because there is a judgment due to sin. We were not designed that way, not originally, but we are that way now.

Keep in mind that as with all things that spiral out of control, the effects of sin are imposing themselves randomly throughout creation. Sometimes good people get cancer and bad people get away with murder. Jesus said that any personal avoidance of the consequences of sin should not produce pride in us but repentance: **"Or those eighteen on whom the tower in Siloam fell and killed them: do you think that they were worse offenders than all the others who lived in Jerusalem? No, I tell you; but unless you repent, you will all likewise perish"** (Luke 13:4–5).

- *Sin is behind every sickness problem in our souls.*

  We're not just broken in our bodies, but our souls are sin-twisted. The part of us that lives forever is broken. The Bible actually pronounces us already spiritually dead (Ephesians 2:1–3). The fact that we die physically is God's consequence for our sin. Our spiritual death has the same cause. Our inclination is to do wrong every time. All of us. Every breach of God's law, every violation of another person, every self-exalting, others-debasing, wounding action is because of sin. We pick up a newspaper and read the results of sin on every page—the greed, selfishness, pride, quest for power, sexual sin, and perversity are running rampant and getting worse. Sin provokes every casual indifference to God's truth, every prideful God's-Word-doesn't-matter-to-me thought. Scripture says that evil men will grow worse and worse until God Himself steps back on the world stage and rights all that is wrong. Until we understand the pervasive infection of sin everywhere, nothing else makes sense. Wouldn't it be great if we could stick with sin in the newspaper? Sadly, though, we must choose to turn our gaze toward self until we see sin in the mirror.

We Are All Sinful

Romans 5:12 says, **"Therefore, just as sin came into the world through one man, and death through sin, and so death spread to all men because all sinned."** We are sinful by birth; we are sinful by nature; we are sinful by actions. Sin is in our genes. If anyone doubts that, just go back to the Ten Commandments.

God laid down a summary of His law in Exodus 20, and we have been lawbreakers ever since. God built some authoritative walls of protection around us with just ten rules. To go outside one of these walls is to say, "I know what God told me to do, but I'm not going to do it."

Exodus 20:3 says, **"You shall have no other gods before me."** God wasn't just talking about golden calves and tiki dolls. "No other god" means nothing is more important than Him.

To distort His priority is to twist the very purpose for which you and I were created. God not only deserves to be first, but He demands to be first—all the time. Anything else is sin. Having God first in our lives is such a battle because we want the job of being most important! We're insatiably self-centered!

Here's another law: "**You shall not take the name of the LORD your God in vain**" (Exodus 20:7). *Oh, I would never do that!* OK, maybe you wouldn't say blasphemous words, but "in vain" also means that you should not minimize the importance of God by what you say or by what you do. Don't speak flippantly about Him or trivialize anything about Him or what He's doing. Don't be indifferent about His work around the world, in your church, or in your heart.

How is that going for you?

"**Remember the Sabbath day, to keep it holy**" (Exodus 20:8). God made it a law—one day a week for rest and to focus on Him and His priority in your life. No work, no checking e-mail, no "just this one thing and then I'll relax." The Sabbath is intended to be devoted to you and God, doing the things that help you connect and grow in that relationship. Nothing should get in the way of that.

How's that going? Are you setting a pace for your life that is unhealthy or unsustainable? If you are, it's sin.

"**Honor your father and your mother**" (Exodus 20:12). *Yeah, well, you don't know my mom and dad.* I don't see any disclaimer here. Regardless of your parents' success rating, regardless of how you may feel, God commands all of His people everywhere to honor their father and mother. It does not say "Honor good parents" or "Honor your father and mother until you leave for college." Honoring your parents is an attitude accompanied by actions. It means to give them grace and respect and to speak well of them, both directly and to others. To do otherwise is sin.

"**Do not murder**" (Exodus 20:13 CEV). *Finally, a check mark!* But Jesus said if you hate someone, you're a murderer in your heart. If you have a deep-seated, ongoing, unresolved anger toward someone, you've already murdered them. You're just lacking the courage or the opportunity to do what your heart has already strategized. If you hate, in God's eyes you have already done the deed.

"You shall not commit adultery" (Exodus 20:14). *Check*. Again, Jesus looks beyond the action and to the heart. He said if you look on a woman and lust after her in your heart, it's only a fear of the consequences that keeps you honest. It's not your respect for God that keeps you from choosing sin; it's fear of fallout. If you could do it and get away with it . . .

"Do not steal" (Exodus 20:15 CEV). Don't ever take anything that isn't yours, ever. Not objects, not applause, not someone's reputation.

How's that going?

"Do not tell lies" (Exodus 20:16 CEV). Ever. About anything, even to yourself. Don't ever say anything deceitful or 'destructive about anyone, ever. Don't say something to hurt someone else. Don't tear down what God is building up. Don't ever put someone's reputation in a bad place to put yourself in a good place. Don't say things that aren't true. Lying is serious.

"You shall not covet" (Exodus 20:17). Don't want what isn't yours. Don't want your neighbor's house. Don't wish you had his car. Don't wish you had his wife. Don't wish you had anything that belongs to someone else that you didn't earn yourself.

That's just the top ten. How's that going? Not well? I thought so; me neither! We're all sinners. The consequences of these sins are grave and eternal. Sin is serious. We don't need any more evidence that we're sinful, broken, and bent! To fail in any of these, even once, is to be guilty of all. James 2:10 says, **"For whoever keeps the whole law but fails in one point has become accountable for all of it."**

What the Bible Says About Our Sin

For sure, someone reading this is thinking, *All this talk about sin . . . aren't you overdoing it a bit? I mean, no one's perfect. Isn't sin something only theologians wrestle with?*

Actually, I think it's a huge issue at your house and in your life too. If you remain unpersuaded, take to heart these five truths the Bible asserts about our sin:

1: *We are determined sinners.*

Very little can stop our passionate pursuit of sin. David said in Psalm 51:5, **"Behold, I was brought forth in iniquity, and in sin did my mother conceive me."** Nothing in this world can equal our devoted desire to sin. We are loyal to it. Our minds constantly gravitate toward it . . . *How can I get what I want? I was created to crave God, but now all I want is my own thing.*

We come by it quite naturally. We've never needed a pep talk on sinning. No one has ever had to coach us: "Keep that sin thing going, man. Don't get discouraged. I know it's hard, but keep it up!" It is our constant condition; furthermore, we ignore the solution.

On the flip side, we need a lot of input to maintain our focus on the *right* direction. Leave us alone for a while and off we go in our sinful bent, whatever that is. We all have different patterns of sin. My personal weaknesses are different from yours.

It baffles me how some people can be totally indifferent to how they will spend eternity. How can they sit passively by as though these were not issues of the greatest urgency? We are hard like stone, and it is only by the grace of God that our rocky hearts are broken and we become tender toward Him.

This is the way it truly is. We are determined sinners.

2: *We are diseased sinners.*

Sin is a spiritual disease. Genesis 6:5 says, **"The LORD saw that the wickedness of man was great in the earth, and that every intention of the thoughts of his heart was only evil continually."** Sin is a virus of the soul. It's gangrene of the heart. It eats away at the fabric of our being and will continue until it consumes us. And there is nothing we can do to stop it.

We are diseased sinners, and our condition is terminal.

3: *We are deceived sinners.*

Ironically, each of us is blind to the reality of the truth we now hear. Even as you read this, something inside you knows it's true but struggles to admit it. Some of you are thinking, *this really doesn't apply that much to me.* Jeremiah 17:9 says that our own heart will deceive us. For example, we will glance at something that is not righteous to pursue, and then we will see it and savor it and seek it until we convince ourselves that it is OK. That's self-deception, denial—sin. We each have a stunning capacity to deceive ourselves into thinking that darkness is light and wrong is right. It's because we're bent and twisted, and we don't work right.

You know, James, this isn't really a comfortable conversation. Yeah, as though your comfort is the highest good. Even reading this you're looking for little loopholes: *I think I can dodge that . . .* We convince ourselves that we're better than that, or we ask, *What about the guy over there?* Anything to dodge the diagnosis of our sin.

4: *We are desperate sinners.*

We grasp for our sin. Jeremiah 17:9 continues, **"The heart is deceitful above all things, and desperately sick."** This is not some small problem. This isn't something a good shower will wash away. You cannot scour the effects of the sin nature from your spirit. Sin is a desperate disaster. Nothing but the grace of God can stop us. We are frantic in our longing and searching for something to satisfy our sinful inclination.

We fail where we need to succeed. Like a quarterback with a broken shoulder. Like an accountant who cooked the books. Like a banker who embezzled. Like a lawyer who lied under oath. We fall where we *should* stand, and we're desperate because of it. We have no way out of this condition on our own. We can't solve this problem. We can hardly even diagnose it, let alone fix it.

5: *We are destined by sin.*

The natural end to this progression is spelled out in Romans 6:23, **"For the wages of sin is death."** That's not going to be a desirable paycheck when you get what you deserve for what you've done. Had there been no sin, there would be no death. Adam and Eve would still be walking the earth today with all of their descendants in joyful fellowship with the God who made them had it not been for sin. Everything happening in the universe and in your heart that is sordid and sideways is because of sin. And **"the soul who sins shall die,"** reports Ezekiel 18:20. That doesn't just mean a physical death, since we know that we're all going to die. The soul that sins will die spiritually.

Do you get it? Does your heart feel the weight of this pronouncement? You and I have got a sin problem that we can't fix, soften, or solve. And the consequence is certain, forever!

The Problem Is Sin; the Prognosis Is Death

Let's go back to John 3:16. We all love the first part, **"For God so loved the world that He gave his only Son."** But the least emphasized and most important hinge phrase is, **"that whoever believes in him should not perish."** *Perish* is a serious reality that has to be solved. Do you see that the promise of God's salvation is conditional? *You must believe.*

The promise is equally true that everyone who *does not* believe in Him *will* perish. *Perish* means to suffer in hell, to experience the wrath of a holy and just God. *Perish* equals an eternal death sentence.

It's shocking to me the degree to which people ignore the reality of death and hell. Hebrews 9:27 says, **"it is appointed unto men once to die"** (KJV). We get one chance at this life—one chance on God's timetable. A lot of people exit early. *Man, I did not see that off-ramp coming.* James 4:14 says, **"yet you do not know what tomorrow will bring. What is your life? For you are a mist that appears for a little time and then vanishes."** We don't know if we have another week or another month or even another day.

No one knows how long he has, and everyone thinks he's going to heaven. People assume God grades on the curve. Since they know a lot of people who are worse than them, they feel they don't need to worry. But listen—God's not our college professor. If you think the door to heaven swings that way, you are tragically misinformed. Only when we rightly understand sin and rightly understand God's holiness does the rightful judgment of hell not surprise us. Jesus said, **"Enter by the narrow gate. For the gate is wide and the way is easy that leads to destruction, and those who enter by it are many. For the gate is narrow and the way is hard that leads to life, and those who find it are few"** (Matthew 7:13–14). Almost every person you know is going to perish.

People are so slow to embrace the brevity of this life. You feel a pain in your chest or a lump in your breast, and all of a sudden the doctors are sliding you into one of those tubes or taking chest X-rays. "Am I going to die, doctor?" And the straight answer is "Yes—it's only a question of when." The doctor has little control over it. He might be able to help with *when*, but in the end, he can't determine *if*.

So many spend all of their energies working to prolong the temporary, yet they disregard the reality of the forever that follows this short event called *life*. They fix their eyes on *when* but spend no time at all thinking about the most defined reality of all: the moment of their final breath. Why do folks act so surprised and sadly unprepared when death arrives? They have frittered away their chances to choose, and all of a sudden it's too late. Can you feel the truth zeroing in on you?

This is the big deal—not what happens to you in the next ten minutes but what happens to you in the next ten thousand years! What will you do in these minutes to prepare for an endless eternity? That's what really matters. Matthew 10:28 says, **"And do not fear those who kill the body but cannot kill the soul. Rather fear him who can destroy both soul and body in hell."** That's the message that the world won't tell you about—the greatest message of all. You have a choice to make that can change the location of your eternal residence!

Let me interrupt this line of thinking for a moment and ask what you're thinking about all of this. I believe some will say, "This chapter sounds an awful lot like one of those hellfire and brimstone sermons." Perhaps so. But answer these questions honestly:

- What would you think of an accountant who didn't tell you, "You will be bankrupt in three weeks"?

- What would you think of a lawyer who didn't tell you, "If you go into court with that story, you'll go to prison for the rest of your life"?

- What would you think of an oncologist who told you, "You'll be fine! Go have a picnic," when he knew you had two weeks to live?

Well, they'd be worthless, wouldn't they? You're right. Yet people line up to hear preachers tell them that everything is going to be fine, even as they are running like lemmings over a cliff into a bottomless pit.

Preachers who only want to tell you the good news but never ask you to face the reality of your own sinful condition before God are the worst kind of worthless. Why would you want to avoid a decision about the eternal destiny that is racing toward you this moment? How can I not tell you that apart from being reconciled to God through His Son Jesus Christ, you are without God and without hope in this world? This is the way it really is. I'm telling you the truth because it's only the truth that sets you free.

It's a fact that we don't hear a lot about hell these days. Regardless, hell is an actual place and settled certainty. Now, I don't believe we have the capacity to comprehend fully what hell is like. But God, in His mercy, describes it for us throughout His Word. I say "in His mercy" because to pull back the curtain and glimpse its horror helps us to quickly get over our own denial. Hopefully it even compels us to run faster to God's throne of grace. Hell is the place of God's wrath and judgment that will never end. Hell is a place of punishment, where the flames never cease and the thirst is never quenched. Hell is a place of eternal, conscious torment, and people you have known are there right now (Matthew 13:42, Luke 16:24, 2 Peter 2:4, Jude 13, and Revelation 20:10). As awesome as heaven will be, hell will be that awful, and if you understood it biblically, you would not wish it on your worst enemy!

Here are some of the stark pictures the Bible gives us about hell:

- *Hell is a place of torment.*
  Matthew 8:12 and 13:42 says, "**There will be weeping and gnashing of teeth.**" Revelation 14:11 speaks of agony: "**And the smoke of their torment goes up forever and ever, and they have no rest, day or night.**" The smoke never stops! The fire never stops! The darkness never stops! The torment never stops! The falling never stops!

- *Hell is a place of bondage.*
  Matthew 22:13 reads: "**Bind him hand and foot, and cast him into the outer darkness. In that place there will be weeping and gnashing of teeth.**" Second Peter 2:4 speaks about the fallen angels being held in "**chains of gloomy darkness.**" Revelation 14:11 says there is no rest in hell. Daniel 12:2 describes hell as a place of "**shame and everlasting contempt.**" Sinners take all their shame with them to hell, and they relive their lives moment after moment after moment.

- *Hell is a place of memory.*
  The rich man in Luke 16 remembered his life. For all eternity, people in hell remember they didn't have to be there. They remember the opportunities they rejected.

- *Hell is a place of desires without hope of satisfaction.*
  The first desire of the rich man in hell (Luke 16) was for Abraham to take one drop of water and place it upon his tongue. He didn't get it. He still desires it today. He cried out for mercy but didn't get it. He pleaded for someone to go tell his brothers about hell. For all eternity the people in hell will never be granted even one of their desires. For all eternity they will be like drug addicts going through withdrawal.

- *Hell is a place of separation from God.*
  Second Thessalonians 1:9 (KJV) says, "**Who shall be punished with everlasting destruction.**" Destruction does not mean annihilation but ruination, separation from God. So this verse is saying, "Who shall be punished with everlasting ruination, separation from the presence of the Lord and from the glory of His power!"

Enough? I don't know about you, but it's almost too much information to bear. Hell will go on forever because no amount of punishment for sin can justify the choice to reject the forgiveness God so freely offers.

When we were in high school, many of us read the Shakespearean play *Macbeth*. Lady Macbeth is an ambitious woman who wants to be queen, so she tricks and traps her husband into killing the king. As he stumbles away from the murder, he stupidly brings back the bloody knives instead of planting them in the servants' quarters per her instructions. So she takes care of business herself, hiding the knives on the unsuspecting fall guys.

All progresses as planned. Her husband becomes king and she the first lady. But their scheme unravels as she increasingly is consumed by the weight of guilt for the sin that she chose. By Act 5, Scene One, Lady Macbeth sleepwalks around the castle, reliving the murder scene and wringing her hands as if washing them. The bloody stains, physically washed away long ago, are spiritually still obvious. She pitifully moans, "Out, damned spot!" She cannot get her conscience clean.

Lady Macbeth is just like you and me. She cannot clean her sinful self, and neither can we. No amount of goodness can wash away sin. No amount of human kindness can resolve the debt of our own violation of God's law. Nothing in us can wipe that away.

We need God's forgiveness for the sin that hangs in the corner of our consciousness and cannot be washed away by itself. And like Lady Macbeth, we will take our sin to the grave and into hell itself apart from some external cleansing agent.

In summary, then, the problem is sin, and the prognosis is hell. Unless God steps in, this is our future and nothing can alter the course. What if the book ended right here? What if there were no good news? You cannot appreciate the good news until you embrace the reality of the bad news. We've got a serious problem that we can't fix. We've got a future that is as grim as it can be. But God . . . but God!

Ready for the good news?

God's Prescription for the Disease of Sin

> ONCE YOU SEE YOUR DESPERATE PROBLEM, THE WONDERFUL NEWS OF ETERNAL RELIEF IS THAT GOD IS A FORGIVING GOD.

Unimaginably, God has provided a way of escape. You and I can be forgiven of the sin that rightly condemns us to hell. *Really? You've got to be kidding!* You can be absolutely changed. You can be forgiven! Good news! You don't have to go to hell—but only if you choose it. Once you see your desperate problem, the wonderful news of eternal relief is that God is a forgiving God.

Can I remind you of what God's Word says about His forgiveness? I have prayed that as you read the following scriptures, the hope of God's mercy will wash over your life. You will know as a fact that you have forgiveness in Christ Jesus. There can be a restoration of your relationship with God. You can know relief from the weight of guilt. Soak in what Scripture says about you and God, and what He would like to do for you, if you will choose it.

The Fact of God's Forgiveness

- Exodus 34:6–7*a*: "The LORD, the LORD, a God merciful and gracious, slow to anger, and abounding in steadfast love and faithfulness, keeping steadfast love for thousands, *forgiving iniquity and transgression and sin*, but who will by no means clear the guilty" (emphasis mine).

- Psalm 86:5: "For you, O Lord, are good and *forgiving*, abounding in steadfast love to all who call upon you" (emphasis mine).

- Micah 7:18: "Who is a God like you, *pardoning iniquity* and passing over transgression for the remnant of his inheritance? He does not retain his anger forever, because he delights in steadfast love" (emphasis mine).

Choosing God's forgiveness means something because God's love expresses itself in forgiveness. Among the certain things God has told us about Himself is, "**I will forgive**" (Jeremiah 31:34).

The Extent of God's Forgiveness

- Psalm 103:12: "**As far as the east is from the west, so far does he remove our transgressions from us.**"

- Micah 7:19: "**He will again have compassion on us; he will tread our iniquities underfoot. You will cast all our sins into the depths of the sea.**"

- Ezekiel 36:25: "**I will sprinkle clean water on you, and you shall be clean from all your uncleannesses, and from all your idols I will cleanse you.**"

God won't just take your sin away from you; He'll put it so far away you can't find it anymore. That's how forgiven you'll be. He's not going to say the next morning, "Oh, yeah, I was thinking about that forgiveness thing last night . . . And I spoke a little too soon. Now I'm mad again." God's not tentative about forgiveness. He will never remind you of your sin again.

> GOD WON'T JUST TAKE YOUR SIN AWAY FROM YOU; HE'LL PUT IT SO FAR AWAY YOU CAN'T FIND IT ANYMORE. THAT'S HOW FORGIVEN YOU'LL BE.

The Blessing of Forgiveness

- Ezekiel 36:26–27: "**And I will give you a new heart, and a new spirit I will put within you. And I will remove the heart of stone from your flesh and give you a heart of flesh. And I will put my Spirit within you, and cause you to walk in my statutes and be careful to obey my rules.**"

- Psalm 32:1: "**Blessed is the one whose transgression is forgiven, whose sin is covered.**"

It's so true, isn't it? Think of the crowd of people on the broad road carrying their sin with them, and compare them to the few people who chose the forgiveness of their sins in God. How eternally blessed is the one whose sins are covered! *I'm forgiven by God. It's my identity.* Everything begins to fall into place when you have made that choice.

Don't you want to be forgiven? Don't you want to have all of that sin washed away? Are there not many things hanging in the attic of your conscience that you long to have wiped clean? Do you long to know that the God who made you and loves you has provided a way to forgive you completely?

You Can Choose God's Forgiveness

God offers us *grace*: grace is when we get what we don't deserve. God offers us *mercy*: mercy is not getting what we do deserve. Because of God's grace and mercy, we can be forgiven.

You're like, *This forgiveness thing sounds like a pretty good deal. God is going to just wipe away my sin? God will say, "Oh, it's OK, never mind about your sin"?*

No. That's not it at all. Because of God's holy, pure, and righteous character, He could never lightly dismiss sin. Sin is not a trifle—it's a terror. So you have to get this next part.

The Payment for Our Sin Is Christ

All of God's anger for sin; all of God's wrath for all the selfish, prideful things we have done; all of the good that we *should* have done but we've left undone; and all of our indifference to God—God placed the sum of it squarely on Jesus Christ. As it says in 1 John 4:10, **"In this is love, not that we have loved God but that he loved us and sent his Son to be the propitiation for our sins."** You don't really get Christianity until you understand Christ is the payment for sin. If you think Christianity is going to church and carrying your Bible and getting your check mark, you don't get it.

By the way, evangelical churches are filled with people who don't get it. Even more shocking, many people who go to your church are going to perish. *What?* Yes, it's true. Church attendance doesn't count. Neither does leading a small group or serving in Sunday school. Jesus said many people will come to Him and say, "I did all these things for You . . . ," but He's going to respond, **"I never knew you"** (Matthew 7:23). You were just some religious person going through the motions of what you thought would save you. Hanging around church doesn't get it done. Getting it done happens when you've personally turned from your sin and embraced Jesus Christ by faith for your forgiveness.

Now we're on the bull's-eye of the gospel. This is what separates biblical Christianity from all false religions of the world, including aberrant Christianity. In all false religions, there is this one thread: *I will get to heaven on my own. I will prove to God how good I am. God has to reward my performance.* In every aberrant religion you find people cutting themselves, walking on their knees, doing penance, kissing rings, bowing down, making a journey to some sacred location, and trying to do for God what God has already done for us in Christ.

The glory of the gospel is that God loves you! The greatest proof of that love is when Christ stood in for you (Romans 5:8). He took God's wrath for your sin. All of God's righteous anger was placed upon Christ. The Bible says that Jesus is the Lamb slain before the foundation of the world (Revelation 13:8). Rather than some tragic turn of events, this was God's plan from the start. He knew we would choose the wrong, so even *before* we chose the wrong, He chose the right. God's love made a way out for us. That's what John 3:16 is all about. *Whoever chooses Christ will not perish.*

His love for you is so great that He did for you what you could not do for yourself: He sent His Son Jesus Christ into the world to die a substitutionary death on your behalf. Jesus put Himself in your place and took upon Himself the punishment for your sin.

Isaiah 53, written one thousand years before Jesus Christ, prophesied about His life and declared He would bear our sin, **"All we like sheep have gone astray; we have turned—every one—to his own way; and the LORD has** laid on him the iniquity of us all" (v. 6). Second Corinthians 5:21 says, "For our sake he made him to be sin who knew no sin, so that in him we might become the righteousness of God." Jesus paid a debt He did not owe because we owed a debt we could not pay. What would drive Him to such a sacrifice? First John 4:10 says, "In this is love, not that we have loved God but that he loved us and sent His Son to be the propitiation [payment] for our sins."

This is the gospel, my friend.

The only way to have our sins forgiven is to throw our arms around the gospel with our whole heart. Someone had to pay, and God's love sent His Son to get it done for you.

It's Your Choice

The choice is yours to believe on the Lord Jesus Christ and be saved, says Acts 16:31. No one can do this for you. This is not some shallow mental assent, such as, *Oh, yeah, I'm good with that,* or a casual, half-hearted, *Oh, yeah, I'm in with Jesus.* That's not believing. When you believe on Him, you give Him everything. You give Him your life. You trust in Him completely, so that if you were to die today and stand before God, and He asked you, *Why should I let you into heaven?* you'd answer, "You shouldn't, Lord. I can't believe I'm even here. But I trust in what Jesus did on my behalf on the cross. I'm here because of Him. His work is the total basis for my forgiveness. It's because I accepted Jesus' payment for my sin. Nothing in my hands I bring, simply to His cross I cling. I believe that's why You'll let me in!" If that's not your answer, you do not believe in Christ. You actually believe in something or someone else to gain acceptance before God.

Titus 3:5 drives home the point that "he saved us, not because of works done by us in righteousness, but according to his own mercy." And Ephesians 2:8 makes the definitive statement, "For by grace you have been saved through faith. And this is not your own doing; it is the gift of God."

To really believe, you have to overcome the obstacle of pride. *I'm not going to go that Jesus route,* pride murmurs. *That might be good for some people, but I'm going to go my way.*

I'll never forget a funeral held at our church several years ago for a woman not tightly connected to our church. Her family said, "We've brought this boom-box, and during the service we're going to play the Frank Sinatra song 'My Way.'" And I said, "Well, no, we're not going to be doing that." They were outraged. They couldn't believe that we would not want such a wonderful song sung by Frank Sinatra to be played inside our church walls. They had their reasons for wanting Ol' Blue Eyes to sing at the funeral. After all:

- Famous artists—from Pavarotti to Willie Nelson, from Sid Vicious and the Sex Pistols to U2—have performed versions of the song.

- Even Elvis Presley released a number one hit version of "My Way" a few weeks before he died.

- "My Way" has been the most frequently played song at British funeral services.

- William Shatner opened the AFI Lifetime Achievement Award tribute to George Lucas by reading the words to "My Way."

- The former Serbian president and indicted war criminal Slobodan Milosevic was said to be a huge fan of the song, playing it repeatedly in his prison cell at The Hague, awaiting execution.

I doubt if there is a more universally recognized song than this one. So why would we not allow it to be played at our church? You can probably remember most of the lyrics. Think of it as an alternative answer to God's question, *Why should I let you into heaven?*

Here's my CliffsNotes version of the song:

Verse 1: I'm confident I can make a case for my life as I face death— my way!

Verse 2: I've pretty much gone everywhere and done anything—my way.

Verse 3: I do have to admit some regrets, but they're hardly worth mentioning because they involved things I just had to do. I'm not willing to call them sins. They're just my way.

Verse 4: I planned and chose the careful course I took as long as it was my way.

Interlude: Sometimes I may have been in trouble, but I stuck it out or bluffed my way through 'cause, after all, I was doing it my way.

Verse 5: When I sum up all the highs and lows of meaning in my life, the only word that comes to mind is *amusing*. It's all my way.

Verse 6: So, God, listen, can I just get credit for saying, "I did it my way"? Is there any other way than my way?

Postlude: Hey, God, I'm all I've got. There's nothing else, is there? I certainly refuse to face death with the humility and faith of someone who kneels because that's not my way!

The arrogance in the final verse is difficult to miss:

> For what is a man, what has he got?
> If not himself, then he has naught.
> To say the things he truly feels;
> And not the words of one who kneels.
> The record shows I took the blows—
> And did it my way![1]

I did it my way. That, my friend, is the proud anthem that they sing in hell. "My way" is the highway that takes you to an eternity separated from God. "My way" creates an obstacle of pride that has to be overcome in order to choose God's gift of the forgiveness of your sins. The alternatives to forgiveness won't work. Some people think, *Well, God will weigh up the good and the bad that I did.* God doesn't use the curve nor does He use a scale to judge our lives. The standard is perfection, and we can't measure up by ourselves. Others say, "Well, will it really be that big an issue if I show up in heaven and I'm sincere? I don't need Jesus; I'll just do my best and get there on my own." Let me tell you a story to make clear what a bad plan that is.

Imagine for a moment that I am very close friends with your son. In the course of my life, I get way off track and commit an awful crime. I go to court and am sentenced to death. But your son and I are the best of friends, and he does a crazy thing. He was broken-hearted about the situation my choices had put me in. He appeals to the judge: "Is there any way possible that James wouldn't have to die for this crime?" Incredibly, the judge says, "The crime was done, and someone has to pay for it." And your son says, "Well, what if I paid? What if I stood in for him?" The judge concedes and says, "Then you would die, and he would go free." To everyone's amazement, your son steps forward and says, "Then I'll do it—my life for his."

Now, you didn't hear the news until it was too late. Your son gave his life for me, and I was released. To add to your grief, you overhear someone ask me, "How did you get free? I thought you got the death penalty?" And I say, "Well, they looked at my life and decided I wasn't so bad after all. I had done some awful things, but overall, I was a pretty good guy—maybe even better than most. So they gave me a break."

You would think to yourself, "My son gave his life for you and you're telling yourself and others you were released on your own merit?" And your heart would break with grief and outrage.

God and My Way

Let me tell you, hell is not deep enough to contain the wrath of God for those who think they don't need Jesus. If you reject His only provision for forgiveness in Christ, then there is no hope for you. God has given only one solution for the forgiveness of your sin—one way only. Hebrews 10:29 says, **"How much worse punishment, do you think, will be deserved by the one who has spurned the Son of God, and has profaned the blood . . . and has outraged the Spirit of grace?"**

> **THE SURPRISING THING IS NOT THAT THERE IS ONLY ONE WAY TO HEAVEN; THE INCREDIBLE THING IS THAT THERE IS A WAY AT ALL.**

Why shouldn't God be outraged when His Son Jesus freely extends to you His nail-pierced hand of forgiveness, but you slap it away and say, "No, I don't want Your forgiveness. I'll find my own way. I'll get up there, you'll see." But sadly, you will not.

The surprising thing is not that there is only one way to heaven; the incredible thing is that there is a way at all. It's amazing that God would even care about saving our sorry selves and giving us forgiveness.

The choice you must make is to believe. The obstacle you must overcome is pride.

The Time Is Right Now

My heart's desire is that every person reading these words will choose God's forgiveness if you have not done so already, or if you are in doubt about your standing before God.

So I have to ask you, *do you understand?*

Do you understand that sin is your problem and hell is your future?

Do you understand that forgiveness is your need and Christ is your provision?

Do you understand that faith must be your choice, and you must make the choice now?

Deuteronomy 30:15 says, **"I have set before you today life and good, death and evil."** So choose . . . choose life.

Are you ready to choose God's forgiveness? Your choice will establish your identity with God, who has loved you with an everlasting love.

How awesome it is that by God's Spirit, you and I can connect now, one-on-one through this book. As though God were pleading through me,

I implore you: be reconciled to God through faith in Christ. The choice isn't my way or your way; it's God's way and our only hope.

Some of you reading these words may feel very sure that you're not forgiven. You know that you don't have God in your life. If you were to die today, you would fall straight into hell. That can all change for you right now. God loves you, and He will forgive you if you get over your pride and run to Him in repentance and faith. You can be forgiven right here and now. You can get your eternal destiny settled once and for all.

Others of you are not sure if you have been forgiven by God. This doesn't happen by accident—you've got to be certain about this. You say, "I've prayed a prayer or walked an aisle, but my life is not the life of a follower of Jesus. My heart is so filled with selfishness. I'm not certain that I know Jesus Christ." Whether you know that you don't or don't know if you do, you can settle that right now.

What is more important than this? What else will matter a hundred years from today? Do you know Him, whom to know is life eternal (John 17:3)? Did you find in Him the forgiveness of your sin that you couldn't earn and you didn't deserve but only receive because of God's great love and the gift through His Son Jesus Christ? Can you say, "I ran to Him and threw my arms around Him and found in Him everything I had been looking and longing for?" If not, do you want to make that faith-run right now? God loves you. His arms are open. He will receive you.

If you want to know that your sins are forgiven; if you accept the fact that you're a sinner; if you believe that Jesus died to pay the penalty for your sin; and if you want to confess Christ now, personally, pray to Him now in your own words, something like this:

Lord, I know that I'm a sinner. This isn't news to me; I admit it. I know I've broken Your law. I know I've failed You in ways that I do not even know. I know I've not been the person that You want me to be. I know that I deserve Your judgment. I deserve hell. I'm not resisting that reality. My pride is broken. My stubbornness is melting. I just want to know that I'm forgiven. I want to receive the gift of eternal life that You are offering and I am receiving. I choose God's forgiveness. I need it. Come into my life, Lord Jesus. I want to settle this once and for all. Forgive me, Lord Jesus—wash me and make me clean. Grant to me according to Your mercy the gift of eternal life. I receive it now, and I thank You for forgiving my sin. In Your Holy Name. Amen.

In this chapter, you have had set before you life and death, heaven and hell, forgiveness and punishment, Christ or your own way. Now you're responsible to choose. This is the most important choice you can make. And with all my heart I tell you that it will change your life forever.

Make the choice. Say it from your heart: *I choose God's forgiveness.*

A Choice to Make

Acknowledge the Choice

- What is your answer to God's question: Why should I let you into heaven?
- What would it take for you to admit that you can't provide a reason in your behavior or character that would merit acceptance under a perfect, holy standard?

Consider the Choice

- How would you feel about introducing yourself to someone with the phrase, "Hello, my name is _____, and I'm a sinner"?
- What do you find most appealing about the possibility that God forgives sinners?
- Given what you have read and thought about up to this point, how do you think your life would be changed if you accepted God's forgiveness?

Make the Choice

- Say the prayer above on your knees with your hands open and your eyes lifted to God.
- Call two friends and tell them what you prayed and why.
- Allow God's forgiveness to eclipse your will and become your identity.

A Choice Prayer

Loving and forgiving God, thank You for loving me enough to let me see enough of who I am to realize I need You. Thank You for Your promise to forgive me, particularly when I see how unworthy I am. Thank You for the ongoing experience I can have of relying on Your faithfulness every morning, knowing that Your love and forgiveness go with me throughout the day and are just as available when the evening falls as they were when the day began. And thank You for all You did, Jesus, to make forgiveness a reality I can choose. And I claim it in Your name. Amen.

PART II

MY AUTHORITY CHOICES

Choice 3: I Choose Jesus Christ as Lord

Choice 4: I Choose the Bible as God's Word

We're continuing to build a strong foundation of good choices. The first two walls were identity choices: I choose to believe that I am loved by God, and I choose to believe that I am forgiven by God. These are foundational because whenever we struggle with doubts about our place in this world, we can anchor our hearts to our identity in God and what He declares to be true about us.

Now to the other two walls of the foundation—authority choices.

The concept of authority has fallen on bad times in recent years. Just say the word, and people wince. In some ways that's not surprising. A shameful parade of professors, politicians, and, tragically, pastors and priests have abused their authority and betrayed their followers. As a result many are wounded, and most are suspicious at best regarding people in authority.

The sad fallout from the abuse of authority is that good authority and God's authority are routinely questioned too. We need to recognize that godly authority is one of the great gifts God has given humanity. God's authority is a protection in this world from the dangers we are deaf to and the devastation we are blind to. God's authority is expressed to us in the person of His Son and in the blueprint He has written called the Bible. The alternative is not escaping authority, for everyone is under the authoruty of someone or something. Everyone is making choices based upon some reference point. This is only about choosing *who* your authority is going to be, rather than stumbling into it. Making these two authority choices puts us in a position to be protected no matter what happens and to prosper in every important way. They are the next two choices that will change your life forever.

Beginning Prayer

Father, I ask for Your help in understanding what it means that Your Son, Jesus Christ, and Your Word, the Bible, are my authority. By Your Spirit, cause it to become so real to me that I can embrace my choices with confidence. I pray, God, for my own blessing and benefit, that Your Spirit would seal this truth in my heart. Reshape my thinking with Your thoughts. Work in my spirit. Apply Your Word in my life. Guide me in Your truth so that I would discover safety and happiness under the umbrella of Your authority. In Jesus' name. Amen.

[Jesus] is the image of the invisible God, the firstborn of all creation. For by him all things were created, in heaven and on earth, visible and invisible, whether thrones or dominions or rulers or authorities—all things were created through him and for him. And he is before all things, and in him all things hold together. And he is the head of the body, the church. He is the beginning, the firstborn from the dead, that in everything he might be preeminent. For in him all the fullness of God was pleased to dwell, and through him to reconcile to himself all things, whether on earth or in heaven, making peace by the blood of his cross.

—Colossians 1:15–20

I Choose Jesus Christ as Lord

*Everyone serves someone, even if it's himself. Jesus Christ
is the only one who loves me unconditionally and forgives
me completely. I choose Him as my Lord.*

Everybody serves somebody. Everybody has somebody in charge of his life.
I'm not sure that Bob Dylan got a lot of things right, but he was right on
target when he wrote the song, "Gotta Serve Somebody."

You remember Bob Dylan? A cultural idol of the '60s, Dylan sang lyrics
laced with edgy social commentary, religious language, and philosophical
themes. In 1999, *Time* included him among its hundred most influential
people of the twentieth century. In 2004, *Rolling Stone* ranked him as the
number two recording artist of all time. He's been nominated several
times for the Nobel Prize. His most recent album, *Modern Times*, entered
the *Billboard* charts at number one in 2006, which made him the oldest
person ever to have reached that mark. So the guy is a musical icon with
major impact.

Gotta Serve Somebody

After a motorcycle accident in the late 1960s, Dylan began a spiritual search.
In the '70s he claimed to be born again, and soon after he wrote "Gotta Serve
Somebody." In classic Dylan style and rhymes, he described the various roles
a person may have that might look like ultimate human independence—

from rock-stardom to career superstar—but it all comes down to serving somebody. Dylan even drew the ultimate distinction between serving the devil or the Lord; everybody's gonna serve somebody.

When the song was released, it became an immediate Grammy nominee and a platinum hit. But the song and rumors of his religious conversion really upset his peers. John Lennon, within months of eternity himself, countered Dylan's song with his own, titled "Serve Yourself."

Dylan's conversion may not have been genuine because within a couple of years, he was telling David Gates of *Newsweek*, "This is the flat-out truth: I find the religiosity and philosophy in the music. I don't find it anywhere else. Songs—that's my religion. I don't adhere to rabbis or preachers or evangelists and all of that. I believe in the songs."[1] His lyrics may have pointed out that people serve either the devil or the Lord, but he later seemed to indicate there might be other "somebodies" who ultimately could be served.

So who is he serving? Who is his final authority in life? It is difficult to tell. The point is, he's right: everybody is serving somebody. What's more, we all choose whom we will serve. Let's look at some common choices:

- *Some people choose an esteemed person to serve.*
  They look to an authority figure, a pastor, a professor, or a politician. The choice is dangerous, of course, because if they look closely enough, they will see that person's massive imperfections and become disillusioned: "Why am I serving *him*?" Then they will flee to find some other idol to emulate.

- *Some people serve a close relationship as their ultimate authority.*
  "I just do whatever my wife wants." Or, "My son has to be happy; if he's not happy, then I can't be either." Psychologists have written a lot about the lack of health in that approach to life (some call it codependency), where you're so wired into another person that your life goes sideways if his gets offtrack.

- *Some people decide to serve a mission, a value, or an organization.*
  My company, my club, my church—we feed the poor, we save the trees, or we elect the best possible candidates. I'm sure you live near or work with people who are always raising the flag for some important cause.

- *Some people serve a personal agenda.*
  This is very common. People set their eyes on accomplishment. *I'll get this degree; I'll reach this milestone; I'll break this record; I'll build this company; I'll establish this priority.* Of course, that's just a thinly veiled version of the most common one, the goal that most people are pursuing . . .

- *Most people serve themselves.*
  Lennon was right, or at least he was honest—serve yourself, suit yourself, help yourself, and take care of yourself. This is said or thought billions of times a day. Most people live by this philosophy. *At the end of the day, I'll do what works for me. I'm the one who's in charge here.* That's the religion of the masses.

If you have never made a choice, a real choice, for Jesus Christ as Lord, you probably are on this last agenda by default. You may not feel like you chose, but by not making a deliberate, conscious choice, you have been swept up in the cultural current and carried along in the whitewater of living for self.

You Choose Who You Serve

Before we go any further in this discussion, I think it's important to establish that *you* choose whom you serve. The most powerful aspect of this assertion is that since your life can be different, your choice to change it is right within your grasp. This is far truer than people are willing to admit. The person who adamantly claims he has no choice is at that moment making the choice to articulate his frustration about the pressure from others to choose what he wants. Still, we choose whether or not to accept the pressure.

Forget about all the excuses—you choose whom you serve. You don't fall into servitude; it's not an accident. You don't enter servitude by default from your environment or from something in your background. You choose whom you serve. Your mama doesn't choose for you. Your pastor can't choose for you. As much as someone might love you, he can't choose for you whom you will serve. Even God, who loves you perfectly, will not choose for you. There are simply some crucial decisions you have to make for yourself. The ball is in your court. Joshua was right when he challenged Israel, **"Choose this day whom you will serve"** (Joshua 24:15).

There's no better way to illustrate this fact than by the now-infamous poem "Invictus," written by William Henley more than a hundred years ago. This poem is a troubling celebration of *I am in control of my life.* Among those who have used it to define their lives was Timothy McVeigh, the Oklahoma City bomber, who wrote out the words to this poem as he sat on death row. He left it on the table as he walked out to be executed for his murderous actions. He must have known the words by heart:

> Out of the night that covers me,
>   Black as the Pit from pole to pole,
> I thank whatever gods may be
>   For my unconquerable soul.
>
> In the fell clutch of circumstance
>   I have not winced or cried aloud.
> Under the bludgeonings of chance
>   My head is bloody, but unbowed.
>
> It matters not how straight the gate,
>   How charged with punishments the scroll,
> I am the master of my fate:
>   I am the captain of my soul.[2]

As McVeigh scribbled those words on the exit ramp of life, he was flat-out choosing. He made the final choice not to change whom he served, and then he went to account for his choices. He was the lord of his life.

Though not as obvious, most of the people we meet are on that program, whether they could quote the poem or not. Oh, it's unlikely they will ever act out their philosophy in such a horrific way as did McVeigh, but their self-centered universe is the same. Contrast this attitude with a young woman named Dorothea Day, who once was mesmerized by "Invictus." It characterized her life and her mission until she met Jesus Christ as Lord. She was so repulsed by what she had formerly believed that she wrote a poem in the early twentieth century to parallel her old master of self and declare the new choice she was making. Her poem is entitled "Conquered":

> Out of the light that dazzles me,
> Bright as the sun from pole to pole,
> I thank the God I know to be,
> For Christ—the Conqueror of my soul.
>
> Since His the sway of circumstance,
> I would not wince nor cry aloud.
> Under the rule which men call chance,
> My head, with joy, is humbly bowed.
>
> I have no fear though straight the gate:
> He cleared from punishment the scroll.
> Christ is the Master of my fate!
> Christ is the Captain of my soul!

"Invictus" and "Conquered" are not opposite sides of the same coin. These two people made completely different choices about whom they were going to serve. And those choices led to radically different outcomes. You choose every day who is going to be in charge.

Jesus Christ Is Lord

One day we will all stand before Jesus Christ the Lord. It's important you know now just who it is you're going to meet. Let's read a couple of Bible passages that bear this out.

The formal title of the last book in the Bible is "The Revelation of Jesus Christ." It begins with the writer, the apostle John, having a personal encounter with Jesus:

> Then I turned to see the voice that was speaking to me, and on turning I saw seven golden lampstands, and in the midst of the lampstands one like a son of man, clothed with a long robe and with a golden sash around his chest. The hairs of his head were white, like white wool, like snow. His eyes were like a flame of fire, his feet were like burnished bronze, refined in a furnace, and his voice was like the roar of many waters. In his right hand he held seven stars, from his mouth came a sharp two-edged sword, and his face was like the sun shining in full strength. When I saw him, I fell at his feet as though dead.
>
> —Revelation 1:12–17*a*.

That's Jesus Christ the Lord.

Revelation 19 describes the Second Coming of Jesus Christ. Someday our eyes will look upon this:

> Then I saw heaven opened, and behold, a white horse! The one sitting on it is called Faithful and True, and in righteousness he judges and makes war. His eyes are like a flame of fire, and on his head are many diadems [crowns], and he has a name written that no one knows but himself. He is clothed in a robe dipped in blood, and the name by which he is called is The Word of God. And the armies of heaven, arrayed in fine linen, white and pure, were following him on white horses. From his mouth comes a sharp sword with which to strike down the nations, and he will rule them with a rod of iron. He will tread the winepress of the fury of the wrath of God the Almighty.

On his robe and on his thigh he has a name written, King of kings and Lord of lords.

—Revelation 19:11–16

Get all the kings of the earth together. Get every person who has ruled with authority. Get everyone who was ever in charge of anything together—Jesus rules over all of them. He stands supreme. Jesus Christ is the King of kings. He's the Lord of lords—yes, the *true* Jesus is Lord!

But Are You Following the Right Jesus?

Quite often, people hear those passages we just read and say, "Well, that Revelation description of Jesus is not the Jesus I know. The Jesus I believe in would never dress in those clothes or act that way." If your response runs along those lines, you might be embracing a caricature of Jesus.

Have you ever been to the fair or to the circus and seen the artists who offer to draw a caricature of you? You'd definitely recognize yourself in the picture, but the style exaggerates certain features, and you end up with a distorted version of who you are.

Many people are following a caricature of Jesus—a distorted picture of the real Jesus, with certain features exaggerated or twisted from the true Savior of Scripture. You need to make sure you have not embraced a man-made, unbiblical picture of the real Jesus. The consequences of that choice are eternal and devastating. Are you following the real Jesus with no features avoided, no features neglected, and no features exaggerated? You have to get this right.

In fact, if you need to do a check on what caricatures you must reject, I've made a list of some distorted versions of Jesus in our day. There'll be some similarities to the real Jesus, but none of these represent Him accurately. None of these caricatures ever spoke to the wind, hung on a cross, or rose from the dead. And not one of these caricatured versions of Jesus will take you to heaven. None of them will change your life.

- *Caricature #1: Jesus is my buddy.*
  Yeah, Jesus and me, we're on cool, casual terms. Listen, Jesus is not our pal. His idea of hanging out usually involves a significant amount of discomfort and pain. No, Jesus may call us His friends in John 15, but if He showed up right now, I guarantee we would not be slapping Him on the back or offering to high-five Him. If He ever appeared in your vicinity, you would fast be on your face in deep humility. The real Jesus is Lord.

- *Caricature #2: Jesus is my safety net or my good luck charm.*
  Jesus is there when I need Him. If I fall, I'll call out to Him, but other than those rare occasions, He and I are pretty much on a don't-call-us-we'll-call-you kind of program. He's like a good luck charm that I wear around my neck. No, Jesus is not lucky; He is Lord. Does He take care of His own? Absolutely. But He is so much more than a safety net.

- *Caricature #3: Jesus is my religious artifact.*
  Jesus is over at the church. He knows His place, and I'm sure He wouldn't be comfortable out in the world where I live. There are pictures of Him that I kiss, and every day we go through a little ritual with candles and jewelry, and I get some vague sentimental feelings. I can't explain—so don't ask me. I like the warm feelings, and I like to look at the sweet Jesus. No, that's not the biblical Jesus. He is alive. If death and a rock-hewn tomb couldn't hold Him, He certainly won't fit in any display case we construct. He is the one who is working and stirring in people's hearts through His Word and by His Spirit. He is Lord.

- *Caricature #4: Jesus is my meal ticket.*
  I used to be messed up until I learned that Jesus wants to heal all my diseases, fill my bank account with money, and answer my every prayer. Jesus makes everything perfect for me. As long as He is taking care of my needs and making life good, I'll call Him anything He wants to be called. No, if this is the Jesus you're following, you're in

for a world of disappointment. Jesus isn't a magic genie who shows up every morning while you're having coffee and asks, *Is there anything I can do for you?* Jesus doesn't serve us, we serve Him! He is the Lord. If the reason you're following Jesus is because you want to be healthy or wealthy, you are still serving yourself.

Jesus is not the key that unlocks the door to every longing in our sinful hearts. This is such a North American, Western world, last century distortion of the real Jesus Christ. It's true that the Lord has done great things for us, but His blessings are only part of His greatness and authority.

- *Caricature #5: Jesus is my social conscience.*
  I don't really want to hear about the Cross or the empty tomb. Keep heaven and hell to yourself, and for sure, don't tell me about my need for the forgiveness of my sins. Jesus is my motivator toward horizontal goodness. He was the nicest man that ever lived, and I want to be a nice person, too, and so I think about Jesus and the nice things he did. Jesus is our example, and He does help us love our neighbor, but the political, Peace Corps Jesus won't take you far in this life, and He won't get you to any place good in the life to come.

The problem with a caricature is that the truth is in there, but it's distorted by an emphasis of one thing to the exclusion of others. Make sure you're following the real Jesus. Who is He? I would love to tell you!

Jesus Christ Is Lord

When you think *Jesus is Lord*, start with Colossians 1:15–20:

He is the image of the invisible God, the firstborn of all creation. For by him all things were created, in heaven and on earth, visible and invisible, whether thrones or dominions or rulers or authorities—all things were created through him and for him. And he is before all things, and in him all things hold together. And he is the head of the body, the church. He is the beginning, the firstborn from the dead, that in everything he might be pre-eminent. For in him all the fullness of God was pleased to dwell, and through him to reconcile to himself all things, whether on earth or in heaven, making peace by the blood of his cross.

Let's look closer at these verses for insight into Jesus' lordship.

- *Jesus Christ Is Lord: He Is Unique.*
  "He is the image of the invisible God" (v. 15). There have been many imposters and pretenders, but there is only one Jesus Christ the Lord. He is unparalleled. He is unprecedented. There is no one else like Him. He stands in the solitude of Himself in unbreakable solidarity within the Triune God. To compare anyone else who has ever lived out a life in this world to Jesus Christ is foolishness. He stands alone.

  Colossians 1:15 says, **"He is the image of the invisible God."** You can easily substitute the word *icon* for the word *image* in this description, which is the word used in the Greek New Testament—*eikon*. It means that Jesus is the exact replica of God. It's way more than, "Hey, you look like your mom." The term goes to the core of His being; Jesus is the icon, the visible representation of eternal God. Looking like someone is one thing; *being* exactly like someone is another thing entirely—that's Jesus.

  Jesus is the only God we'll ever see. No one can see God the Father and live. I don't understand all the dynamics of the Trinity, but I believe there is one God eternally existing in three persons. Jesus is the only person of the Godhead that we will ever see—which is OK because seeing Jesus will be enough. Hebrews 1:3 says, **"[Jesus] is the radiance of the glory of God."** John 1:14 and 18 explain, **"And the Word became flesh and dwelt among us, and we have seen his glory, glory as of the only Son from the Father, full of grace and truth . . . No one has ever seen God; the only God, who is at the Father's side, he has made him known."**

Colossians 1:15 goes on to say He is **"the firstborn of all creation."** That phrase has been problematic in the church over the centuries. The Arians in the first century and the Jehovah's Witnesses in the last century have taken that word *firstborn* and mistakenly interpreted it to mean that Jesus is not God. They say, "Jesus is not God Himself. He's just one of God's best creations." That's a misunderstanding of the word *firstborn*.

In our day, there are few cultural rules related to birth order, but in the Old Testament world, the firstborn male in the family got half of everything, and the rest of the children had to split up the leftovers. That was the way the inheritance system worked for millennia. This concept was so ingrained in society that eventually *firstborn* came to mean "unique in rank and privilege."

For example, the description *firstborn* was ascribed to things other than family order. Israel was called God's firstborn in Exodus 4:22. It wasn't the first nation, but it was unique in rank and privilege. In Psalm 89:27, David is called the firstborn, although he was the eighth child (and the youngest) in his family. David was also unique in rank and privilege.

So when Colossians 1:15 says that Jesus Christ is **"the invisible God, the firstborn of all creation,"** God is confirming in His Word that Jesus Christ the Lord is the second person of the Trinity. He's not a guy like us who got a good break. He is God of gods. No one can be compared to Him. If this challenges your capacity to comprehend, welcome to the club. Many people a lot smarter than you or me have been humbled by the mystery of Jesus' deity but have accepted it rather than deciding: *Well, if I can't fully understand it, it must not be true.*

- *Jesus Christ Is Lord: He Is the Creator.*
Who created the universe? Out of whose mouth did the words, **"Let there be light"** come (Genesis 1:3)? Colossians 1 goes on to say, **"For by him all things were created"** (v. 16). Jesus Christ, the preincarnate second person of the Trinity, spoke the entire universe

into existence. It was Jesus who breathed life into Adam. It was Jesus who took Adam's rib and made Eve. God the Father did it all through Jesus. Get that into your head when you're thinking about whom you are following. Jesus made it all.

He made it all. Can we possibly comprehend what's captured in the word *all*? Do you have any idea how big the universe is? I love reading about science. So here's my latest round of research to help us blow our minds on the creation Jesus spoke into reality.

If we could get into a spacecraft and leave right now from Earth to travel to the end of our solar system at the speed of light (186,000 miles per second), the trip would take seven hours. Those solar system maps that we used to have in our grade school classrooms were not even close to scale. The idea of a cozy little cluster of planets hanging out in space is a little misleading. In order to construct our planetary neighborhood to scale, we would have to make Earth the size of a pea and put Jupiter, about the size of an orange, a thousand feet away. Pluto, as big as a grain of sand, would be a mile and a half away. That's just *our* solar system.

Scientists now number the galaxies at 140 billion, each of them filled with billions of stars, each one representing an innumerable variety of solar systems. The vast Milky Way galaxy is merely one gathering of star-suns similar to ours. Hebrews 1 says that Jesus Christ stood in eternity past and looked over the void of nothing and spoke—and the worlds were formed. That's the Jesus whom you and I are supposed to be following.

- *Jesus Christ Is Lord: He Is Our Goal.*
  "For by him all things were created, in heaven and on earth, visible and invisible, whether thrones or dominions or rulers or authorities—all things were created through him and for him" (Colossians 1:16). For whom was the universe made? It was made *for Him*, for Jesus. He is the ultimate reason everything exists. He owns it and made it for His purposes.

  When the apostle Paul wrote the letter of Colossians to the early church, Jesus' lordship was being questioned. Some were saying that Jesus was an angel—albeit a really good angel. This explains the list in verse 16 that says that Jesus created everything, **"whether thrones or dominions or rulers or authorities"**—all referring to the angelic realm. Jesus not only wasn't an angel, He *created* the angels. Don't get it confused, Colossians proclaims to the early church and the church today. We were made for Christ.

Everything hinges on this: Are you following the biblical Jesus?

- *Jesus Christ Is Lord: He Is the Source.*
  "All things were created through him and for him. And he is before all things" (vv. 16, 17). Jesus Christ always existed. **"He is before all things"** (v. 17). Before there was time, there was Jesus. There was never a time when there was not Jesus.

"And in him all things hold together" (v. 17). What an awesome assertion. In Jesus Christ, the universe is held together. We've talked about the macro-universe; now let's talk about the micro-universe.

This staggers the imagination. Do you know how small an atom is? (Just say no.) Atoms are the building blocks of molecules, which are the building blocks of matter. Everything is made up of molecules, and molecules are made up of atoms. Atoms are so small that half a million can hide behind a single human hair.

Back in high school science class, we learned that one of the smallest living organisms is a paramecium. We would place a drop of stagnant water under a microscope and see a tiny world of life busily swimming around. But if we wanted to see a paramecium with our naked eyes, we would have to blow up the drop of water (and everything in it) until it was forty feet across. To allow the atoms from which that paramecium are made to come into view, we would have to expand that single drop of water until it was fifteen *miles* wide.

Here are more stunning insights from science class. If you drill down to the center of an oxygen atom, you'll see a nucleus with eight positively and eight negatively charged particles. Coulomb's law states that like charges repel one another. Given this law, scientists can't figure out why the nucleus of every atom isn't flying apart. Everything made of atoms (in short, every single thing) should be exploding this moment.

In fact, Karl Darrow, a physicist at Bell Labs, says this: "Do you grasp what this implies? It means all the mass of nuclei have no right to be alive at all. Indeed, they never should have been created, and if created they should have blown up instantly. Yet there they all are . . . Some inflexible inhibition is holding them relentlessly together."[3] Yes, and that would be Jesus. I would submit to you that the creative force of Jesus Christ is still at work in the universe in this moment, holding together something that stymies and mystifies scientific fact itself. In Him all things are held together.

Someday Jesus Christ will remove His hand and His hold from the earth. Second Peter 3:10–13 warns us of the day when Jesus the Lord will withdraw His sustaining influence, and the earth itself will melt with such fervent heat that it will make a nuclear explosion seem like a Bic lighter. Our earthly existence is being held together this moment by the second person of the Trinity. This is the Jesus whom we love and are serving. This is Jesus Christ the Lord.

- *Jesus Christ Is Lord: He Is the Head.*
  Colossians 1:18 continues, **"He is the head of the body, the church."** What do you call a body without a head? A corpse. We would all agree that a body without a head has no future. I'd say things are pretty well over once you lose your head. The head is the control center: all of your thinking, smelling, tasting, speaking, hearing, and seeing happens right there above your shoulders.

  Think about Christ's church worldwide—all of His followers everywhere. He's the head of the body, the focal point. Jesus owns the world as its Creator, but He maintains a special relationship with His church as Lord, as head.

- *Jesus Christ Is Lord: He Is Preeminent.*

Lastly, and very importantly, **"that in everything he might be preeminent"** (v. 18). The NASB translation says, **"that He Himself will come to have first place in everything"** (v. 18). Jesus Christ must be honored, worshipped, and adored. He has to be our total focus, our number one authority.

He's got to have first place in our church.

He's got to have first place in our family.

But none of those things will ever be possible unless He has first place in our hearts. He can't be first anywhere for us until He's first *in* us.

People read this amazing profile of Jesus, and they sometimes wonder, *Doesn't it miff God the Father to see all the attention going to the Son?* That makes me smile. Our family loves to play games, and like most people, I like to win. But it pleases me more when my kids beat me. I have so much joy in seeing them succeed and prosper. Granted, this is just an accommodation to our understanding of how almighty God feels. But don't worry about God the Father—He wants nothing more than the exaltation of His Son. Honor coming to the Son gives the Father great pleasure and divine satisfaction.

Colossians 1:19 explains, **"For in him all the fullness of God was pleased to dwell."** Jesus wasn't speaking in hyperbole when He said, **"I and the Father are one"** (John 10:30). The better we know Jesus, the better we know God the Father (John 14:7). Jesus also said, **"Because I live, you also will live. In that day you will know that I am in my Father, and you in me, and I in you"** (John 14:19b–20). If all of the above is true, wouldn't it make sense to acknowledge Jesus as Lord now and continuously? God's Word tells us that God gives us sufficient reasons to recognize His lordship in this life or we will be convinced in the next when it's too late. This is because . . .

Someday Every Knee Will Bow to His Authority

Someday Jesus Christ will step onto the world scene and bring this whole unfolding drama to a conclusion. His presence and appearance will bring all of us to our knees; every knee will bow (Philippians 2:9–11). I'm not sure *when* it will happen, I'm not sure *how* it will happen, I just know it *will* happen.

Nothing will stop that day from coming. In fact, compared to what Jesus Christ has already done throughout history, including the creation of the universe itself, getting all of the people from this tiny planet in our little solar system to bow before Him will be a nonissue.

Every person who exits this life in a sin-darkened state will bow before Jesus Christ, only then to be separated from Him. Every suicide bomber horrified not to meet a harem in eternity, every addict who chooses his substance over his Savior, and every religious person who thought he could get to God on his own terms—every knee will bow. No one is going to wander around hell wondering how he got there. They will know. They will realize that they admitted Jesus' lordship too late to do them any good.

Romans 14:11 says, **"As I live, says the Lord, every knee shall bow to me."** God demonstrates great patience and long-suffering as He bears with the rebellion of a dark, wicked, stubborn human race. But He will not do so forever.

Remember who we've seen Jesus to be? Yes, it's true He became a man and lived among us, but that was one piece of the story. Philippians 2:5–11 puts that in perspective. Before He came, **"Christ Jesus, who, though he was in the form of God, did not count equality with God a thing to be grasped"** (v. 6). In other words, He didn't have to grasp for it; He had equality with God. And He didn't have to hang on to it for dear life. He demonstrated His equality with God by stepping down!

For Jesus, stepping down from equality with God was a giant step: **"but made himself nothing, taking the form of a servant, being born in the likeness of men. And being found in human form, he humbled himself"** (vv. 7–8a). The second person of the Trinity, the Creator of the universe, became a man, with all of the indignity and limitations of humanity. But He didn't stop there. **"He humbled himself by becoming obedient to the point of death"** (v. 8*b*). And as if that wasn't enough, **"even death on a cross."** What did God the Father think about all of this? I'm sure God the Father was counting the seconds till He could get Him back up where He belonged.

Now and for all time, **"God has highly exalted him and bestowed on him the name that is above every name, so that at the name of Jesus every knee should bow, in heaven and on earth and under the earth, and every tongue confess that Jesus Christ is Lord"** (v. 9–11). Every person is going to say it: *Jesus Christ is Lord.* "Well, I'm not much of a public speaker," you might reply. Oh, but you will declare Jesus is Lord. You will account for yourself. You will answer for the choices you have made.

The Lordship Debate

Some people say that bowing to Jesus' lordship is a salvation decision. Other people say it's a second decision. First you receive Christ as Savior, and then you come back a while later or down the road at a summer camp when you make Him Lord.

First, to clarify, *we* don't make Jesus anything, especially Lord. Jesus *is* Lord. I think we've seen already that Jesus is bigger than anything we can do to affect Him. You also don't need to feel sorry for Jesus. Some people quip, "Oh, poor Jesus, out there knocking at the door of your heart. He must be so cold out there. Won't you let Him in?" We've also got to lose that "invite Jesus into my heart" language that is so appealing to children but is completely unattested in all of God's Word. Jesus is Lord. You fall on your knees before Him in a crisis, and you embrace all that He is.

The whole debate revolves around whether you can be saved without knowing that Jesus is Lord. I'm not really into that debate, but here's what I know for sure. If you are a true follower of Jesus when the reality of His lordship or aspects of His lordship dawn upon you, you cannot reject it and still claim to be one of His followers. You may have had a moment when you acknowledged the lordship of Jesus Christ, when you understood with your mind and you embraced it with your heart, but lordship is a lot more than throwing a stick in the fire, walking the aisle, or raising your hand. The lordship of Christ in your life is the litmus test of a truly transformed heart. Jesus Himself says in Matthew 7:21, **"Not everyone who says to me, 'Lord, Lord,' will enter the kingdom of heaven, but the one who does the will of my Father who is in heaven."**

Your life needs to match your acknowledgement of Jesus' lordship by choosing one moment at a time that He is in charge of your life.

We can recover eternally despite some bad choices, but we cannot get this one wrong. We can avoid God, but not for more than a lifetime. Jesus Christ is Lord, and someday every knee will bow to Him as the rightful ruler. The Master. The One in charge. He is our ultimate authority.

We Can Bow Willingly Now

If life is about one thing, it's about getting this ultimate authority relationship figured out. Nothing is more important to settle in our lives than to acknowledge and bow to Jesus Christ as Lord. No matter what we accomplish in this world, a hundred years from today, if we didn't get this figured out, we will have nothing. You and I must get this settled.

We have but one mission in life: to figure out who's really in charge. It's not Washington, or Hollywood, or Wall Street, and it's not you and me. It's Jesus Christ the Lord.

You can choose Jesus as Lord today. How tragic if you reject His rightful place in your life and someday in hell look back on today and realize that you had your chance to choose differently . . . *I was reading that James what's-his-name's book, and there was that moment when I knew. I knew I needed to choose Jesus as Lord, and I remember I chose not to choose.* Don't be deceived into thinking you have plenty of time to decide; your opportunity to choose Jesus Christ as Lord is now. Hebrews 3:15 warns, **"Today, if you hear his voice, do not harden your hearts."**

Bowing to His Authority Is Obeying His Commands

You say, "James, I will bow, I want to bow. How do I choose His authority?"

Well, in every decision there is a crisis and a process. The crisis is a decision. I understand it with my mind: Jesus Christ is Lord. Then the process: bowing to his authority means obeying His commands. Knowing it, saying it, and living it are all part of a life in which Jesus is Lord.

At the end of the day, the ultimate test of lordship is not the crisis of deciding that you believe this but the process of allowing your will to submit to His at the point of pressure, the place where He and you might disagree on what to choose. He becomes Lord in your life as you choose His choices above your own. Jesus as Lord is chosen in a thousand daily decisions, each one taking your life to a better place:

> THE ULTIMATE TEST OF LORDSHIP IS NOT THE CRISIS OF DECIDING THAT YOU BELIEVE THIS BUT THE PROCESS OF ALLOWING YOUR WILL TO SUBMIT TO HIS AT THE POINT OF PRESSURE, THE PLACE WHERE HE AND YOU MIGHT DISAGREE ON WHAT TO CHOOSE.

- If I were in charge, I would do _____ with my life. But Jesus is Lord, and I choose His way, day after day in every area.

- If I were in charge, I would do _____ with my finances, but Jesus is Lord, and this is how I will save/spend what I've been given to use for Him.

- If I were in charge, I would do _____ right now in

my marriage, but I'm not in charge. He is Lord, and I will do what His Word says.

- If I were in charge, I'd go in Monday morning and tell my boss a few things I've been wanting to tell him for a long time, things he deserves to hear. But Jesus Christ is Lord, and I am His representative, so I will not say what satisfies my flesh. God help me, I will do what my Master would want me to do. He is Lord.

In this moment, I am concerned about you coming to the crisis of agreeing that Jesus is Lord. I want you to have that now, if you've never had it before. But I'm equally concerned about the process of living out His lordship on a daily basis. He's the Master. When He says jump, I say, "How high?" This willing obedience is foundational to a lifetime of good choices. All the good that God wants to bring into your life comes from this place of submission.

God loves you.

God forgives you.

He will be the authority in your life. Don't stiffen your neck to that—embrace it as the good news that it is. Do it now while you can. Jesus Christ is Lord.

A Choice to Make

Acknowledge the Choice

- How did you respond to the discussion about authority in the early part of this chapter?

- What do you think about when you hear the phrase, *Jesus is Lord*?

- What would it mean personally for you to say, "Jesus is Lord"?

Consider the Choice

- Who are some of the somebodies you have served in your life? What have you learned from those situations?

- If you were to review the way you are responding to Jesus as Lord, what areas of your life do you realize might have to be significantly changed?

- What, if anything, stands in the way of your choice to recognize Jesus as Lord of your life? How valid is that barrier?

- How have you handled the thought that Jesus is Lord whether you choose or not? He is not affected by your choice; you are. Your choice gives you access to the benefits of His lordship, and you escape the results of trying to live outside His lordship.

Make the Choice

- Settle in your heart and mind that "Jesus is Lord" matters to you and the way you live, and then, perhaps, bow before Him in a declaration of allegiance to His authority.

- Give someone permission to point out when you are not living like Jesus is Lord.

- Read more about Jesus Christ the Lord, beginning with the dialogue by S. M. Lockridge titled "That's My King" in appendix A.

- Put into prayer your desire to recognize and live under the authority of Jesus Christ as you meditate on this:

I want to be a Christian who demonstrates the reality that Jesus Christ is Lord. I don't want people to see a battle in me. I don't want to be one who rationalizes little sins around the edges and defends my position by comparing myself to others. I want Jesus to be Lord of everything.

Lord of my disappointments.

Lord over the things that have hurt me that in my flesh I would hold onto, but by God's grace I can release.

Lord of my family.

Lord of my heart, my thoughts, my dreams, and my plans.

Lord of my relationships, my finances.

I choose Jesus as Lord . . . Lord of everything.

A Choice Prayer

It's true, Lord, I offer no resistance. In my heart I believe it—You are Lord. You are the Master. You are the authority. You are the One in charge. Be the Lord of everything.

Lord, thank You for Your Word. Thank You for the clarity of what You've said. We don't have to wonder about the truth—You've made it very clear through Your Word and Your Spirit who You are.

I ask You for the strength and the grace to embrace the real You. Forgive me where I've distorted You or allowed unbiblical teaching or my own selfish thoughts to soften Your character. You are the Lord. You are the ruler of the universe. All that I am belongs to You. All that I have belongs to You. You are my purpose. You are my reason. You are my future.

Lord, You are everything to me. Amen.

The law of the LORD is perfect, reviving the soul; the testimony of the LORD is sure, making wise the simple; the precepts of the LORD are right, rejoicing the heart; the commandment of the LORD is pure, enlightening the eyes; the fear of the LORD is clean, enduring forever; the rules of the LORD are true, and righteous altogether. More to be desired are they than gold, even much fine gold; sweeter also than honey and drippings of the honeycomb. Moreover, by them is your servant warned; in keeping them there is great reward.

—PSALM 19:7–11

I Choose the Bible as God's Word

When God's Word is my authority, it can change the
direction of my heart, mind, and feet. It is God's offering
of satisfaction for my every longing.

Our church has just emerged from a several-year process of building a new worship center on one campus and doing major building improvements on another. We now have one entire room dedicated to housing hundreds of blueprints with thousands of pages of architectural drawings with details covering every single aspect of these huge projects. I know more than I ever wanted to know about construction.

In the construction world, nothing good is built without a blueprint. The necessity of a plan is a universally accepted assertion that you'd have to be nutty not to know. Any time there is a problem or question, builders examine the blueprints. Every time there's an uncertainty or a perplexity, every time there's a question about what to do next, they go back to the blueprints.

Interestingly, though, the principle is not just true in the construction world. It's also true in life.

You can't build your finances without a blueprint.

You can't build your family without a blueprint.

You can't build your future without a blueprint.

You can't build your faith without a blueprint.

It's amazing to me how professionals in the construction trades would never try to build anything of value without a blueprint, but all the time people try to slap together some sort of life without a pattern or a plan. They reach for materials, cut without measuring, and hurriedly nail a bunch of stuff together randomly. *Bang! Bang! Cut, Cut!* And up goes all kinds of craziness in their lives—"Hey everyone! Look at what I built!" Even when things go wrong, they never go back to the blueprint—because they don't have one! Even as the horror at what they're building grows before their eyes, most never stop and say, "I've got to get a clear plan for my life. I've got to consult the blueprint."

You say, "Well, don't Christians get that?" Most people, even a lot of Christians, don't get the importance of operating from a blueprint—much less God's blueprint—as they build their lives. Christians create special problems because they know they have a blueprint, but they refuse or forget to check it for direction.

God Wrote the Blueprint for Human Happiness

God Himself authored all of the manufacturer's specifications for your happiness. He knows how you're put together; He knows how you work. He knows what will make you happy or miserable. He knows what will satisfy you and give you joy. He wrote the blueprint for your complete happiness.

When Jesus was just beginning His ministry, He went through an extraordinary experience that bears this out. In Matthew 4:1, "**Jesus was led up by the Spirit into the wilderness to be tempted by the devil.**"

Notice that He was led by the Spirit. God wanted Him in the wilderness. He wanted Jesus sifted and tested so that Hebrews 4:15 could say He "**in every respect has been tempted as we are, yet without sin.**" God Himself led Jesus up into the wilderness to be tempted by the enemy.

Part of the test included a forty-day fast. Just think, how hungry would you be after fasting for forty days and forty nights? Most of us miss a meal and get cranky. When I'm preaching on Sunday, I notice some people's eyes get a little crazy if I go over even by ten minutes. They're fussing, "I don't know how much longer I can sit here. What is he thinking, going on and on like this? We're hungry!" If we miss a meal, we go insane. If we miss a whole day's worth of food—well, let's just say most of us make sure that never happens!

So when we encounter Jesus in the wilderness, He has been fasting forty days. Some people question the forty-day thing, countering that there is no possible way Jesus could fast that long. But check this out: in Ireland in 1981, a group of people went on a hunger strike to protest British domination of Ireland. They drank water but ate no food. The first person died on day forty-seven. The last person in the hunger strike died on day seventy-six. So Jesus' forty-day fast is totally possible.

Let's put to rest right here the allegation that Jesus was a weak man. If we had no other evidence, this scenario proves Jesus' physical strength. On day forty, though, He was weak and He was very, very hungry. Look at Matthew 4:2: **"And after fasting forty days and forty nights, he was hungry."** Don't you love the way the Bible understates things? Of course He was hungry.

Jesus had a need, and Satan saw his opportunity. **"And the tempter came and said to him, 'If you are the Son of God, command these stones to become loaves of bread'"** (v. 3). Notice Satan's first taunt was to Jesus' identity (*"If* you are the Son of God . . ."). Next came the temptation to end the trial that the Spirit had led Him into—but end it on His own terms, in His own time, using His own power to usurp the authority of the Father.

To me, this whole scenario of Satan tempting Jesus Christ the Lord, the second person of the Trinity, is outrageous. It reminds me of something that happened recently when one of my good friends, Scott Pierre, and I were playing a round on a golf course—a golf course Scott owns.

He called me one summer night and said, "Hey, let's go play a few holes." When we arrived, we just jumped in a cart and off we went. We didn't have to go to the pro shop or sign up or pay for the time—we just went. Why? He owns the course.

So we got to this one hole, and the people there were playing it slowly, so we scooted around them and headed for the next hole. Not many people were on the course, and, well, he can do that because . . . he owns it.

The two of us could play faster, and by leapfrogging the slow pokes, neither they nor we would be inconvenienced, or so we thought. Some golfers don't like it when you go around them. One member of that foursome saw us teeing off for the next hole and walked over, screaming and cursing. "Who do you think you are? You can't jump around us. I'm so sick of people like you." And then he added the most amazing line as if on cue. He said, "What do you think, you own the course?"

I won't forget that great moment for a long time. I didn't say a single word, but my friend very calmly answered, "Well, sir, as a matter of fact, I do." The argument might not have been over, but the point was made. Ownership does have privileges.

Now, I recognize in comparison to Jesus' place in the scheme of things, this is a poor illustration, but climb up to what's happening here. Satan, the author of sin and all that is dark and evil in this world, taunts Jesus Christ, the Lord, the second person of the universe. *If you really are the Son of God.* Just think what *could* have happened in that moment. Jesus created and owns the universe; He holds it together. One of His creations, the chief fallen angel, was trying to tempt Him. He could have just lost it and obliterated all of creation in a moment, including Satan. But that wasn't the plan. Jesus, wanting to submit to His Father, handled the temptation the same way we must handle temptation. He gave us an example. If you want to defeat Satan, use the blueprint.

Notice what He did with Satan's goad, *If you are the Son of God, command these stones to become loaves of bread.* For a man who hadn't eaten in forty days, Satan's suggestion was probably pretty tempting. Remember Jesus' first miracle? He turned the water into wine so tasty that people said it was the best they'd ever had. Imagine the bread Jesus could have made from rocks. Would it have been a crusty French roll? Would it have been a piece of hot sourdough bread with butter dripping off the side? Jesus probably didn't think about it too long because His response to Satan was amazing and immediate. He handled the temptation the way that we need to handle it—with the Word of God.

When Satan lured Him through His hunger, Jesus answered, **"It is written"** (v. 4). Don't miss the way Jesus used God's Word to defeat temptation. When he replied, "It is written," He was referencing Deuteronomy 8:3, which described the way God dealt with the children of Israel on the wilderness journey: **"And he humbled you and let you hunger and fed you with manna . . . that he might make you know that man does not live by bread alone, but man lives by every word that comes from the mouth of the LORD."**

When you and I are confronted with temptation, we should immediately reference the blueprint. We should say, "The temptation says I should do _____ , but God's Word says I should do _____. I choose to follow the blueprint!"

Jesus was tempted three times, and each time He referenced the Scriptures (vv. 4, 7, and 10). Finally, He dismissed His enemy with scripture. *Be gone, Satan! For it is written.*

The power to dismiss the enemy is the power of the Word of God. When Satan stands in front of you and lies, *I think this would make your life go better,* you say, "Well, let me check with God's Word because it's the blueprint for human happiness. It is the manufacturer's specifications for all things that bring joy to the human heart. You think I should do _____, but here's what God's Word says."

The power to say no to temptation is the power of the Word of God. If you

> **THE POWER TO DISMISS THE ENEMY AND THE POWER TO SAY NO TO TEMPTATION IS THE POWER OF THE WORD OF GOD.**

find yourself in a situation where some temptation is being pressed upon you, don't even try to stand against it yourself. You don't have the power to resist it in your own strength. When James 4:7 says, **"Resist the devil, and he will flee from you,"** it doesn't mean get out your boxing gloves. It means draw the sword of the Spirit, the Word of God (Ephesians 6:17). Apply some truth to the error that's clouding your thinking. Satan is the father of lies—that's all he ever does. God's Word, however, is the true blueprint for human happiness. Without God's Word, you are lost and wandering in the darkness. With it, you can find everything that your heart has been looking for and longing for.

> **WITHOUT GOD'S WORD, YOU ARE LOST AND WANDERING IN THE DARKNESS. WITH IT, YOU CAN FIND EVERYTHING THAT YOUR HEART HAS BEEN LOOKING FOR AND LONGING FOR.**

"Man shall not live by bread alone" (Matt. 4:4). Most people live almost exclusively for their body's satisfaction. But even as a man, tempted with the exact things we are, even as a hungry man who hadn't swallowed a piece of food in forty days, even though weakened by extreme hunger, Jesus knew that body satisfaction is the B-version of human satisfaction.

There's another level called *soul* satisfaction where your heart finds its joy in obedience to God and its delight in God's Word, in His ways, and in His purposes for your life. This kind of satisfaction goes way beyond food. No food anywhere, no matter how hungry you are, can touch that place of soul satisfaction. No bread can give you the joy you feel when you're in sync with the God who loves you.

But what does God's Word offer to bring such satisfaction? My own experiments and experiences have led me to five deeply satisfying and practical gifts I find in God's Word. Each can be stated in a word. You can chase these five words all over Scripture:

- *Heaven*
  If you look to the future and are perplexed with what will happen to you at the end of this life, in God's Word you find heaven. You see the plan on how to go to heaven—you can't work for it or earn it, and you don't deserve it, but you receive it by faith. You get who's going to heaven and who's not. You see Jesus dying to give you heaven. You get the confidence **"to be absent from the body, and**

to be present with the Lord" (2 Corinthians 5:8 KJV). The fact of heaven is all over God's Word. So is the sobering message that everyone is going to hell unless they believe what God's Word says about how to go to heaven—that God loves you and sent His Son to die for you, and if you'll embrace Him by faith for the forgiveness of your sins, you can receive the free gift of eternal life.

Heaven will be beyond anything we could ever ask or imagine. Not just streets of gold and amazing food but things so mind-blowing God can't even describe them to us. **"Eye has not seen, nor ear heard, / Nor have entered into the heart of man / The things which God has prepared for those who love Him"** (1 Corinthians 2:9 NKJV).

God's Word gives us heaven.

- *Hope*

Another deeply satisfying gift I find again and again and again in God's Word is hope. Psalm 118:18 says, **"The LORD has disciplined me severely, but he has not given me over to death."** In other words, God is not done with me yet. Hope is the confident expectation that better things are ahead. I find most of us can identify an area of life in which we desperately need to hear God's promise of hope. We need to know that good things can still come for our future. We haven't so messed up our life that everything good is now past and all opportunities are gone.

I was not a great student in high school. I was distracted and lazy. But each September I entered the new school year wanting to work hard and get better grades. However, by Christmas it was like, *Yeah, that's probably not going to work out this semester.* That's the way it is with some people—they think, *Man, the midterms are already done. Even if I ace the final, I still won't get a good final grade.* The Bible gives us hope that it doesn't have to be that way. God's not done with us yet, and by making better choices, we can get to a better place. Today could mark a turn-around in your life.

Hope is the idea that it's not too late, no matter how many mistakes you've made. Your life could be better. Some of the things you've dreamed about can still be yours. You don't have to be trapped in this cycle of failing and falling and fumbling all the time. You can rise up and be who God wants you to be. That is hope. Do you feel it rising in your heart? Hope is found in God's Word. Hope isn't even that hard to find when you choose to find it in God's Word: **"But this I call to mind, / and therefore I have hope: / The steadfast love of the LORD never ceases; / his mercies never come to an end; / they are new every morning; / great is your faithfulness. / 'The LORD is my portion,' says my soul, / 'therefore I will hope in him'"** (Lamentations 3:21–24). Hope is in God's Word; it's there now, waiting for you.

- *Help*
  Here's another very practical component of soul satisfaction I find in Scripture. I find help. I find wisdom. I find direction. I find counsel and guidance on every important subject. God's Word is Resource Central. Psalm 118:21 says, **"I thank you that you have answered me."**

  I can't tell you how many times I've been perplexed, uncertain, and confused until the exact moment when God's Word has helped me. *What should I do? How could I ever get out of this? Where will this go, exactly?* I would not be where I am today if not for the help that I have found in God's Word. Have you learned what to do when your mind is confused and distorted and you're heading in the wrong direction? If you will get alone, open God's Word, and start to read, the Scripture will wash over your mind. It will clean up your faulty thinking, set your feet on a rock, and send you out in a good direction. Have you discovered this principle in your life? *What is the way, Lord? Show me the way.* Psalm 119:105 says, **"Your word is a lamp to my feet and a light to my path."** We get help from God's Word.

- *Healing*
  What a big deal this is—God's Word heals! Most of us have been

hurt by things that have happened in our lives. Everywhere we go, we carry around the disappointment of people or situations that have wounded us and circumstances that have developed differently than we planned. We wonder how we will ever get past these things. The idea of soul satisfaction seems foreign and very distant.

I would not be living my life today if it weren't for the healing that I find in God's Word. Certain situations and seasons in my life have been so painful, so disappointing, and so disillusioning that I absolutely would not have been able to continue if it weren't for the healing that I have repeatedly found in God's Word. Think for a moment about Psalm 23. Those six familiar verses are filled with healing balm. Let some of the phrases run through your mind: **"He restores my soul . . . your rod and staff, they comfort me . . . You anoint my head with oil"** (vv. 3–5). The oil mentioned in verse five is healing oil. Every night, when the sheep passed under the shepherd's hands into the fold, he treated the wounds of the day with oil for healing. You can let God's Word be a healing oil every day, for every hurt.

When I get disappointed with people and become disillusioned about the way situations unfold and frustrated with my own failures and weaknesses, I go back to God's Word.

God's Word washes my mind.

God's Word renews my spirit.

God's Word cleanses my heart.

God's Word is medicine for your soul. If you take it and apply it liberally, you can't believe the healing that you'll experience.

- *Happiness*
Finally, I find sheer happiness in God's Word. Now, the world has tried to hijack this word. So to be clear, when I say happiness, I don't mean some little oh-I-just-had-a-Big-Mac-meal-I'm-so-happy-right-now. True happiness is not some shallow, giddy, short-lived pleasure. Like we said, God wrote the blueprint on human happiness. Psalm 1:1–2 says, **"Blessed is the man / who walks not in the**

counsel of the wicked, / nor stands in the way of sinners, / nor sits in the seat of the scoffers; / but his delight is in the law of the LORD." The word *blessed* means happy—real happiness, not the horizontal, worldly substitute that flashes by in a heartbeat. *Blessed* is the person who knows God's kind of soul satisfaction that lasts and flourishes in our hearts.

Yes, this kind of happiness can be yours.

These are some of the things that I find when I choose God's Word: the assurance of heaven, the promise of hope, the hand of help, the comfort of healing, and the real kind of happiness. How are those things going in your life?

Do you want to change your life forever? It's time to make a choice.

Hold in your hands the Word of God.

It is God's owner's manual.

It is God's manifesto for human happiness.

It is the manufacturer's specification for soul satisfaction.

It is the authoritative Word from the Creator of the universe about how life really works.

God's Word Is My Authority—I Choose It

Matthew 8 includes the story of an enemy soldier, an officer in the Roman army. He was very distraught and appealed to Jesus for help: **"Lord, my servant is lying paralyzed at home, suffering terribly"** (v. 6). Maybe this employee had been part of his life for a long time. If you found out that one of your most loyal companions was suffering, you'd be suffering too.

I can totally relate. Just this past summer our staff gathered at our church camp for a retreat. One afternoon we were trying out a new zip line—down a steep incline and off into space over a creek and brush. We have a great staff of risk-takers who eagerly lined up to experience the rush—including my assistant of almost twenty years, despite the fact that she's a grandmother of unpublished age. Just as she was sprinting down the runway to take off, her foot rammed a stump, and her ankle twisted and shattered. All we could do was watch helplessly as she flew down the line with her mangled foot pointing in the wrong direction. It took several agonizing hours to get her to the hospital for help. I worried and fussed and did all I could. I just couldn't be OK until she was OK. I completely understand the centurion's urgency—even reckless abandon—to go to any length to find help for his beloved servant.

Jesus understood the man's anguish. Immediately He said, "**I will come and heal him**" (v. 7). *No problem. Where do you live? I'll come over to your house.*

"**But the centurion replied, 'Lord, I am not worthy to have you come under my roof'**" (v. 8*a*). Do you see the immense humility in that? "**Only say the word and my servant will be healed**" (v. 8*b*). The centurion got it: *I know who You are. I know what You can do. You don't need to walk over to my house and put Your hand on my servant—just say the word, and I know it will happen.* He understood something about the word Jesus would speak that I wish more believers would experience.

He went on to explain himself in verse 9. He said, "**For I too am a man under authority, with soldiers under me. And I say to one, 'Go,' and he goes, and to another, 'Come,' and he comes, and to my servant, 'Do this,' and he does it.**" Basically, he said, *I know how the authority thing works. Jesus, You're the authority, and You're the Lord. If a word comes out of Your mouth, it will happen. You don't need to be there in the room. I don't want to waste Your time. I don't deserve Your time. I'm not worthy to have You under my roof.*

This was incredible to Jesus. Verse 10 says that Jesus marveled. I can just imagine Him thinking, *I haven't seen people with this kind of faith even in Israel, and you're a Roman! You don't find many people very often that get it. You get it!* He then rewarded the centurion's faith in verse 13: "**'Go; let it be done for you as you have believed.' And the servant was healed at that very moment.**" The Roman centurion grasped the power of God's Word. Do you? Do you realize the power you hold when you hold your Bible?

This Is the Word of God

Every word of it comes from the mouth of God (Matthew 4:4). His word
came through "holy men of God [who] spoke as they were moved by the
Holy Spirit" (2 Peter 1:21 NKJV).
It is God-breathed (2 Timothy 3:16).
It will outlast heaven and earth (Matthew 24:35).
It is about all things pertaining to life and godliness (2 Peter 1:3).

You will never have the power to live a full and fruitful, godly life until
you choose God's Word as your final authority. Do you want power over
temptation? Do you want power over that draining and difficult circumstance that you can't conquer on your own? God's Word has the power. Ask
God to help you become more like that Roman centurion and say, "Just
give me Your word, that's all I need."

The Bible is the decree of God. God has eternally determined that what
is written there *will happen*. That's why, in the face of temptation, Jesus
said, *It is written . . . it is written. It will be as God said.*

So let me ask you: Have you made the choice that God's Word will be
your authority?

Haven't all Christians accepted the Bible as their authority? Well, no,
they haven't. Oh, I know we have a lot of Bibles around, but the Bible can't
really do much for you until you choose it for what it really is. Sadly, instead
of making the Bible their authority, many people treat the Bible as one of
several sorry substitutes:

- *Some People Treat the Bible Like an Hors d'oeuvres Tray.*
  If Kathy and I came over to your house for dinner, I bet you that
  we wouldn't be in the door five minutes and you'd offer us a tray of
  some hot goodies. I'd look at the tray and say, "That one right there
  looks really good. I'm not sure what that one is, but it probably has
  too many calories . . . *There*, that's the one I want."

This is how a lot of people treat the Bible. They pick and choose whatever suits their taste: "I really like that part in Romans 8 about how much God loves me, and I really like that part in 2 Corinthians 12 about how '**My grace is sufficient for you**' [v. 9], but I don't like the part over in Galatians 2 about '**I have been crucified with Christ**' [v. 20]. I'll skip the part about forgiveness, or repentance, or hell."

The Bible is not your authority as long as you're picking and choosing the parts you like.

- *Some People Treat the Bible Like Rental Car Insurance.*
  I would guess that most people waive the extra rental car insurance. If you're like me, you think to yourself, *The rental car costs plenty already. Now they want me to add $35 a day for the insurance? I haven't had an accident in ten years. What are the chances that I'm going to have an accident today? Slim. No, I don't want the insurance.*

  A lot of people treat the Bible like that. *I guess in an extreme emergency I'm going to want the Bible, but I doubt I'm going to have a crisis today, so I think I'll pass.* Technically, you should get up and spend some time in God's Word, but instead, you grab a cup of coffee and rush out the door. *I'll probably be OK today without it.* Some people treat the Bible like rental car insurance.

- *Some People Treat the Bible Like a Seat Belt.*
  Do you wear your seat belt? Yes, of course you do—but why? *Well, because it's the law.* I think it's because of that crazy bell that won't quit ringing until you click it. If you could get behind the dashboard and rip that bell out, I think you'd wear your seat belt a lot less. The manufacturer makes you wear your seat belt.

  Some people treat the Bible like that: *Yeah, I read the Bible because it's the law. And also because I can't get the guilt to quit ringing in my ears if I don't.* So to silence the alarm in your head, you spend a few minutes in the Bible every day. But then the Bible isn't your authority—it's a nuisance you have to handle.

- *Some People Treat the Bible Like an Algebra Equation.*
  I could never figure out math. Consequently, I hated it. I warn the
  parents in our church not to waste their time asking me to tutor
  their children in math. I hated algebra like I hated all things I
  considered useless. I remember throwing my algebra textbook
  against the wall when my dad tried to help me. I just couldn't
  understand it. To this day I wonder what algebra is good for. I have
  never once faced a problem in which algebra delivered the solution. It was so much work for so little benefit.

  Some people see the Bible like that. They decide, *It's really
  complicated, and I guess I'm supposed to need it sometime in the
  future, and I know it's really good for my mind, but I've never really
  figured out what the Bible has to do with life.* I'm sorry if you think
  the Bible is like an algebra equation. My underlying purpose in
  this entire book is to help you cross the bridge to see how incredibly
  valuable and practical God's Word can be in your life. That's why
  we are using God's Word for every choice chapter. The Bible is no
  algebra equation. It helps you figure out life!

- *Some People Treat the Bible Like It's Their Hobby.*
  My mom is a hobby person of the extreme category. She had all
  kinds of crazy interests when I was growing up. I remember this one
  phase she went through with "liquid embroidery." She took what
  looked like a toothpaste tube filled with paint and squeezed it onto
  T-shirts. "Look, James, I can put your name right on your shirt."
  Yeah, no thanks.

  Another craft was decoupage. You do decoupage when you get
  a wedding invitation from someone you like and feel guilty about
  throwing it in a shoebox. So you get a piece of wood and you burn
  the corners of the invitation so it looks old and then you slather this
  lacquer over the invitation, sealing it to the board, and the whole
  house reeks because of it. That's decoupage.

  Next, my mother really got into ceramics. We had a kiln in our
  basement and shelves full of molds and greenware. My mom
  taught classes on ceramics three nights a week. Then that phase

passed. My mom is the absolute greatest—and I have no issue with hobbies, not even with switching them up. But some people treat the Bible like it's a hobby, a passing interest: *Man, there was a time in my life when I first came to Jesus Christ that I was so fired up about the Bible. I was digging into it and marking the pages. I couldn't get enough of it. It was so satisfying to me! Then somewhere along the line I just stopped using it, although I keep carrying it around.*

If the Bible was a phase that you went through, if it was a hobby, today's a great day to come back to the Bible.

Instead of an authority to guide your life, these are the ways people minimize the Bible:

An *hors d'oeuvres tray*—where you can pick or choose.
Rental car insurance—that you're glad to have, but only in an
    emergency.
A *seat belt*—a nuisance that cramps your style.
High school algebra—technically accurate but practically, nothing.
A *hobby*—like a fun phase you go through.

How sad. If this characterizes your thinking in any way, come back to the priority of God's Word in your life, and let it be your authority.

God's Word Is My Correction—I Challenge Myself with It

How will I know when the Bible is my authority? Here is a sure indication: when it can stop you dead in your tracks. *I was going in one direction that I thought was the right way, then God's Word was held up to me as a mirror, and I realized I was going the wrong direction. This isn't what God wants for me. This is not the kind of person God wants me to be. These are not the kinds of priorities God wants me to have. This pursuit is not what I'm supposed to be passionate about. I saw the truth and* e-r-r-r-k! *Stop the bus, I'm getting off.* God's Word is not your authority unless it can change your direction.

Proverbs 14:12 says, **"There is a way that seems right to a man, but its end is the way to death."** We all have a propensity to go the wrong way. God's Word has become your authority when it can change your direction. You also know the Bible is your authority when it can help you recognize and break a a negative pattern of thinking in your life—a lustful thought, a selfish habit, or destructive way of looking at someone or something. Your thinking was skewed and taking you down the wrong path. God's Word stopped your spiral and corrected your direction.

> ## GOD'S WORD IS NOT YOUR AUTHORITY UNLESS IT CAN CHANGE YOUR DIRECTION.

God's Word puts your feet back on course. **"Your Word is a lamp to my feet and a light to my path"** (Psalm 119:105). It keeps you from falling in the sin ditch. It keeps you from stepping in a hellhole. God's map keeps you from speeding up the freeway ramp into the oncoming traffic. It keeps you from devastating your life and the lives of the people you love.

You are probably thinking, *If you want me to actually let the Bible alter my direction, I'm going to need some evidence that the Bible is God's book.*

No problem. There is immense evidence for the Bible as God's Word. It's some of the lowest hanging fruit in the intellectual universe. Proofs of the Bible's authoritative reliability are available to you. They are not even that difficult to find. I've actually written a book on this subject called *God Wrote a Book*, which details what I can only summarize here.

The Evidence for God's Word

I've repeatedly heard it said that the Bible is a human, fallible document. Have you heard that? Well, two strikes on that one. It's not human, and it's not fallible. The Bible is a lot more than an ancient book that has survived the passage of time. To begin our defense, let's look at evidence outside the Bible.

The Bible Is Preeminent Among Literature

The fact that we call the Bible a book is almost a misnomer by itself because it is so completely unlike any other book that has ever been written. First, the Bible is preeminent in its circulation of more than seven billion copies. In second place is Mao Tse-tung's *Little Red Book*. The Communist Chinese government printed 900 million copies and required by law (unsuccessfully) that everyone would have one. Next in line is *Webster's Dictionary*, with 100 million copies sold. I've already told you that I'm not great at math, but calculate how far apart 100 million and seven billion are.

The *New York Times* doesn't even put the Bible on its bestseller list. It's number one every week. There would never be a *New York Times* number one bestseller because it's always been the Bible. All you'd ever see on that prestigious book list is the number two bestseller because the Bible is and most likely always will be number one. No other book comes even remotely close to the Bible.

The Bible Is Preeminent in Its Influence Too

Do you have any concept of the number of books that are written and published every year about the Bible? The lexicons, dictionaries, commentaries, and Bible study aids—it's a river that never ceases. People are giving their lives around the globe in every language to the study of God's Word. The majority of scholars who are studying languages that have never been written down are doing so partly with the goal of translating the Bible into those languages.

The Bible Is Preeminent Among Religious Writings

The Bible is so preeminent that even secular scholars study the language, the beauty, the simplicity, and the power of the Bible. Take the Book of Mormon and the Koran and put them alongside the Bible. They're not even worthy to be compared. The Bible is the Sears Tower, and all other religious writings are like three-story walk-ups. The difference between these books is pitifully obvious. Go ahead and satisfy your intellect, if that's a barrier to you, but you'll find that the treasure God has given to us in His Word is absolutely preeminent among literature. There's nothing even close to second place.

How did the Bible get to this place, considering it is continuously and always under attack?

Preservation Under Fire

It goes without saying that the Bible is ever and always under attack. Since the Old and New Testaments were written, people have given their lives to attack God's Word. The irrefutable record of the Bible's survival is evidence in itself that it is a supernatural book.

No other book has been so burned, banned, and defamed as the Bible. From Roman emperors to communist leaders to college professors, everyone seems to take it upon themselves to attack God's book. Why are people always attacking the Bible while giving deference and respect to the Koran and the Book of Mormon? It's because the Bible declares who is the authority, and everyone who has chosen other authorities instinctively lashes out at God's Word. Their hearts hate the book that calls them to their only source of hope.

In spite of countless attacks, the Bible has been uniquely preserved throughout human history because almighty God wrote it and He is taking care of it. Anybody who sets himself out to destroy the Bible is not going against man but against God. I certainly wouldn't want to spend my life trying to get God's book out of circulation.

Preservation Against Time

Some ask, "How can we know for sure that we have the Bible as it was originally written? Hasn't it been altered and changed through the centuries?"

Those are very good questions. They can be answered by looking at three factors: 1) the vast collection of manuscripts, 2) the age of the manuscripts, and 3) the demonstrable accuracy of the manuscripts.

More than 24,000 early, whole or partial manuscripts of the Bible currently exist. These are usable manuscripts in identifying the original text. Scholars have available almost a hundred times more ancient Bible documents than the next most commonly copied ancient written work.

The sheer quantity of Bible manuscripts brings up the issue of variants. As scribes copied, maybe they didn't copy it accurately. Do we really have an accurate transmission of the Bible as it existed? Sir Frederick Kenyon, one of the greatest authorities in the field of New Testament textural criticism, said, "No fundamental doctrine of Christian faith rests on a disputed reading."[1] None. So as scholars look at all of the manuscripts used to make up the Bible we use today, the differences are infinitesimal (for example: punctuation and one-word differences) and easily explainable. But none of the textual issues affect any doctrine of the faith. Not one truth is called into question. God has preserved His Word with amazing accuracy. People used to say, "We don't know what the real Old Testament said." Then in 1948 the Dead Sea Scrolls were found, which included a complete copy of the book of Isaiah that was one thousand years older than the previous oldest manuscript. This was their finding: in a thousand years of copying and recopying, only one word in Isaiah 53 was questioned, and it doesn't change the meaning of the sentence at all. So why would Isaiah 53 be important? It is one of the clearest prophecies about Jesus Christ: **"He was wounded for our transgressions, / He was bruised for our iniquities; / The chastisement for our peace was upon Him, / And by His stripes we are healed. / All we like sheep have gone astray"** (vv. 5–6a NKJV). The time gap of a thousand years was closed. It turned out Christians *hadn't* gone back and "added" Christ to the Old Testament over the years—He was there all along! God Himself is standing behind His Book, and nothing will alter its priority in this world. It is everything that God had claimed it would be. As Jesus said, **"Heaven and earth will pass away, but my words will not pass away"** (Luke 21:33).

Proof from Archeology

The Bible speaks of actual places. You can visit them. The people were real people. They lived and died and had families and jobs just like us. Revisionist scholars (people who attack the Bible) say that Bible stories of Israel's origin are fiction—they never happened. Yet archeologists have recently discovered King Solomon's seal, King David's name in stone, and a bull the Canaanites worshipped. In 1998, *Christianity Today* referred to "two leading Egyptologists"—not even believers—who "are marshaling evidence from the land of the Pharaohs to answer the question did the Exodus ever happen?"[2] The answer is yes; it did happen.

William Albright, known as one of the world's foremost archaeologists, says, "There can be no doubt that archaeology has confirmed the substantial historicity of the Old Testament." He adds, "The excessive skepticism shown toward the Bible by influential historical schools of the eighteenth and nineteenth centuries has been progressively discredited. Discovery after discovery has established the accuracy of innumerable details and has brought increased recognition to the Bible as a valuable source of history."[3]

All of this is written by people who don't intend to promote Jesus. They are simply reporting the archeological evidence of places, events, and people in the Bible that used to be ridiculed by critics as inventions of the ancient writers. Israel is not the biggest country in the world, and only 1 percent of the available land mass has actually been studied archeologically, yet almost every single historical figure in the Bible has already been confirmed by empirical data.

Archeology will no doubt continue to uncover facts that prove secular scholars are wrong. Scripture is as God says it is: true and accurate, completely reliable in all that it asserts. The Bible is not a human document, it's a supernatural book.

The Bible Is Not Fallible

This topic really gets me going sometimes. Some people casually claim, "The Bible is so full of contradictions," to which I counter, "Name one."

Their eyes usually glaze over because they have assumed their statement was self-evident. Usually they are just echoing generations of biblical neglect and criticism. And the contradictions they occasionally come up with are superficial and silly.

All the Authors Agree

The history of the writing of the Bible is staggering in time and scope. Forty *different* authors wrote over a span of two thousand years and were as varied as farmers, kings, shepherds, wise men, and fishermen.

What's more amazing to me is that they all agree. If you put four people from your street on different corners of the same intersection and ask them to watch something happen, you're going to get four completely different stories. People just see things from alternate perspectives. Yet, how is it that forty people can write over a period of two thousand years and agree on everything they wrote? I'll tell you how—God was guiding their hands. Every single word in His Book is breathed by the Spirit of God Himself. There were many writers but one mind; one Author was behind the Book, always present during the writing.

The Supposed Contradictions Are Silly

From cover to cover, the consistency in the Bible is remarkable. Challenge anyone who brings up contradictions, and with study or perspective you will find an explanation every time. When people bring up this argument, it usually points to what seems a difference between the Old and New Testaments. But usually the contradiction is a completion or an update. For example, when people say, "Well, here's a huge problem. In the Old Testament it says an eye for an eye, and in the New Testament it says to turn the other cheek." If you read to them the New Testament reference (which they have probably never seen), you can show them that Jesus said, **"You have heard that it was said, 'An eye for an eye . . .' But I say to you . . ."** (Matthew 5:38–39). That's not a contradiction, it's an update. Jesus was pointing out that a civil law given to preserve societal order was not meant to apply the same way in the interpersonal relationships of people who wanted to live for God.

The next time somebody says the Bible is full of contradictions, just type his question into your search engine, and in about four minutes, you'll have fifteen answers about why the Bible stands true. He'll just say, "Never mind," and then walk away. The new and startling problems with the Bible turn out to be the same ones that have been responded to for the last couple of millennia!

Those of us who chose the Bible as our authority don't have to be defensive. We hold a supernatural book.

All of the Prophecies Concerning Christ Came True

We could also go into the whole subject of prophecy and how multiple hundreds of prophecies about Jesus Christ—about His life, about His death, about His ministry that were foretold hundreds and even a thousand-plus years before He was born—all came true. Just try to stack that up against Jeanne Dixon or Nostradamus. The Bible invites examination; it claims perfect accuracy when God foretells what He will do. It practically dares us to trust it.

The evidence inside and outside the Bible points to the fact that the Bible is a supernatural book. When I plead with you to choose God's Word as your authority, I'm not telling you to check your mind at the door. The truths of God's Word have satisfied the greatest minds in human history.

So here's the key question. It's not whether the Bible can satisfy your intellectual integrity but whether the Bible can correct *your* wrong thinking! Want to make a choice that will change your life forever? Let God's Word challenge and alter your thinking. Recommit to it as the blueprint for your life.

You may say, "James, I've got to be honest. When you were going through that stuff about the seat belt and the Bible as an obligation, I've got to tell you, that's how it feels to me so often." If you feel like you've never really gotten all that much out of the Bible, I want to give you three steps that will help you get more from it:

Step 1: Discipline

"Do your best to present yourself to God as one approved, a worker who has no need to be ashamed, rightly handling the word of truth" (2 Timothy 2:15). You're going to have to discipline yourself to get into God's Word, and it's going to feel like you're starting to work out on a treadmill. In the beginning it'll take getting up in the morning and making yourself do it.

Here's the workout plan: I challenge you in Jesus' name to discipline yourself to spend thirty minutes every day in God's Word for a month. During those thirty days, set aside the first half hour of every day, before you get in the shower, before you dress for work, before you drink a cup of coffee (or at least simultaneously). Commit: *I will not do anything else until I get thirty minutes with the Lord in His Word.* It will feel like hard work, and that's OK—it won't stay that way for long. For some reading this book, God's Word has never been more than an obligation. That's been your Christian history for many years. You can choose for that to change.

Break the frustrating pattern. Get a friend to hold you accountable. Call each other every morning, and start and stop at the same time. Go after this choice that will change your life forever. Thirty minutes for thirty days. It starts with discipline.

Step 2: Desire

The next step is when God's Word becomes your desire. This step involves another thirty days. No longer is this just a discipline; now you can't wait to throw the curtains open and get to your desk and sit there before the Lord with a pen in your hand, saying like David, **"As a deer pants for flowing streams, / so pants my soul for you, O God"** (Psalm 42:1). I want it; I desire it; I hunger for it.

You will wonder how you lived without it. You'll recognize how famished and impoverished your soul has been and how difficult the Christian life has been with no grease on the wheel or gas in the tank. It won't be a big burden. It won't be an obligation. It won't be like the treadmill anymore.

You get that after thirty days of discipline and thirty days of desire. After these sixty days, you'll never look back spiritually. You will say, "I chose God's Word as my authority, and my life has been changed forever," because now you're going to step 3, and it will blow your mind.

Step 3: Delight

In the third thirty-day step, you will begin to experience what David observed about the blessed man, **"But his delight is in the law of the LORD, / and on his law he meditates day and night"** (Psalm 1:2). David confessed in Psalm 119:97, **"Oh how I love your law! / It is my meditation all the day."**

When you begin to delight in God's Word, the time spent in His Book will be the greatest moments of your life. It will be the favorite part of your day and the best part of your week. The most treasured time that you spend on this earth will be the time that you have alone with Him to dig into His Word, letting His Spirit feed you. And the effects will seep into every part of your day so that you will find God's Word running in the background of your thoughts constantly.

Jeremiah 15:16 says, **"Your words were found, and I ate them, and your words became to me a joy and the delight of my heart."** Delight is like what the disciples experienced on the road to Emmaus in Luke 24:13–35. Do you remember? They were walking along with Jesus but didn't know that it was Him. The Bible says that Jesus was expounding from the Scriptures all things concerning Himself. Then when He was recognized and disappeared, the disciples looked at one another and said, **"Did not our hearts burn within us while he talked to us on the road, while he opened to us the Scriptures?"** (v. 32).

Choose God's Word, and invite it to become your delight, your treasure that you cherish.

Choosing God's Word

You may say, "James, I'm going to do this. I'm going to do this, God help me, discipline for thirty days. Now what?"

Here are five practical aspects of acting on your choice of God's Word:

1: *Read it.*

Where should I start? Most Bibles average around 1,400 pages. Think of the Bible as a pantry full of healthy spiritual food. You will not be able to consume it all at once. But a steady diet of God's Word will do wonders for your whole being. In order to make sure you comprehend the power of what you are reading, savor it like you would your favorite dessert—take a bite or two, then put your spoon down. If you read it for thirty minutes each day, you could finish reading the Bible in six months, and you will be so incredibly blessed you would want to start all over again. It's really not as intimidating as most people make it.

As for *where* to start, use any of the suggestions mentioned earlier or go to the gospel of John, the fourth eyewitness account of Jesus' life. As you read it slowly, every time you see the word *believe*, underline it and ask yourself: *Believe what?* After that, read 1, 2, and 3 John, then another Gospel. Those sections will keep you busy reading for a while. Try reading a chapter from the book of Proverbs to coincide with the day of the month. Pray before you begin reading each time. Ask the Lord to open your mind and heart to His truth, and then believe that He will. Make a note of words whose meaning you have to guess, and use a Bible dictionary to improve your basic comprehension. Also, don't lie down when you read the Bible. It's not a magazine or a novel—it's God's Word. If you give it the respect it deserves, you'll understand it better.

2: *Question it.*

Here are some prompts I use; over time, you can develop your own:

- *What portion of my reading stands out to me?* After you read two or three chapters, you will feel drawn to a certain part. Go back to that part and ask the following questions:

- *Why does this part have my attention?* What is it about these verses that caught my attention? To help you answer that question, use the remaining questions.

- *Is there an example for me to follow?* I can't tell you how many times God's Word has impacted my life just from asking this question. All of a sudden something jumps right off the page. "I should be more like that!" I love it when God's Word calls me to be more of what the Lord requires.

- *Is there an error for me to avoid?* It's very comforting to know that if I have unknowingly stepped in a wrong direction or made an unwise decision, God's Word can reveal my error to me. It's easy to see the mistakes others make, but it's much harder to see our own mistakes. This is where the Word of God becomes a mirror (James 1:23–25).

- *Is there a duty for me to perform?* Is God's Word calling me to act? Am I neglecting something in my home, or where I work, or in my personal life? If so, I want to know what it is so I can work on it.

- *Is there any promise for me to claim?* God's Word can bring you strength and encouragement. As you study the Bible, you will hear the Lord committing Himself to certain things or to act in certain ways. As you come to those promises, you acknowledge, "Yes, God! You are like this, and You've promised to be this way for all my life. I trust You." Your heart will be thrilled as you learn and review the promises of God. Parts of Scripture will easily become a dialogue of prayer between you and the Lord.

- *Is there a sin for me to confess?* You won't read the Bible long before you come across passages that reveal sins in your life. One promise that helps me with this is, **"If we confess our sins,** he is faithful and just to forgive us our sins and to cleanse us from all unrighteousness" (1 John 1:9).

3: *Plan and pray it.*

To benefit from the Bible as much as you can for the rest of your life, you must have a plan as to how you will apply what you are learning. Have a journal open beside your Bible, and write some notes in it. Get in the habit of writing your thoughts in the margin of your Bible. Date your notes to track spiritual growth. When the Word convicts you about anger or deceit or selfishness, have a specific and measurable strategy to deal with those sins. The results will amaze you.

You'll also discover an incredible power when you pray God's Word back to Him. By doing this you can be confident you are praying according to His will and that God will respond to what you are asking if the direction truly comes from His Word. For example, you can personalize passages like Psalm 23 as you pray them back to God—*Lord, You are my shepherd, so I know I will never want for anything.* You will find many of the Psalms were written for this very purpose.

4: *Memorize it.*

One of the greatest decisions I've ever made in my life and ministry was to memorize God's Word. The greatest treasures I have are the scriptures that I've memorized.

"I have stored up your word in my heart, / that I might not sin against you" (Psalm 119:11). God often brings His Word to my mind in moments of temptation. God can't bring anything to your mind if you don't store it in there. If it's not in your heart, He can't remind you of it. You say, "Well, I always struggle with Bible memory. I just don't seem to be able to get it down." Forget how you've done it in the past.

Do this: write the scripture down on an index card, and read it out loud seven times a day for a couple of weeks, and you'll never, ever work at memorizing. "The Lord is my refuge and strength . . ." Dwell on it; think about it. Let it renew your mind. Put it in a box, take it out and read it three times a year, and you'll have it for life. That's how memorization works. You don't have to work at it. Just go over it and over it and read it out loud. God will put it in your heart.

Meditate on it too. Make memory cards of scriptures that give you comfort, and put them on your car dashboard. Instead of just sitting at a traffic light, read them over and think about the verses. Go over it and over it until it changes you. Soon enough you will actually look forward to red lights and traffic delays. You'll be driving along and think, *I hope the light turns red. I can't wait to stop and start on a new verse!*

5: *Share it.*

Hebrews 10:24 says that we should **"consider how to stir up one another to love and good works."** You're taking a giant step forward in your own spiritual life when you decide to teach God's Word to others. This is an important bridge that many Christians never cross. I guarantee you, giving God's Word to other people will change you forever.

My wife, Kathy, is teaching a woman's Bible study this year. She has been a student of God's Word since she came to Christ at fifteen years of age, but it's fantastic to see her when I come home at night with her Bible open and her notes in front of her as she's digging into Scripture for herself. What's driving her to spend all of this extra time in God's Word? She's teaching and entrusting to other people what she's learning.

No matter where you are, God's Word can reach you. The Bible can reach others too. It's not for religious people; it's for everyone. It's not for perfect people; it's for you. No matter where you've been or what you've done—the Bible is for you. Choose it.

Here is the story, in his own words, of a man who made that choice and e-mailed me his exciting news:

I would like to tell you how much my life has changed in just the past month. My friend Frank, who happens to be the [overnight delivery] driver at my shop, started talking about religion. It was an honest, simple chat about how much God meant to him, how he has been dealing with a troubled marriage, and yet has an honest joy and sense of peace that he obviously carries with him. Until recently, I was agnostic. I believed there was someone, but I didn't know what to call that person. Allah, Buddha, God, Jesus—I didn't know—and unfortunately at that time, I really didn't care either. I thought the Bible was in the same section of the bookstore as *Gone with the Wind* and *War and Peace*—good books, but fiction nonetheless.

Frank and I would have these short conversations every day while he would pick up or drop off packages. One day I was in a serious amount of pain with my rheumatoid arthritis. He asked if he could say a prayer for me with me. That kinda set me back. I figured, *Why not?*—couldn't hurt, right? So he did and went on his way. The next day he brought me a New Testament. I started to read it and was astounded. When I told Frank about my response, he gave me a study Bible. Next, I told my wife about my interest in maybe reading the Bible: "I don't want you to think I am gonna become a holy roller Bible thumper or anything like that, I just wanna read it." She, of course, thought it was a good idea.

When Frank gave me my Bible, I was shocked, especially considering he would not take a single penny in payment. He just told me to pray to God to have Him open my heart to understand the Word with my heart as well as my mind. I did. What followed was what I can only say has been nothing short of amazing. I thirsted for the Word, read all the time—on breaks, at lunch, after work, and at home. My wife was visibly happy with what was going on. I felt a completion that I had never known. I didn't know I needed anything . . . boy, was I wrong.

Frank also told me about Christian radio, and I listened to *Walk in the Word* almost every day. I was excited one day when I found out that you had a church out in Chicago. I told Frank I wanted to go on a field trip to see who I had enthusiastically been listening to on the radio for about a month. I didn't think my wife would go, but I was wrong. She insisted we all go, and she wanted to buy a Bible so she could bring it to church. Then my youngest son wanted a Bible too! My older son had one from Sunday school. *Wow!* I thought, *That's a bunch of money I just dropped on Bibles—this better be worth it!* (LOL—I actually thought that!)

So we went to Harvest on 11/11/07. That night blew me away. The months since then have been filled with lessons and changes. So many things I see in a different light, in a different perspective, a different every-thing. I realize just how selfish and sinful I was, and now I am, every day, trying to be a better person for my family, myself, and, of course, God.

People are starting to look at me differently, which is fine. If they ask me why I am in a good mood, I tell them my story. On the way to church each week, we chat about whatever, usually the excitement about what we think is gonna happen. But on the way home, we reflect and discuss what we heard, how we were convicted with the circumstances and words presented to us that day. It has just been awesome.

It's unbelievable how this short time has made such a change in my heart, my life, my perspective, everything. I just figured I would tell you how your radio show snowballed into changing my life and making me realize how truly lost I was. I thank God for being such a presence in my life. I know now He has always been there. I just now know I can worship and praise Him for everything He has done in my life . . . but the best thing is that I know this is only the beginning, and it's only going to get better.

—Thom[4]

I choose God's Word as my authority. You can do the same. That's a choice that will change your life. It's right in front of you. Your time is yours. The opportunity is here.

You have to choose what will be your authority. Choose God's Word.

A Choice to Make

Acknowledge the Choice

- How would you describe your personal history with God's Word?
- What would have to change in order for you to make the choice to treat the Bible as your authority?

Consider the Choice

- Think through the three steps described in this chapter, beginning with *discipline* in God's Word, moving to *desire*, and then developing *delight* in God's Word. In what ways does that process speak into your spiritual life right now?
- Review the five aspects of acting on your daily exposure to God's Word explained above. Are you ready to begin?

Make the Choice

- Today, choose the Bible you will use and the passage where you will start.
- Start your first thirty-day period tomorrow morning. Expect it to be work—you can do it.
- Mark on your calendar, thirty days from now, this question: Have I begun to desire God's Word?
- Mark on your calendar, sixty days from now, this question: How am I delighting in God's Word as never before?

A Choice Prayer

God, You have given me so much of Yourself in Your Word! I admit I fall short in treasuring it and giving it the attention it deserves. I casually say I don't hear from You or can't sense You directing my life, when all along You speak truth and guidance into me from Your Word. Lord, as other people reading this are deciding to choose Your Word as their authority, may Your Spirit be a persistent presence these next days as they begin to put into practice the basic steps of reading Your Word that will lead to desire and then delight. May this decision turn out to be, in years to come, a definite choice in the road of life that they eventually realize made a huge difference in every way.

I know You want Your Word to have life-changing significance for me, and that when I choose it, I bring honor and delight to You.

In Jesus' Name, the Living Word, I pray. Amen.

PART III

MY CAPACITY CHOICES

Choice 5: I Choose to Forgive

Choice 6: I Choose to Trust

As we continue with *10 Choices: A Proven Plan to Change Your Life Forever*, we are ready to build on the foundation created by the earlier choices. If you have been following along, you have made some of those big choices already.

The first two are identity choices. *Who am I?—I choose to believe I'm loved by God. I choose to believe I'm forgiven by God.* You already know those are not soft, stale truths but life-transforming points of identity that form the first two walls in the foundation.

The next two walls are authority choices. *Who's in charge?—I choose Jesus Christ as Lord and I choose the Bible as God's Word.* I'm not in charge anymore; I'm not in the driver's seat. I choose Jesus. He is the Lord of my life. His Word is the script I'm operating from, and I do what He tells me to do because He promises a good result.

Two identity choices and two authority choices form the firm foundation upon which we can now build our lives. This construction project continues with our capacity choices.

In our youth we tend to believe that we are invincible. Nothing can shake us, nothing can stop us, very little can even slow us down. The fact is, though, you start to learn differently. Life has a way of revealing our immensely limited capacity. Now into my mid-forties, I find myself confessing much more frequently, *I can't change that, I can't fix that, I can't settle that, not now, not today, not with the current strength I have.* As soon as possible, you need to get to the place where you choose to admit your limited capacity.

Nowhere is this more important than in the arenas of past and future. God did not make us with the capacity to carry the disappointments of yesterday or the uncertainties of tomorrow. If the Bible is now your blueprint, if you have chosen that for your authority, you need to know that it calls you to focus on today. It's all you really have capacity for. These next two choices are about choosing to accept your limited capacity and following God's plan for how to get yesterday into the past where it belongs and keep tomorrow from creeping into today. If you make these important capacity choices, I promise you, it *will* change your life forever.

Beginning Prayer

Lord, I only have enough capacity to carry today what You say I can. I've tried to lug around my past, but it crushes me. I've tried to bear all the questions I have about tomorrow, but the worry drives me crazy. Lord, here at the start, I draw upon Your strength and choose to forgive those who've hurt me. I give you all my trust for all of life's uncertainties. Please open my heart to the truth of Your Word, and help me to run to obey. Amen.

"Therefore the kingdom of heaven may be compared to a king who wished to settle accounts with his servants . . . one was brought to him who owed him ten thousand talents. And since he could not pay, his master ordered him to be sold, with his wife and children and all that he had, and payment to be made. So the servant fell on his knees, imploring him, 'Have patience with me, and I will pay you everything.' And out of pity for him, the master of that servant released him and forgave him the debt. But when that same servant went out, he found one of his fellow servants who owed him a hundred denarii, and seizing him, he began to choke him, saying, 'Pay what you owe.' So his fellow servant fell down and pleaded with him, 'Have patience with me, and I will pay you.' He refused and went and put him in prison until he should pay the debt . . . Then his master summoned him and said to him, 'You wicked servant! I forgave you all that debt because you pleaded with me. And should not you have had mercy on your fellow servant, as I had mercy on you?' And in anger his master delivered him to the jailers, until he should pay all his debt. So also my heavenly Father will do to every one of you, if you do not forgive your brother from your heart."

—MATTHEW 18:23–35

[Choice 5]

I Choose to Forgive

*I have a limited capacity to go forward in life without
getting free from unforgiveness, so I choose to forgive
those who have hurt me.*

I remember as a kid watching the British comedy program *Monty Python's
Flying Circus*. The show became famous for its silly and often boorish skits.
In one memorable vignette, a very large man, clearly stuffed to the limit, is
seated in a restaurant. He is rejecting a waiter's persistent offer of an after-
dinner mint. "Not another bite," he pleads, but the waiter will not relent. Of
course, the tiny mint is what exceeds his maximum capacity, and the poor
man actually explodes to hilarious effect. Do you ever feel like you are going
to explode? Like you can't lift another load or take another step?

I don't know about you, but I have had a hard time admitting that I have
a limited capacity. I want to be able to do it all. But I can't.

I can't see it all. I can't say it all. I can't be it all.

I can't solve it all. I can't carry it all. I can't fix it all.

I just can't.

Yesterday was a milestone. It marked twenty-five years since Kathy and I
first voyaged out into ministry, twenty-two years since we moved from
Canada to Chicago. Soon we'll celebrate twenty years at the church we
planted, Harvest Bible Chapel. We laugh now at the stories and pictures
from those days and shake our heads at how young we were "back then"—
how wonderfully clueless.

In those early years, I didn't realize how life has a way of piling up on you. You just don't see it when you're young. But by the time you've flipped a few pages on the calendar, you begin to look back on choices you wish you had made differently and choices others made that you hoped would have turned out better. All of a sudden, a few years have gone by, then a few decades, and stuff has started to pile up. Life moves so fast. It's easy to just stick unresolved conflicts and hurts into a mental drawer. Then something else happens, and since the drawer has filled up, you find a spot on a shelf somewhere. And let's say you move to a new place, so now you pack up all that crud and put it in a box in the attic of your new place. Before you know it, you need a serious garage sale—but I'm not talking about dumping old lamps, baby clothes, and exercise equipment. You need to get rid of all the times that people have disappointed you, all the rejection you've stuffed away, and all the situations that unfolded in unexpected and painful ways. If you don't do something with all those accumulated hurts, they just get packed inside emotional suit-cases and stuffed in the attic. Moving away won't help because unresolved hurts are like carry-on bags—you bring them with you.

I realize I may be stirring up some feelings of discomfort and despera-tion. Many of us know we're lugging around too much baggage from the past. But we also have a sneaky suspicion that we're stuck with it. How do we get rid of what seems like part of us? The garage sale plan is a nice idea, but it won't sell—I mean no matter how much I mark down my emotional junk, no one is going to buy it! And putting it out on the curb with a "Free for the Hauling" sign on it—horrors! Our emotional issues on display out there for the neighborhood to see? That would cause people just to detour around our lives, wouldn't it? Many of us then conclude deep down that we're absolutely stuck with our emotional baggage from the past.

The Truth About Capacity

Has anyone ever told you that God didn't make you with the capacity to carry forward the residue of all the negatives from your past? He doesn't expect you to store it or ignore it. We call it emotional baggage, but parts of our past are really more like toxic trash or radioactive waste. It's unstable and explosive. We can't throw it in a mental hall closet, lock the door, and hope for the best. If we try, the pressure will build until the closet explodes, throwing serious shrapnel on everyone around us.

Forgiveness is what God gives to free us and others from the weight of relational failure. Forgiveness disposes of the glowing green sludge of hurts, betrayals, and disappointments. Forgiveness is God's solution to capacity issues. The older we get, the more we realize we've got to become skilled at forgiveness. If we want the kind of life that God promises us, we must find a good way to deal with the wounds that happen to us and the weights that life heaps on us. We need to become the experts at forgiveness in our families, the experts at forgiveness in our churches and on our jobs, and the experts at forgiveness in our neighborhoods with this all-important biblical, necessary, required skill—forgiveness.

What honest person among us wouldn't say, "If I could do the past ten years over, I'd do some things differently"? I count myself in on that. But we can't go back, and God didn't make us to carry forward the weight of the past. So we have to make the good choice to forgive today.

I Choose to Forgive

Everyone knows the Lord's Prayer, right? In Matthew 6:9–15, Jesus was teaching on a number of spiritual disciplines. Luke's account of this prayer includes the detail that Jesus was fielding a request the disciples made, **"Teach us to pray"** (Luke 11:1). You recall Jesus' response:

> Our Father in heaven, hallowed be your name.
> Your kingdom come, your will be done,
> on earth as it is in heaven.
> Give us this day our daily bread, and forgive us our debts,
> as we also have forgiven our debtors.
> And lead us not into temptation, but deliver us from evil.
> —Matthew 6:9*b*–13

What do you think was going through Jesus' mind when He was teaching this model? Was He hoping, *Man, prayer is a really big deal. I hope they get this.* Or maybe, *I wish I couldn't see into the future because some people are going to make this into a ritual prayer, and that's so not what I'm talking about.* Actually, we don't have to wonder at His thoughts, we can see them right in the text. He didn't say, *Pray these exact words over and over.* He began His answer, **"Pray then like this"** (Matthew 6:9), as in, *Here's a pattern you can use and some important issues to keep in mind.* Based on His immediate comments on the sample prayer, we can tell He wanted to clarify the part of the prayer that deals with forgiveness. *They'll get stuck there. They're going to struggle in their hearts with the forgiveness part. I need to help them see how critical it is.* So He went on: **"For if you forgive others their trespasses, your heavenly Father will also forgive you, but if you do not forgive others their trespasses, neither will your Father forgive your trespasses"** (Matthew 6:14–15).

Now how clear is that? That is scary-clear! As a preacher committed to teaching through every verse of the Bible, I often come to a passage that is flat-out difficult to understand. That's not an issue at all in Matthew 6:14–15. God makes it crystal clear: if you don't forgive, God's not going to forgive you. Read it again and notice the conditions: you forgive; you get forgiven—you don't forgive; you don't get forgiven.

Those are serious verses. We need to get this right. If God makes such a big deal about forgiveness, we need to treat it as a major deal too. That's why choosing to forgive is one of the ten choices that will change our lives forever.

The word *forgiveness* is used 143 times in the New Testament. It's a legal term that means "to release a person from an obligation." In financial contexts, it's the idea of canceling a debt. Forgiveness always involves a choice!

To clarify, Jesus isn't saying that you get forgiven by forgiving. He's saying that people who are forgiven by God become increasingly forgiving people—not perfectly, not entirely, but more and more so. He is pointing out that when you release others through forgiveness, God can free you from the weight and captivity of unforgiveness. As the love of Christ penetrates your heart more deeply and more genuinely, you become more forgiving. You ought to be the most forgiving person at your workplace. When your name comes up in conversation, your coworkers should say: "He's not a guy who holds grudges. He doesn't find fault." "She doesn't try to make people pay,

she just lets it go." "He's not a score-keeper—he's just not like that. He's forgiving, that's what he is." They may not understand why you forgive or how you forgive, but it should provoke at least some of them to ask you, "What makes you such a forgiving person?" That's what should come to mind when people think of you. *You forgive.*

> **PEOPLE WHO ARE FORGIVEN BY GOD BECOME INCREASINGLY FORGIVING PEOPLE.**

But it's downright hard to pray, *Lord, please forgive me the way I forgive other people.* I hardly know anyone who sincerely thinks or feels that way. We definitely want God to forgive us a lot better than we forgive others. *Go ahead, God. Be out in front on this one. Give me the lead, and I'll try to follow.* But every time we mouth the Lord's Prayer, we give God permission to leave us under the weight of unforgiveness as long as we are unwilling to forgive.

Forgiveness is a decision. It's an act of the will. It's a choice.

This is going to sound odd, but right where you are, please set the book down for a moment and raise your right hand, then continue reading.

You were probably thinking one of two things: 1) *What? Well, why not—maybe something fun is coming,* or 2) *That's crazy. Why? He can't even see me. I'm totally not going to do it.*

Whether or not you raised your hand was your choice, an act of your will. Forgiveness is just like that decision. Don't glamorize it. Don't make it bigger than it is. Forgiveness is a choice that you make to release a person. It opens the cage you put them in when they hurt you. *Now, go free.*

Free from what? When someone hurts you, they're taking something from you that isn't theirs. That creates an obligation.

If I took your wallet, your lawn mower, or your promotion at work, you have a choice to make. Even if you got the item back from me (the obligations we call emotional baggage can't be returned), the choice would remain.

You have two options: First, you could hold that debt over me. Every time you see me for the rest of the year or for the rest of the decade or for the rest of your life, you could think, "There's that guy that took my _____." Or you could choose to forgive me. Forgiveness is a decision to release a person from the obligation that resulted when he injured you. The obligation is that I owe what I took. Your choice is to cancel the debt.

It's easier to release someone when the obligation is a tangible loss:

- You took my place in traffic.
- You borrowed my hedge clippers for two years, but then you brought them back after I bought a new pair.
- You took my customer in Cleveland.
- You took my friend, Cindy.

Each of these can be instantly released. It doesn't take much thought to realize that forgiveness is the better choice.

The intangible losses are much harder to forgive. Believe me, I know firsthand that the intangible hurts are harder to forgive:

- You took my right to fairness.
- You took my dream for a happy marriage.
- You took my dignity as a person.
- You took my confidence in you.
- You took my safety.
- You took my purity.

When you have been robbed of something precious but insubstantial, releasing the person from the obligation becomes much more complex.

What was taken can't be seen, nor can it be returned. The damage is done. The offense feels deeper; the desire for reparation stronger. Forgiveness seems to fly right in the face of our need to keep that person under obligation for what they stole from us.

Sadly, this dark world offers many occasions for that kind of forgiveness. Offenses happen all the time. Intangible loss is often devastating. I've been a pastor a long time, and I've seen more than I would ever want to recall. Don't think for a moment that I haven't thought of every horrific possibility that may be coming to your mind when we talk about how others have hurt you; I can picture every possibility as I call you to

> **FORGIVENESS IS A DECISION TO RELEASE A PERSON FROM THE OBLIGATION THAT RESULTED WHEN HE INJURED YOU.**

choose to release them from the obligation that resulted when they injured you. I won't minimize the unspeakable pain. I understand how immense the task is just to *consider* forgiveness.

But what choice do you have? You cannot change the past, and God did not give you the capacity to carry it forward. Unforgiveness is a cancer in your soul. You carry it around with you as it eats away at you from the inside. The only choice that remains for you is to forgive. If you don't, the bitterness will eat away at you like an acid.

Unforgiveness is:	Forgiveness is:
You owe me!	You don't owe me.
I'm going to make you pay for what you did by hating you, slandering you, and returning in kind what you did to me.	I'm not looking for payment.
I'm going to recruit other people to my bitterness.	I'm not trying to even the score.

| In the end, I will get my revenge. | I'm writing it off; I'm letting it go. |
| I will make you regret your actions. | God didn't make me so I could carry all this. |

The choice between forgiveness and unforgiveness is a fork in the road of life.

The Bible repeatedly refers to people's shock and surprise when they meet Jesus. Their direct experience is often the flip side of their expectations. It is especially true when it comes to the issue of forgiveness.

> **UNFORGIVENESS IS A CANCER IN YOUR SOUL. YOU CARRY IT AROUND WITH YOU AS IT EATS AWAY AT YOU FROM THE INSIDE.**

The same is true today. In spite of what God's Word has said, many people march forward with the notion that they can experience the Lord's forgiveness and still not forgive other people. They think, *Oh, God will understand. That was just too difficult for me. He'll waive the obligation.* Let me give you a reality check—that's a very bad plan. You have been deceived into thinking you're going to beat the odds. When you stand before God, every choice you've made, every relational transaction that you have lived out will be right there for all to see. If you're an unforgiving person, no matter what you say about knowing Jesus, the reality of your relationship gets called into question. Matthew 6:14–15 bears itself out: **"For if you forgive others their trespasses, your heavenly Father will also forgive you, but if you do not forgive others their trespasses, neither will your Father forgive your trespasses."**

Do you get it? I've been praying these three things for you as you read on:

- That you would understand *with your mind* God's forgiveness of you and what God's Word says about your responsibility to forgive others.

- That you would agree *in your heart* that you have a limited capacity to go forward in any good way in life without choosing to free your heart from unforgiveness.

- That you would *engage your will* and decide today that you will deal with whatever unforgiveness lingers in your heart.

Forgiveness Is a Crisis and a Process

You say, "James, I can make that choice here today, but you just need to know that by Thursday I'll have the offense or wound on my back again. I'll remember it. It will still hurt." I understand that. Forgiveness happens in a moment of crisis, and it continues in a process.

The Crisis

The first step is to see your unforgiveness as sin. You have to know that God is not going to forgive you if you don't forgive others. Stop explaining it, defending it, holding on to it, cherishing it, or reviewing it. You've got to say, "I don't want this for my life. I choose to forgive. My deep desire for God's forgiveness outweighs any desire to hold on to unforgiveness."

The Process

This means on Sunday when you see that person at church who said or did that hurtful thing to you, your injury is going to come back to mind. You've got to promise yourself that you won't bring it up to him, you won't bring it up to other people, and, by far the hardest, you won't bring it up to yourself. Don't review it; don't get yourself worked up about it. Don't let it roll around in your mind. In the crisis, you decided you would forgive him; in the process, you live out your choice not to extract payment for the pain he caused you.

When You Fail in the Process, You Have to Return to the Crisis

You're going to fail at completely letting go at first. The memory of the offense will come out of nowhere, and suddenly you will be right back in the hurt of it. Satan will plant a thought inside your head, and you'll stand in the shower for forty-five minutes staring straight ahead, caught in the negative mental loop.

You failed in the process. So you've got to return to the crisis. Get before the Lord and pray, *God, forgive me. I want to be a forgiving person, and here I am holding on to this again, Lord. Help me again. I commit afresh to let it go.*

I can never excuse or justify my unforgiveness again. I can't go back to being that hateful, slanderous, harsh person I once was. When God points out to me that I'm circling back into unforgiveness, I will repent and go through another crisis and process cycle.

Crisis/process. Crisis/process. Crisis/process. Over time, with God's help, you'll let go of the offense, and God's mercy will wash over you and give you release. There will come a time when you can think of the person or the pain and it will no longer trigger the old response. You will know that forgiveness has taken hold in your life.

You Won't Forget Until You Forgive

No matter how deep the wound, God can bring you to the place where that person's sin doesn't hurt you anymore. You may remember it, but it won't hurt you anymore. God allowed it to happen, and He's using it for good. He loves you. He's making you into an amazing person through the difficult things in your life. You don't need to hang on to it and cherish the hurt anymore. No, you'll forget the pain through the crisis and process of forgiveness.

Crazy Reasons Why We Don't Forgive

Sometimes we fail in the crisis and the process because we cling to crazy rationalizations for not forgiving. For example, some say . . .

1: *The hurt is too big.*

I don't minimize the pain of what happened, trust me, but the size of the offense is no reason to hold on to it. Anyone who loves you will tell you the truth—the bigger the hurt, the more you've got to get rid of it. The pain won't get any smaller because you withhold forgiveness. In fact, it will only increase. Instead, you should approach this like the patient who says, "Doctor, doctor. Get the tumor out! Put me under and get it all. I don't want that in me."

2: *Time will heal it.*

Here's another reality check: time heals *nothing*. The offense is not going away just because you flipped some pages on the calendar. How many people go day after week after month gathering the disappointments and the pain of the past and tucking them away to rehearse later? Whether the hurt is big or small, time heals nothing. If waiting and wallowing in your hurt won't heal it, then clearly the time to forgive is *now*.

3: *I'll forgive when she says she's sorry.*

Sorry, that day isn't coming any time soon. In fact, your life isn't long enough to wait for that day. She's probably not coming back to tell you she's sorry. More than likely, she's off doing the same thing someplace else, and she's not thinking about you at all. She sinned against you because she is selfish, but **"we are convinced of better things concerning you"** (Hebrews 6:9 NASB). God is putting you on the high road where you are going to a better place with your life. Don't hold on to unforgiveness, thinking that somehow you're going to punish the person who hurt you. *She's going to see the resentment in me; it's going to make her feel bad, and then she's going to say she's sorry.* Yeah, quit dreaming. In fact, you're going to endanger other relationships if you continue to hold on to your bitterness.

Bitterness functions like its own whip. There is nothing so bitter as being bitter. It's like a burning coal in your hand. The tighter you grip it, the more you'll get burned.

4: I can't forgive if I can't forget.

You have that backward. You won't forget until you forgive. Unforgiveness is the choice to cherish the injury—"I'll never forget it."

Forgiveness means you will let God heal it, no matter what it is. He can bring you to the place where that doesn't hurt you anymore. It may come to mind and there might be a scar, but it just doesn't hurt anymore. You'll have a perspective on the offense like you haven't had before.

Remember Joseph in the Old Testament? He should be the poster boy for forgiveness, considering what his brothers did to him. Genesis 41:51 tells us, **"Joseph called the name of the first-born Manasseh. 'For,' he said, 'God has made me forget all my hardship and all my father's house.'"** God will help you forget the pain through the crisis and process of forgiveness.

5: If I forgive him, he's only going to do it again. Someone has to make him pay.

I agree, someone has to make him pay—and justice would be God's job. If you're one of His children through faith in Jesus, you can entrust the ultimate settlement to Him. Second Thessalonians 1:6 tells us, **"Since indeed God considers it just to repay with affliction those who afflict you."** God loves you—He's the one responsible as the authority in your life. Romans 12:19 cautions, **"Beloved, never avenge yourselves, but leave it to the wrath of God, for it is written, 'Vengeance is mine, I will repay, says the Lord.'"** You don't want to get between the hammer and the work when God keeps His promises. Let God do His thing. You focus on giving evidence to God that the love of Jesus has penetrated your heart by choosing to forgive.

"But, James, if I forgive, he's just going to do it again." Let's be clear; forgiving someone doesn't mean you put yourself in the position to be injured again. It's fine to say, "Hey, we're not going there anymore." This is a different conversation than bringing it up to him as you rehearse what he's done to you. You should raise the issue again only if it would be to his advantage to remember it.

What about Luke 17:3? Some people hold to Luke 17:3 as a reason to withhold forgiveness. **"If [your brother] repents, forgive him."** They think you're not to forgive someone until he repents.

That's very bad theology. On the cross, Jesus said, **"Father, forgive them"** (Luke 23:34), and the people crucifying Him were a long way from repentance. In Acts 7:60, Stephen also says, **"Lord, do not hold this sin against them,"** even as the crowd was stoning him unjustly.

There are two parts to forgiveness: vertical and horizontal. I am sure you have seen people on television come on after some horrific crime and say, "Even though he killed my daughter, I forgive him." That's sounds noble, but it does no good. In fact, it only cheapens sin.

The Bible calls for immediate, unilateral forgiveness as it relates to your communication with God. Relying on God, you release that person from the obligation he created by injuring you, and you tell God, *I choose to forgive him.* The next time you see that person, you interact with him in kindness, but you should not verbalize your forgiveness. Yes, release him from his debt to you, but only communicate forgiveness to him when and if he repents. If he acknowledges his sin and turns from it, accepting responsibility for his choices, then you can tell him the choice you made earlier to forgive him.

God brings stuff up to me all the time. Within my local church, I've been very open about some areas where God is growing me. When I get into a pressure-cooker situation, I can feel my temperature rise. The Lord will convict me with, *James, watch out! You're going to blow it here if you're not careful!* I don't respond with, "Why are You bringing it up again? I thought You forgave me. I thought You forgot about my sin. I thought You cast it in the depths of the sea" (Micah 7:19). I know He's reminding me of it because He loves me and doesn't want me to fail in this area anymore.

That brings up a good question: *Can God forget stuff? What does God do with the sins when He forgives?* No, He doesn't forget, He does something better. He treats me like it never happened. Forgiveness is treating the person as though the offense never happened. I only bring up a past offense if in doing so I help someone not fall into it again. That's how forgiveness works.

Forgiveness Has No Limits

As I preach, I maintain steady eye contact with the people in the audience. Often I'll say something in the message that makes their minds drift. Their eyes change a little. I see them go off for a moment or two, remembering something from their experience, and then I see them return. I'm sure those brief, thoughtful departures happen to all of us.

That's what happened to Peter in Matthew 18. He was listening to Jesus teach on forgiveness when his mind stopped dead in its tracks. Jesus said, **"If your brother sins against you, go and tell him his fault, between you and him alone. If he listens to you, you have gained your brother"** (v. 15). As Jesus went on teaching, from verse 16 all the way through verse 20, Peter didn't go with Him; he was stuck back on verse 15. He was thinking, *But what about _____? He sins against me a lot. Where is Jesus going with this? Go work it out with the guy? I can't just let him keep doing this same thing to me over and over and over again.*

Peter was caught in a rationalization loop. So the first chance he got, he asked a question: **"Then Peter came up and said to him, 'Lord, how often will my brother sin against me, and I forgive him?'"** (Matthew 18:21).

In the Jewish culture, it was magnanimous to forgive someone three times for the same offense. The religious thinkers of the day had everything distilled into a spiritual recipe when it came to forgiveness: three strikes and you're out. So Peter thought, *Jesus always maxes everything, so instead of three, I'll go six, no, seven.*

"Jesus, my brother sins against me all the time in the same way. How about if I forgive him *seven* times?" Peter was getting ready to receive the

Disciple of the Year award when Jesus replied, *How about seventy times seven.* People debate whether He meant 77 times or 490 times. Doesn't matter—it really means *don't count.* Stop keeping score. Nothing can happen in your life that forgiveness can't conquer. There's nothing that you can't be free from in your past through forgiveness.

What is the manner of your life when it comes to keeping count of offenses? Do you try to put a limit on forgiveness?

- *What You'll Forgive*
  You make categories in your mind of what is forgivable and what is not. *Little things . . . OK; big things . . . depends.*

- *Who You'll Forgive*
  Do you classify candidates to receive forgiveness from you? *Family members . . . yes. That lowlife at work . . . absolutely not. A stranger who crosses me . . . nah.*

- *How Many Times You'll Forgive*
  Peter was doing that. *Seven* times, right? "Fool me once, shame on you; fool me twice, shame on me. I'm keeping track, and this is how many times I'm going to make myself vulnerable to you. After that, I'll never trust you again. After that, I don't have to believe in you anymore."

You can't put limits on forgiveness. But the reality is, it's hard not to. Jesus knew that, so He approached the topic from another side.

Why Would I Choose to Forgive?

The short answer is: because I'm forgiven. My awareness and gratitude for the forgiveness I have received is directly tied to my willingness to forgive!

Jesus, the master communicator, wanted to make sure we understood this, so He told a parable in Matthew 18:23–35. He began by establishing the setting of the lesson. **"Therefore the kingdom of heaven may be compared to**

> **NOTHING CAN HAPPEN IN YOUR LIFE THAT FORGIVENESS CAN'T CONQUER. THERE'S NOTHING THAT YOU CAN'T BE FREE FROM IN YOUR PAST THROUGH FORGIVENESS.**

a king" (v. 23). The kingdom of heaven is the place where what God wants to have happen, happens. The following story illustrates how God deals with people. God is **"a king who wished to settle accounts with his servants. When he began to settle, one was brought to him who owed him ten thousand talents"** (vv. 23–24). One talent was twenty years' wages. Let's say his salary was fifty thousand dollars a year. Twenty years of salary (one talent) would be a million dollars in today's economy. So the ten-thousand–talent debt the man owed would be ten billion dollars.

If you are a big sports fan in Chicago, you could buy all the professional franchises in the Windy City—the Bears, the Bulls, the Blackhawks, the Cubs, and even the White Sox for ten billion dollars. Then you could build each team its own personal state-of-the-art stadium and still have plenty left over to buy popcorn for everyone in the stands for every game forever. Ten billion dollars is a lot of money.

In fact, when Jesus said the man owed ten thousand talents, He was really saying he owed an unpayable debt. And since the servant could not pay, his master ordered him to be sold, along with his wife and his children and his liquidated household. That didn't come close to paying the debt, but he'd pay what he could and be a slave for the rest of his life.

"So the servant fell on his knees, imploring him, 'Have patience with me, and I will pay you everything'" (v. 26). It is a bit insane to plead, "I will pay you everything," when there's no chance of that happening. But out of pity or compassion, the king released him and forgave the debt.

Do you understand whom the debtor represents? The debtor is you. The king is God, and you're the one with the debt that cannot be paid (this was part of the groundwork we explored back in chapter 2). Jesus was saying that in spite of the fact that you're a good person, have done a lot of good things, and have tried to make some right choices, before a holy God you owe a debt that can never be paid. It is only the grace of God that keeps you from falling into hell this moment. You can't earn God's favor, you can't pay off your debt, you can't work to change it.

This all revolves around seeing yourself clearly: *I have nothing with which to commend myself to God. I don't deserve His grace. I don't deserve His forgiveness. I can't earn His favor.*

Numbers 14:18 and Nahum 1:3 say God will not clear the guilty. He will not lightly dismiss our sin. Of course, the good news of the gospel is that Jesus Christ came into the world to pay a debt He did not owe because we owed a debt we could not pay. It's outrageous that Jesus Christ took upon Himself the penalty for our sin. It is mind-blowing to think that the God of the universe would love us enough to provide for the forgiveness of our sins through the punishment of His own Son.

All of the punishment for our debt was poured out upon Christ so we could be set free. That is the gospel. The stunning thing is not that this is the only way; the stunning thing is that there is a way at all. Holiness demanded that sin be paid for; love found a way to pay the price Himself (1 John 4:7). Jesus Christ accomplished the way to be forgiven by God.

God didn't send His Son by accident. If you could have solved the problem on your own, He would have let you. The deliberate act of the second person of the Trinity dying as a substitutionary payment so that your sin could be forgiven was the only way.

I deserved judgment, I got forgiveness. I deserved death, I got life by faith in Jesus. I deserve hell, I get heaven . . . all because I'm loved by God and can be forgiven by God.

You've got to let the love of God change you. If God's love and forgiveness are your identity, you will be impacted in countless ways. One of these ways is by an awareness of your need to pass God's blessing on to others.

People who have experienced the forgiveness of God are forgiving people. We don't forgive perfectly, but we are growing in our willingness and ability to forgive. Take Ephesians 4:31–32 to heart and to life: **"Let all bitterness and wrath and anger and clamor and slander be put away from you, along with all malice. Be kind to one another, tender-hearted, forgiving one another, as God in Christ forgave you."** If you really understand that God has forgiven you, you're also giving it away. If you're not giving it away, you don't have God's forgiveness, no matter what you say.

If you're still holding up the barrier of *what was done against me*, you're not able to see what you did to God. If you are focused on the sins of others, you will not see the tragedy of your own. One clear glimpse of our sinful selves before God will eclipse any horizontal wrongdoing, no matter how grievous that injury may be.

It's your choice to allow your life to be altered by this reality. You have to recognize your condition before a holy God. You need to be baffled by His love and rocked by His forgiveness. Throw your arms around what God has done for the salvation of your own soul. Have you done that? It all starts right there—you need to be forgiven through your faith in Jesus Christ (for more on this, reread chapter 2).

When you realize that you possess priceless forgiveness you did not deserve, you'll make the choice to forgive others. Think on this: you have been provided for through all of eternity. Ten thousand years from today, you will be singing the praises of the righteousness of God who loved you enough to give Christ in your place for your forgiveness. This is a life-altering choice, not some Band-Aid you put on an I-feel-guilty sore.

If your life has been changed by the forgiveness of Christ, the truest and surest demonstration of it is that you want to extend that forgiveness to other people.

How's that going? The Bible says that if you don't want to forgive other people, you've never really experienced the forgiveness of God yourself. Perhaps you've gone to church or prayed some self-centered prayer, but if you've really embraced the Lord, one of the things that happens is you increasingly become a more forgiving person over time. God grows in you a greater capacity to extend to others the grace that you've experienced.

Because Unforgiveness Destroys Other People

To withhold forgiveness is a destructive, devastating choice. Jesus had a way of capturing in a sentence or two what we have taken a couple of pages to unpack. The king forgave the unpayable debt and closed the books. Let's go back to the parable in Matthew 18: **"But when that same servant went out, he found one of his fellow servants who owed him a hundred denarii"** (v. 28). Now this was no small amount. It was around one hundred days' wages. So if fifty thousand dollars is a year's wage, then two-fifths of that would be about twenty thousand dollars. The forgiven debtor went after one of his fellow servants who owed him some significant money. First, he grabbed him. Then he started to choke him. Then, having gotten his attention, the speech began, "Pay what you owe!"

Remember, the debtor was just forgiven ten billion dollars, and now he's out choking this guy for a hundred days' wages. He should have said, "You can't believe what just happened to me! I just was forgiven a googleplex of money. Hey—don't worry about what you owe me. Just let it go." That's what we should be like, if we're changed by the forgiveness of God.

Just look at what unforgiveness cost in Jesus' story (and in our lives):

- *First, shattered relationships*
  Once he was done choking the guy, I think that relationship was pretty much over. The barbeque on Friday night was off. "Hey, dude, sorry about that choking thing yesterday. I just lost my head for a minute." No, that didn't happen. Unforgiveness destroyed that relationship.

- *Next, shattered reputations*
  When the forgiven servant refused to listen to his coworker, he had him put in prison. When the other coworkers saw what had taken place, they were incensed. *He was forgiven ten billion dollars, but he's strangling that guy for twenty thousand?* So they squealed on the servant to the king. The forgiven servant lost all of his credibility and integrity with his fellow servants. They probably said something like,

You may have a high and holy thing going on at church on Sunday, but it's definitely not working at the office on Wednesdays.

When he got before the king, the servant was humiliated. This guy was pretty chatty last time, but now the king just says, **"You wicked servant. I forgave you all that debt because you pleaded with me. And should not you have had mercy on your fellow servant, as I had mercy on you?"** (vv. 32–33). He doesn't get to utter a word. He wouldn't know what to say even if he could.

- *Finally, shattered results*
  The king changed his mind and reinstated the debt. *You owe me so much money that you're going to prison until you pay.* This was the same approach the wicked servant had tried on his debtor—put him in prison. Considering how much money you can earn in prison, this decision isn't going to help with the debt at all. At this point, the king was mirroring the attitude of the servant who wouldn't forgive. *I don't care if he ever pays me. I just want to make him pay.* We see here that unforgiveness gradually leaves us with little but a thirst for vengeance. Unforgiveness creates a vortex in the center of life that pulls everything into its destructive vacuum.

Unforgiveness isn't private. People will seethe in silence, insisting, *This is just between me and him.* But that's not true. It's also destructive to innocent people around you. How many people in your life have suffered because of an unforgiveness issue in your heart that has absolutely nothing to do with them? It seeps into the tone of all your conversations. It leaks out in your impertinence and impatience, your short temper and rashness. People who you love, who have done nothing wrong, suffer because of the unforgiveness that you're holding over someone else.

Three Seasons of Forgiveness

Sometime I'm going to write a book called *All the Stuff They Never Taught Me in Seminary.* One of the lessons that people—especially in the ministry—need to learn is the absolutely nonnegotiable need to be a forgiver.

When Harvest Bible Chapel was eight years old, I had a life-changing experience with the Lord. I had not yet taught on forgiveness, and I didn't completely understand it. By this time in our church, I had piled up some fairly significant disappointments with a few people. I had written in my journal, *Lord, I need to learn about forgiveness. I can't carry this forward, God. I don't have the capacity. I can't go on if I can't leave some things behind.*

I wrote down the names of six particular people. I remember very clearly getting on my knees and envisioning a little leather pouch, and after writing out the people's names on little pieces of paper, I put them in the bag and tightened it up. I wrote the word *Forgiveness* on the outside. In my mind's eye, I knelt down and laid that bag at the cross, saying, *God, in view of all that You've forgiven me, I'm letting this go. I'm leaving it behind. I'm releasing them from the obligation that resulted when they injured me.* It was a life-changing decision.

Years later, in the winter of 2002, I woke up in the middle of the night. I couldn't sleep because of unforgiveness. I went to my desk, opened my Bible, reviewed some verses, and did this same exercise again. I wrote out the names of five people. Sadly, one of the original six was still there. (I had failed in the process, and now I was returning to the crisis.) I had to write down his name again. The other original five were gone, but there were four new names to take their place. I prayed, *God, I'm having a crisis here. I'm choosing to forgive. I'm letting it go, God. I'm releasing this to you.*

Another little bag, another kneeling at the cross. What followed were weeks and months of disciplining myself in the process of forgiveness. I did a reality check this week as I thought about this chapter, and, thankfully, all five of those names from 2002 were gone. I can remember them, but they're not painful to think about anymore. I am healed—released—and you will be too.

But the story is not over, and the process goes on. I have five new names on my heart—names of people who hurt or disappointed me or broke a trust. Another crisis for me to confront unforgiveness. Just the other day, I wrote those names down, and I'm now in the process of forgiveness. *I'm having a crisis again, God. I'm committing myself to You for the sake of forgiveness. I'm letting it go. You didn't make me to carry this, God.* I'm making the choice to leave it all behind, thankfully, because it's so destructive.

Because Unforgiveness Destroys Me

Nothing will cut a swath of devastation across your soul like unforgiveness. It is the absolute opposite of the life God calls you to live. You don't have to prove you were right. You don't have to demonstrate the superiority of anything. You've got to let it go.

Notice in the text where it says, **"And in anger his master delivered him to the jailers, until he should pay all his debt"** (v. 34). The language here may refer to more than incarceration—it could be a place of torture. Bible scholars believe this describes not just this life but the life to come— that a person whose life is a continuing pattern of unforgiveness is not truly saved.

This is borne out in Matthew 6:15 (NASB): **"If you don't forgive others, your Father will not forgive your sins."** That's why Jesus closes, **"So also my heavenly Father will do to every one of you"** (Matthew 18:35). Our Father in heaven will deliver every one of you over to the torturer if you do not forgive your brother from your heart. Living in unforgiveness is a barren, tortured existence. Even those of us who have experienced God's love and forgiveness need to be reminded about what we have received because we so easily slide into a self-centered mess of unforgiveness. God knows that sometimes only the crushing weight of accumulated offenses will get our attention, so He lets us pile them up.

The Medical World Recognizes
the Positive and Negative Effects of Forgiveness

In 2004, researchers used MRI scans and found that unforgiveness was destructive to the emotional health of a person. They also found that the hormonal patterns of an unforgiving person mimicked those of a person who is under stress.[1] Another study that same year found that unforgiveness on the part of a victim correlates with the development of psychiatric disorders.[2]

Wellness issues expert Carol Buckley Frazier says there have been about sixty conclusive studies that show a clear connection between the health of the body and the effects of unforgiveness. In one study, vengeful thoughts for as little as sixteen seconds led to an increase in blood pressure, heart rate, and muscle tension, and a decrease in T-cell counts (T-cells are disease fighters). On the positive side, the research shows that when we practice forgiveness, our body's level of cortisol (a vital hormone involved in our response to stress) decreases as the level of anger drops; our ability to love and feel love improves as well as our mental and emotional health. Our immune system also improves as well as cardiovascular functioning.[3]

Get this. Forgiveness can actually make you healthier, happier, and maybe even slimmer. No wonder God says to forgive. The Creator of our bodies knows that we were not designed to hold on to grudges. We do not have the capacity to do this. Unforgiveness is sin. It will eat away at your being until you choose the crisis and commit to the process of forgiveness.

This is an awesome day—you have the choice to change. You have the chance to choose. I wonder if heaven is leaning over you and wondering what choice you are going to make. Your destiny depends on it. To clarify, you are not saved by forgiving, but forgiving is what saved people do. This is one of the litmus tests for reality. Making the choice to forgive is one of the things that prove you truly belong to God.

The Ability to Forgive Is a Gift from God

I do not have unlimited capacity. I can't carry unforgiveness and continue to pastor a church or continue to lead as I'm called to. I could not do what God has called me to do in my life without forgiveness. The burdens would be too heavy, and I would give up.

What if I didn't forgive people in my past? I have a loving wife, a wonderful marriage, and exceptional kids. What garbage would be trashed over my house if I hadn't made the choice to forgive? I love them too much to let unforgiveness spoil what we have together.

Let's Review

When you think, *It's too much, I can't let go*—believe that in God's strength, you can.

When you think, *I won't be able to forget his offense*—believe that with God's help you'll eventually be able to remember it in a very different way.

When you fear, *What if he does it again?*—be ready to remind him he's not going to do it to you again, and turn it over to God to handle.

When you wonder, *What if I go back?*—you will. But when you fail in the process, return to the crisis.

I promise you that someday you'll look back on this hurt and say, "I'm free."

There is such blessing in forgiveness. Forgiveness absolutely is a choice that will change your life forever.

A Choice to Make

Acknowledge the Choice

- What are the warning signs in your life that indicate you are having capacity issues?

- Why do you think unforgiveness has such an effect on our capacity?

Consider the Choice

- How many of the detours and delays over forgiveness that were mentioned in this chapter have you tried in life? How have you discovered their ineffectiveness?

- What are your most vivid and significant personal experiences of being forgiven? How do they motivate your willingness to forgive?

Make the Choice

- Allow the Lord to bring to mind the names and the faces of people you need to forgive, past or present. Take time to think through your family, coworkers, and significant acquaintances over the years. Perhaps you will remember someone you haven't seen for a long time but realize you don't love him because you are holding him accountable for a hurt he caused. Get his face in your heart right now.

  Now the choice lies before you. Will you forgive him? Say, "I choose to forgive _____ (name the person) for _____ (name the offense)." Use the following short prayer to review your reasons to forgive and keep the focus on the way unforgiveness clouds your relationship with God. *God, I need to live in the present. I can't be bound up in my past. I can't carry these things with me. It's hurting me, it's hurting others, and it's hurting You. Forgive me for my unforgiveness and the pain it has caused. Amen.*

Whether you feel anything or not at this moment, believe God hears your repentant prayer. Feelings will follow obedience. Joy comes through obedience. Believe that God loves you, that you are forgiven, that Jesus is Lord, and that His Word is your blueprint for life. Now choose to forgive others because God has forgiven you.

- In Christ, there are no barriers to forgiveness, but sometimes there are limiting factors to reconciliation. Romans 12:18 exhorts us to **"if possible, so far as it depends on you, live peaceably with all."** If you are in a situation where forgiveness has been extended and now you're seeking reconciliation, ask yourself, *Have I done as much as I can do to restore the relationship?*

We are not supposed to pursue a person to try to make him reconciled to us. We are first to forgive the person (or ask for forgiveness), and then we are to turn the other cheek. Go the second mile. Give the person double what he asks. Do everything to work out things, especially understanding that if the person does not follow Christ, he will not have the same priority of obeying Scripture. More information on this topic can be found at www.store. walkintheword.com/p-1045-always-resolve-everything-now-the-key-to-lasting-relationships.aspx.

A Choice Prayer

Father, it must grieve Your heart even more than mine to live in such a dark world where people say things and do things that wound so deeply. But by Your grace I am choosing to forgive. I am simply releasing the pain to You and letting it go. I choose by an act of my will to trust You and Your Word. I'm not going to hold it over the person who hurt me anymore when I have to see him or talk to him. I'm not going to go over it in my mind anymore. I want to handle it as You would. I want to be a forgiving person.

Thank You for being so specific with me and bringing specific people and situations to my mind. By Your grace I leave it here. I'm packing it up in a bag and leaving it at the foot of Your cross. I see the names of those I need to forgive in the bag. This burden belongs with You. You didn't create me to carry this. I do not have the capacity to go forward with this. It's destroying me. With Your help and Your strength, I choose to leave it here at the cross—where I remember all You did for me. Everything comes into perspective and context when I stand here. Forgive me for my pride, my anger, and my pointed comments. Cover me with Your love. Let Your grace displace all that is ugly and angry and unforgiving in me. By Your grace, I choose to forgive.

In His name. Amen.

Therefore do not be anxious about tomorrow, for tomorrow will be anxious for itself. Sufficient for the day is its own trouble.

—Matthew 6:34

And when he got into the boat, his disciples followed him. And behold, there arose a great storm on the sea, so that the boat was being swamped by the waves; but he was asleep. And they went and woke him, saying, "Save us, Lord; we are perishing." And he said to them, "Why are you afraid, O you of little faith?" Then he rose and rebuked the winds and the sea, and there was a great calm. And the men marveled, saying, "What sort of man is this, that even winds and sea obey him?"

—Matthew 8:23–27

I Choose to Trust

I choose to trust God with my future—because I can and because He invites me to and because there is really no other option that works.

I wish my mind were smart enough to only work on things it can affect. Sadly, it is not. Sometimes my thoughts rush to review its perceptions of the future and begins to rev and race about all sorts of uncertainties. These dark clouds seem so close I feel sure it will start to rain soon, but no, the uncertainties never arrive as I see them; they only hang in the distance and cloud my judgment, casting a shadow over my happiness here and now. They are just far enough around the corner so that nothing can actually be done about them now.

It happened to me last night. The clock said 4:10 a.m., and I was wide awake. I was in bed where I was supposed to be at that hour, but my mind was taking a tour of the land of tomorrow. The only thing I knew for sure was that my meandering mind would not be back to sleep until I put the future where it belonged . . . in God's hands.

Why? Because of our limited capacity, which we learned about in the last chapter as it relates to our past. But God did not design our DNA with the ability to carry the future either. The only place to focus my thoughts is on today. So what, then, do we do with these future thoughts that we are so tempted to trade in for the present? That's what this chapter is all about.

The Word on Anxiety

Look at what Jesus said in Matthew 6:34: **"Therefore do not be anxious about tomorrow, for tomorrow will be anxious for itself. Sufficient for the day is its own trouble."** One translation says, **"Each day has enough trouble of its own"** (NASB).

Do you start the day thinking, *I don't have enough on my mind today; I'm going to borrow some trouble from tomorrow and then invent some new problems to load myself up?* Yeah, me neither. The word *trouble* in Jesus' statement means "adverse circumstances, problems, and hardship." Let's just agree with Jesus and each other that every day does have enough of its own trouble.

Jesus says, in effect, *Let's compartmentalize here. You can't carry the weight of the past—that's what forgiveness is for. You can't carry all the uncertainties of the future; you must focus on today. Let's deal with what we can.*

When I was growing up in the 1960s, there were a total of three television channels. Think of your mind being like that. You can set it on channel 1, channel 2, or channel 3:

- *Channel 1 is your past.*
  Not a great channel to tune in to all the time. There's nothing new; it's always reruns—mostly in black and white, with stale storylines.

- *Channel 2 is your present.*
  This is reality TV. Awesome things happen in this up-to-the-minute broadcast. I'm on channel 2 right now as I write this. I'm pouring everything I have into communicating to you the dangers of worry and the positive results of trusting God. I'm not thinking about the last thing I wrote on my blog or about my sermon next week. I'm living on channel 2 right now, and I'm confident I can make a difference because channel 2 is interactive. I can make choices when I'm on this channel.

- *Channel 3 is your future.*
  Major static is the only stuff you see when you tune in to the future

broadcast, so you have to invent what you see. The results are mostly horror TV, full of all kinds of nasty programs to unsettle your heart. You could watch channel 3 all day and fill your imagination with things you don't even need to know or think about. A lot of people spend their whole lives watching channel 3. When you camp on channel 3, you get these three dangerous emotions:

- *Worry.* It comes from an old German word that means "to choke." As your mind drifts to channel 3, worry about the future strangles your happiness, joy, and peace. Your soul begins to hyperventilate!

- *Fear.* This response is more visceral. *Something is coming and it's not good.* It's more of a gut reaction to something uncertain up ahead. Fear is a magnifying glass, enlarging everything you look at. Fear takes a possible threat and blows it way out of proportion, amplifying it so it's beyond rational thinking and overly emotional. Second Timothy 1:7 says, **"God has not given us a spirit of fear"** (NKJV). If you have fear about the future, you've chosen it for yourself.

- *Anxiety.* Jesus Himself mentions anxiety three times right in our text, so you know He was making an important point: **"Therefore do not be anxious"** (Matthew 6:34). *Anxiety* literally means "to divide the mind." Anxiety develops when your mind switches back and forth between channel 2 and channel 3. When you're flipping so often between the present and the future, you can't focus on anything of value, and your mind gets trapped in a cycle that is nearly impossible to break.

We were not made for worry, fear, or anxiety. The manufacturer's specifications do not allow for this. It's no different than if someone poured sand in your gas tank or slipped a virus into your computer. It goes against the mechanics of how those things work. Worry gums up and finally crashes the human spirit. When you constantly keep a tally in your mind of all the unknowns of the future and repeatedly review and extrapolate from your list, the uncertainties become so large that they can crush you. You are defeated before anything actually happens! All of life gets sideways when you're on the anxiety program.

You were not wired for worry.

You were not fashioned for fear.

You were not made for the misery of trembling about tomorrow.

Stay tuned to channel 2. That's the essence of, **"Sufficient for the day is its own trouble"** (Matthew 6:34).

A Lesson from the Country Music World

Do you know who Marijohn Wilkin is? You may not recognize her name — but you probably know her songs.

She grew up in a wonderful, Christian home in Texas; her parents loved the Lord and raised her well. As a teen she moved to Nashville, where she became one of the biggest names in country music, writing songs for Mel Tillis, Johnny Cash, Patti Page, Charley Pride, Patsy Cline, Glen Campbell, and many others. Despite her fame, however, Marijohn was a wreck by the time she turned fifty. She was consumed with fear about the future.

Fear drove her to alcohol. Alcohol drove her to multiple suicide attempts. When life finally got desperate enough, she remembered the God she left behind. Marijohn found a church and met with the pastor, who opened God's Word and directed her back to a life of faith. She realized that she couldn't go on being consumed by anxiety and fear. God didn't make her to work like that.

She left the pastor's office, drove home, and gave her heart back to the Lord. She then wrote one of the most famous country songs of all time. Since it has been recorded by hundreds of singers, you have probably heard several versions of it:

One day at a time, sweet Jesus, that's all I'm askin' from You
Just give me the strength to do every day what I have to do

Yesterday's gone, sweet Jesus, and tomorrow may never be mine
Lord help me today, show me the way one day at a time[1]

Marijohn totally got what we're talking about here: *I'm not switching over to channel 3 anymore. I'm going to live on channel 2.* Sufficient for today are the troubles of today. Marijohn died in 2006 at the age of 86, a happy, contented, alcohol-free, committed Christian, trusting God with her future. She got it! The question is, *Do you get it?* One day at a time—God established the limits of our capacity.

God made you to focus on the things that you can affect, to work on the things you can improve, the stuff that is right in front of you. By narrowing your attention to the present, you will not exhaust your limited capacity. You can't carry yesterday or your imagined tomorrow—you have to trust the Lord today. You'd think that would be an easy thing to admit, but faith is a universal struggle. If you're a worrier, this next part is for you.

I Cannot Control the Future

If you're going to get free from worry, you have to believe with all your heart that you cannot control the future. Jesus told us not to worry about tomorrow because **"tomorrow will be anxious for itself"** (Matthew 6:34*b*). Tomorrow will worry about tomorrow. Maybe you're such a worrier that you're worried about who's worrying about tomorrow. Leave it be; it'll worry about itself.

> **WORRY KEEPS YOU FROM DOING WHAT YOU CAN DO TODAY TO AFFECT A BETTER FUTURE.**

Fear focuses on what you cannot control.

Worry keeps you from doing what you can do today to affect a better future.

Worry chokes your ability to make good choices today.

Fretting about the future does not alter it.

It's time to face the fact that you just can't control your future. Break it down into some categories and say to yourself:

- *I can't control my health future.*

  I might get cancer. I might have a heart attack. I might find out tomorrow that I have MS or Alzheimer's. I might die in a car accident. How sad that would be, but I can't control it.

  Besides, worry keeps me from doing what I *can* do. I can make the best possible health choices today. I can choose what I eat, how often I exercise, and all the things we know very well contribute to health. Worrying about the future doesn't change my health, but it does insulate me from doing the positive things that affect my future today.

- *I can't control my family's future.*

  My kids might rebel and reject God, at least for a season. They might make awful choices that break my heart. In spite of my desire to have a happy marriage for a lifetime, my spouse might turn on me. He might wander away. He might destroy what we have built together, and I won't be able to stop or change it. I can't control others.

  Worry keeps me from doing what I can do today to affect a better future. I can love my family today, first and foremost. I can pray for them, forgive them, and ask forgiveness of them. I can serve them. Worrying about them might help me feel like I'm involved somehow, but all I'm doing is spinning my wheels in the mud. I have to admit I can't control my family's future.

- *I can't control my financial future.*

  I might never get to retire. The stock market could go down in flames this week, and all my investments could be ashes in a matter of hours or days. I might lose my job. I can't control that.

  But worrying about those things insulates me from doing what I

can do today. I can save more money than I spend. I can say no to
things I don't need and pay down that credit card once and for all.
I can work hard at my job and try to be the best employee that I can
be. I can take classes and expand my career opportunities. I can do
a lot. But worrying about the future makes me think I'm busy with
important stuff instead of actually doing what I can do. It insulates
me from the actions today that will ensure a better tomorrow.

- *I can't control my environmental future.*
  We live in a very dark time; temptation is everywhere. Sin and
  solicitations to sin are around every corner and are getting louder.
  I can't change it. I can't control the moral climate that I live in. I
  can't control the outcome of elections. But I can choose to trust
  God and turn to Him for strength and victory.

- *I can't control the organization I work for.*
  *Have you seen the latest quarterly reports? Where is this going
  exactly?* I can't make my job everything I want it to be. I'm not
  smart enough or capable enough to see my career become all I
  have hoped it will be. But I can choose to trust God with my job.

- *I can't control my church.*
  There are some things about my church that I'm just not comfortable
  with, and if I were in charge, I wouldn't do it that way. My church
  is not perfect, and neither am I . . . but I can choose to trust God,
  who wants to show Himself to the world through my church.

- *I can't control my neighborhood.*
  I wish I lived on a better street. I've dreamed of different neighbors. But I can choose to trust God, who loves the people in my
  neighborhood.

Don't Worry

Can you relate to any of those statements? The problem is that worry keeps
us from doing what we *can* do. We can be godly in this immoral climate.

We can vote. We can pray. We can be loving and kind to the people around us. You and I can be the best employees in our company. You and I can be the most faithful, prayerful church members possible, rolling up our sleeves and working and praying and giving ourselves so God's church can be more of what He wants it to be.

Worry costs us a tragic loss of energy and effort. If you've been around me much, you know I say these next two things a lot.

1: *When God says, "Don't!" He means, "Don't hurt yourself."*
For example, when God says, **"Be anxious for nothing"** (Philippians 4:6 NASB), He is issuing a protective statement for you. Obey it and you will be blessed. When you disregard His Word, you open yourself up to the consequences. His commands always have our benefit as their ultimate purpose.

2: *Choose to sin; choose to suffer.*
Need any support for that? Every choice comes with multiple, often unintended consequences. We can't say to God, "I'll choose to sin; Your job is to protect me from the bad consequences of my choices." He loves us too much to accept that arrangement.

Evidence of Anxiety

The consequences of trying to control the future are devastating. Doctors list the following side effects of worry: irritability, depression, insomnia, fatigue, headaches, tightness in the neck muscles, high blood pressure, elevated heart rate, upset stomach, ulcers. Some studies have indicted that worry weakens a person's immune system, making him more susceptible to colds and life-threatening diseases, including cancer. Anxiety can tempt some to overeat or overwork, leading to other health-related issues. Are any of these side effects on display at your house? These are the results of spending your life on channel 3—instead of trusting God.

Have you noticed an increase in the number of drugstores around your town? I know where I live they seem to be sprouting on every corner. This week I found out that they are tearing down my favorite burger joint to put in a drugstore. Why? Because we are consumed with worry about the future. How do we really spell relief? D-R-U-G-S-T-O-R-E!

Here are some of the things that druggists prescribe to stave off the effects of anxiety: Valium, Halcion, Prozac, BuSpar, Ativan, Centrex. At least thirty products are available at the corner drugstore to calm the troubled waters, to quiet minds consumed with fears about what they cannot control. There's got to be a better way than medicating worry.

My friend, you and I were not made for this.

I Will Always Face Uncertainty

Why didn't somebody tell me this earlier in my life? In my idealism, I thought that with due diligence, I could get everything fixed. If there were things up ahead that concerned me, I could just make a plan to solve them. Eventually, I would have it all figured out, and then the automatic pilot of the good life could take over. It's only more recently that I have grasped that life will *never* be "together" this side of eternity. It's hard to accept sometimes that perfect is only for heaven.

There will always be people problems. There will always be financial challenges. There will always be a home burden or a crisis of some kind. Every day I live in this world, there will always be some uncertainty ringing my doorbell. I once thought that if you just worked hard enough, eventually everything would be sorted out, categorized, and put neatly on the shelf. I have never gotten to that day, and what's more, I now know it's never coming.

In Matthew 8:23–24, we land in Jesus' life on a day that perfectly illustrates the imperfections of human existence. **"When he got into the boat, his disciples followed him. And behold, there arose a great storm."** In the original language, the two words *great storm* can be translated to "mega" and "seismic." As in, *And behold, there arose a mega seismic on the sea, so that the boat was being swamped by the waves.* It's worth remembering that this description comes from Matthew, one disciple who was *not* a fisherman. He had the terrified layman's perspective on this storm!

I have a few questions about that whole scene:

1. *Did Jesus not check the Weather Channel?* He totally knew that storm was coming, yet He led them right into it. *Get in the boat, boys.* He knowingly took them into harm's way.

2. *Could Jesus have stopped the storm before it started?* Sure, He could have. But He let the storm come.

3. *So is it true to say that He* wanted *the storm?* I think we could surmise that He was actually looking forward to how He was going to use the storm in the lives of the disciples.

Let's get our theology straight. Sometimes Jesus disguises exciting opportunities for personal growth as difficult circumstances. We would choose to avoid trials at all costs, but Jesus sees the bigger picture.

Remember in John 11 when Mary and Martha were stressed out because their brother Lazarus was sick? They sent the delegation to Jesus with the message: *You've got to get over here right away! The one You love is sick.* John 11:6 says, **"So, when he heard that Lazarus was ill, he stayed two days longer in the place where he was."** Jesus delayed—deliberately.

This was prime teaching time, and Jesus knew where it was going to take them. Later on, when Lazarus had died, Jesus finally said, *Come on, guys, we're going to go wake up Lazarus.* Now the disciples, trying to get out of going near Jerusalem (the Jewish leaders had tried to kill them the last time they were there), said, *Well, Jesus, if he's sleeping, he'll wake up. We don't need to risk getting stoned over it.* Then Jesus turned and said plainly, **"Lazarus has died."** And the shocker—**"and for your sake I am glad that I was not there, so that you may believe"** (vv. 14–15).

Jesus' words offer an awesome insight into what He thinks about your life and mine. *Lazarus is dead, and I'm glad for your sake, so that you may believe.* Glad, Jesus? Yes, glad. The Christian life will always come back to faith. *Will I believe even when the storms blow in? Will I trust Him?* It's always our faith that's on the line.

Back to Matthew 8:23. To emphasize the contrast between faith and doubt, while the storm was brewing, Jesus got in the boat and went to sleep. I bet you He was smiling, too, as He curled up in the bow of the boat. *This is going to be amazing!*

This is a great portrait of Jesus. We see His humanity in that He was tired from a day of ministry. And we see His confidence in that He was able to sleep even though He knew a seismic storm was blowing in. Notice how the scripture says He *went* to sleep—not fell asleep. He was so calm and confident that He intentionally checked out, waiting for the next teachable moment.

We can avoid storms in our lives about as often as we can divert weather patterns over our city. Go stand outside and try. The reality is that there will always be times of uncertainty. In the landscape of our lives, we will enjoy a few blue-sky days, but mostly there will always be a dark cloud gathering somewhere on the horizon of your life, reminding you of the daily need to trust God with tomorrow. You can't set your hope on the illusion that somehow you're going to sort everything out one day. There will always be enough to keep you on your knees. And just about the time you think, *I don't really need to pray that much this week—Wham!* Face it; on this side of eternity, there will never be a day when you won't need to trust the God who loves you.

My future and yours will be ravaged by the waves until we embrace the fact that God allows these storms for our good. He won't let us drown. Can you imagine how it would have wrecked the Gospels if it went down like this: there was a storm, Jesus was asleep, and four of the disciples drowned. Of course not! He would not let them, nor will He let you drown.

But back in the moment, the disciples were wild with fear. Even the professional fishermen knew things were out of control. So they **"woke him, saying, 'Save us, Lord; we are perishing'"** (v. 25). In the original language, it was just this: "Lord, save!"

Notice Jesus' response to them. **"Why are you afraid, O you of little faith?"** (v. 26). Bible scholars debate whether or not that was a rebuke.

Matthew was clearly fond of reporting how many times Jesus said it. First, here in Matthew 8:26, when they feared the storm. In 14:31, when Peter took his eyes off the Lord and began to sink. In 16:8, when they forgot about the miracle of multiplying bread. In 17:20, when they failed to heal the demon-possessed boy. *O you of little faith!*—Jesus said it to them a lot. How often does He say that to us?

> [**NOTHING EVER HAS NOTHING TO DO WITH FAITH.**]

In my mind's eye, I see Him smiling when He says it here in the storm. I think it's tender, as if He's saying, *You don't get it yet, do you?* He's not mad at them, but sad that they didn't think He could take care of them.

Think how you would feel as a parent of anxious kids. What if your child said, "Daddy, what if we run out of money and this is our last month together as a family?" You would smile and shake your head and say, "We'll figure something out, son. Your Mom and I love you, and we're going to take care of you."

In my bent, I would have been tempted to say something smart like, "Well, it's not so much a faith issue, Jesus, as it is a sinking issue, or a too-far-to-swim-to-shore issue." But I would have been wrong. Nothing ever has nothing to do with faith. The issue is always, *Will I trust God? Do I believe He has my best interest at heart?*

I believe that Jesus is ordering the circumstances of my life so that I will come to the place where I will cry out, "Lord, save me!"

I Can Bring My Burdens to the Lord

Let's give credit where credit is due. Here the disciples were in this "mega-seismic" storm, the boat was taking on water, and Jesus was asleep. So they woke Him with, "Lord, save us!" The disciples at least took their burden straight to Jesus.

Remember when I told you about my sleepless night? Instead of just lying awake at 4:10 a.m., I took my cue from the disciples, rolled out of bed onto my knees, and engaged a three-step process, praying something like this:

Lord, save me! Save me from this! You see this burden, it's too much for me. I cannot carry it myself. And Lord, I know who You are. You've made Yourself so clear. You've shown Yourself so faithful.

Then I prayed the second part: *I know who I am, Lord. I know what I can't do. I know what I can't change. I know what I can't work on. Lord, I know my capacity.*

By then, this third thing came easily. I prayed, *Lord, I know that these burdens belong to You.* And I named the burdens, one by one. *You never said I could or should carry these. I trust You instead.*

Well, it was amazing. I got back in bed and in short order, I was asleep. I would commend this practice to you. Psalm 116:1–2 says, **"I love the LORD, because he has heard / my voice . . . / Because He inclined his ear to me, / therefore I will call on him as long as I live."** Heaven is waiting for those moments when you get alone with God and fall on your knees. Jesus will rush to your rescue. As long as you think you can handle the crisis on your own, He'll be sleeping in the front of the boat. But the moment you lift your voice and say, "Lord, save me" is the moment He shows up.

Don't toss and turn and worry and be anxious. Don't waste your time counting sheep; be the sheep who runs to the Shepherd. Prayer is the transaction that transfers your burden to God. The reason so many of God's people are so heavy with anxiety is we're so poor at prayer.

I Choose to Trust

Trust is the antidote to anxiety; it's the resolution of worry and the destruction of fear. Trust is the act of my will to give my burdens to God. It's like a muscle—as you exercise it, trust gets stronger.

Trust is walking forward moment by moment, having rolled your burden onto God. When I sense that I am taking it back on myself, I go back to my knees, get the burden back on God, get on my feet again, and continue to trust. I take the same crisis/process approach with trust that I take with practicing forgiveness.

When you off-load your burden onto God, you can pick up a promise from His Word. Second Peter 1:4 tells us that **"he has granted to us his precious and very great promises, so that through them you may become partakers of the divine nature, having escaped from the corruption that is in the world."** There are literally hundreds of promises that apply to your specific burden. God's Word is filled with treasure.

> **TRUST IS THE ACT OF MY WILL TO GIVE MY BURDENS TO GOD.**

I claimed Isaiah 41:10 that night. **"Fear not, for I am with you; / be not dismayed, for I am your God; / I will strengthen you, I will help you, / I will uphold you with my righteous right hand."** There it is! God is doing this whole thing with one hand tied behind His back. He's not stressed or strained. He's not worried about what to do. He has absolutely no capacity limits!

Isaiah continues: **"Behold, all who are incensed against you / shall be put to shame and confounded; / those who strive against you / shall be as nothing and shall perish. / You shall seek those who contend with you, / but you shall not find them; / those who war against you / shall be as nothing at all. / For I, the LORD your God, / hold your right hand; / it is I who say to you, 'Fear not, / I am the one who helps you'"** (vv. 11–13).

Take a moment to read that awesome promise again. Trust means you anchor your heart in the reality of God's awareness of your situation. He sees more than you can ever see. God, who loves you and is committed to you, will not disappoint you now or in the future if you put your weight fully on Him.

I realized there on my knees in the middle of the night that God is glad for this storm in my life.

I Trust God Statements from Matthew 6:25–34

"Therefore I tell you, do not be anxious about your life, what you will eat or what you will drink, nor about your body, what you will put on. Is not life more than food, and the body more than clothing?" (v. 25). *I trust that God will meet my needs—financially, physically, emotionally.*

"Look at the birds of the air: they neither sow nor reap nor gather into barns, and yet your heavenly Father feeds them. Are you not of more value than they?" (v. 26).

I trust that God cares for me and loves me.

"And which of you by being anxious can add a single hour to his span of life?" (v. 27). "We had to go to the doctor, and things are uncertain." I'm certainly not judging you, and we've had cycles like that too. I've certainly held the hands of those who have gone through deeper valleys than I have. But your days are numbered, and God knows the number, but worrying isn't going to change it.

I trust that God has numbered my days.

"And why are you anxious about clothing? Consider the lilies of the field, how they grow: they neither toil nor spin" (v. 28).

I trust that doing my best is enough.

"Yet I tell you, even Solomon in all his glory was not arrayed like one of these. But if God so clothes the grass of the field, which today is alive and tomorrow is thrown into the oven, will he not much more clothe you, O you of little faith? Therefore do not be anxious, saying, 'What shall we eat?' or 'What shall we drink?' or 'What shall we wear?' For the Gentiles seek after all these things, and your heavenly Father knows that you need them all. But seek first the kingdom of God and his righteousness, and all these things will be added to you" (vv. 29–33).

I trust that seeking God and His kingdom is the best way to win over worry.

And back to our main verse, Matthew 6:34: "Therefore do not be anxious about tomorrow, for tomorrow will be anxious for itself. Sufficient for the day is its own trouble."

I trust God to take care of tomorrow.

It's always interesting to see teaching and writing come together. As I move this content to finished book chapters, my wife and I are in a storm. Every storm feels big when you are in it—but I can tell by the size of the waves and the howl of the wind pressing me to fear that this is a tsunami. We have never been rocked as we've been this past week. I have been fasting and praying for strength to keep trusting. I have been kneeling down many times a day, giving "it" back to God once more. When Kathy and I wake up in the night, we pray together and hand "it" to the Lord yet again. All that to say, I'm living what I'm challenging you to choose, and it's working! It will work for you too.

Your Choice to Trust

OK, James, you've convinced me. I don't want to worry. I know it's not good for me. I know it's sin, and it's destructive. What do I do now?

This whole chapter centers on this moment. Storms are meant to drive you to your knees where you cry out to God for help. If all that you think is, *Yeah—I'm glad that worked for you, but I handle my problems differently,* then I have wasted my time and yours.

I'm praying for you right now to make it your practice to say to God, *Lord, I'm perishing. Save me. I've tried to carry this, God, and it's sinking me. I'm letting it go and choosing to trust You now. I'm picking up Your Word as the basis of my faith.*

Look over the list of scriptures I've included in appendix B. Choose a verse or a passage that God uses to encourage you. Write it out on a card and carry it with you. Put it on the visor in your car. Put it over the sink at home. Put it at your desk where you work. Hang on to the promises of God.

Ask God to develop in you a character of trust. I know I want to be a man who trusts God. If you've read this far, I know you share this passion with me. I don't know how to say it any more clearly, so let me ask you: *Are you choosing to trust?* It's one of the choices that can change your life forever. I choose to give my burdens to God and exchange them for His promises. I choose to trust.

A Choice to Make

Acknowledge the Choice

- What areas of your future have you found the most difficult to entrust to God?

- In what ways is anxiety affecting your relationships with people and your relationship with God?

Consider the Choice

- How are you using the promises of God to deal with trust issues in your life?

- In what ways do you think you would benefit almost immediately by refusing to worry about tomorrow any longer?

Make the Choice

- Get on your knees. Express your dependence on God physically as well as verbally. This is no time to waste time with pride.

- Use a three-step process similar to the one I described on pages 156–157. Start by telling God your need for His help and verbalizing why you are turning to Him. Move on to spell out your acknowledgment of your capacity limits. Then specifically describe each of the problems, people, and possibilities that are creating anxiety in you. Picture yourself placing the burdens at His feet, and watch with amazement as He stands in all His glorious power to speak peace to the storm in you.

A Choice Prayer

Lord, forgive my unbelief, and fill my heart with faith and confidence that You are true to Yourself and true to Your Word. All of Your promises are reliable. This week, as I lean back upon them and choose some specific ones suited to the burdens that I could easily be fooled into carrying, grant me the joy of a liberated heart, free from worry, anxiety, fretting, and fear.

Thank You, God, that You love me. Thank You that You have forgiven me. Thank You that I am known and loved by You. I rest in these promises. You have good things for me and in store for my future. You are faithful and true, and I'm choosing to trust You.

Give me great times of personal prayer with You, unlike what we have had for a long time. Help me to feel again the weight of my own body on my knees and the release of the weight as I give my burdens to You. There's no better place for what I have been carrying far too long.

I choose to trust You and Your Word today. I place my concerns for my future in Your hands. Be a shelter for me, God.

In Jesus' name. Amen.

PART IV

MY PRIORITY CHOICES

Choice 7: I Choose to Love My Family First

Choice 8: I Choose to Be Authentic

Does anyone ever get his to-do list done? *Everybody's ringing my phone, telling me what I should do, or what should matter and what I should emphasize. How do I know what I should focus on?*

Our seventh and eighth choices answer this question. We're focusing on priorities—what's going to be at the top of your nonnegotiable list. If you're going to make good choices, you've got to have established priorities. Established, meaning already decided. Priorities, meaning what are the most important things for you and making sure they come first.

What must be the first things that I give my life to? The previous six choices have focused on your relationship with God and your internal life. These next choices highlight the places where you live out what you believe.

The first one is "I Choose to Love My Family First." I have to give top-priority position to my family relationships every day for the rest of my life. Nothing and no one is as important as they are. You can accomplish a lot in your life—you can build a big company, accumulate wealth, make a name for yourself—but in the end, if you don't have your family, it's all shallow and superficial. I must choose to take care of the people at my house the very best I know how.

Then, in chapter 8, another practical priority is "I Choose to Be Authentic." Let's face it—we can't please everyone. So rather than try to meet everyone's expectations and make myself look good in the process, I choose instead to be real. I'm not gonna let anybody force me into a mold. I choose to live a life that flows from what is true, sincere, and without pretense. I choose to leave hypocrisy behind and press on to authenticity.

Do not lay up for yourselves treasures on earth, where moth and rust destroy and where thieves break in and steal, but lay up for yourselves treasures in heaven, where neither moth nor rust destroys and where thieves do not break in and steal. For where your treasure is, there your heart will be also.

—MATTHEW 6:19–21

I Choose to Love My Family First

*I will establish my family as my highest priority and
choose to love them first and best.*

Choices are most important in the places where the difference between getting them right or wrong is most apparent. If you are like me, your greatest joys and deepest sorrows involve your family. We cannot change the past, and we cannot control the future—what we *can* choose is to put first things first. (Drum roll, please!) Heading the list of human priorities is family.

If you get the family thing right, you can be happy no matter what else is going wrong. But if your family is struggling, or sideways, or stumbling, it's hard to feel like anything is right until that central thing is right. So let's get into God's Word and move decisively toward this truly life-changing choice: the choice to love family first. If you have already made that choice, make it again. Keeping that choice intentional will change your life forever.

Did You Hear About the Guy Who Struck It Rich?

He went after some aggressive business deals, and they all worked out great. He hit it big. I mean, he was rolling in dough and sleeping on cash. If we lived in the 1970s, we'd call him Thurston Howell III or Howard Hughes. In the 1980s we would have called him J. R. Ewing or William Randolph Hearst Jr. In the 1990s, we'd have called him Mr. Burns or Bill Gates. In this decade, television and reality have come together in Donald Trump.

The guy I'm talking about is *that* rich. He had so much money he didn't know what to do with it all. He said, "I don't have enough room in my barns to put this stuff away." So he razed his barns and built state-of-the-art storage facilities—air conditioned, concrete floors, and acres and acres of storage for all of his goods.

Our rich man had a plan for everything, except the unexpected. No sooner did he get up all the barns, pack in all of his stuff, get a glass of iced tea in his hand, and sit down on a lounge chair by the pool, then he had a heart attack and died on the spot. One moment he was on top of the world; the next they were putting him under the ground.

His whole story is told in Luke 12. **"And [Jesus] told them a parable, saying, 'The land of a rich man produced plentifully, and he thought to himself, "What shall I do, for I have nowhere to store my crops?"'"** (vv. 16–17).

What the rich man should have done when he found out that he had more than he needed was to give it away or invest it for future giving to bless other people. He was blessed to *be* a blessing. Why did he have no room to store his crops? Because he hadn't practiced stewardship with everything he got from his abundant harvests.

So Jesus continued, **"And he said, 'I will do this: I will tear down my barns and build larger ones, and there I will store all my grain and my goods. And I will say to my soul, "Soul, you have ample goods laid up for many years; relax, eat, drink, be merry."' But God said to him, 'Fool! This night your soul is required of you, and the things you have prepared, whose will they be?' So is the one who lays up treasure for himself and is not rich toward God"** (vv. 18–21).

The main principle here is the use of money, but the underlying issue is a failure of priorities. The guy was making choices, but he was making bad ones due to misplaced priorities. A lot of people in the world would have been applauding him because he appeared to be doing something substantive with his life. But in the final analysis, his choices were self-destructive. Wrong choices flowed from wrong priorities.

He thought that personal pleasure was the highest good. Notice how many times He said, "I think," or "I will," and how many "*my* crops and *my* barns." He thought that everything he had was for himself. He thought his time on earth was indefinite. He thought, as so many think, that his life would just go on and on and on. *I can choose as I want. I'll never have to account for my priorities.* Sadly, he thought that God could be marginalized and ignored. But neither he nor we can ultimately get away with bad priorities.

Before we're too hard on the guy, though, I think he might have meant well. I think he may have felt, *I can't just waste what I have.* Surely he intended to get to what mattered at some point in his life. A good heart with wrong priorities still leads to bad choices. We've all been there at times in our lives. We want to do the right thing, but our priorities are out of alignment with God's. So when the chips are down, we make bad choices.

Jesus spelled out the application of this parable so we wouldn't miss it. **"So is the one who lays up treasure for himself and is not rich toward God"** (v. 21). We should post a banner over that verse that says: *Priorities—stick to stuff that matters.*

Proverbs 4:26 has really helped me to clarify priorities. **"Ponder the path of thy feet, and let all thy ways be established"** (KJV). In other words, think about your life. Think about where your choices are taking you. Let your ways be sure. Decide beforehand what's important. Establish, write down, and agree within your family or with your spouse that this is the pecking order for priorities. Notice how Joshua could speak for himself as well as his family when he challenged a nation: **"Choose this day whom you will serve, whether the gods your fathers served in the region beyond the River, or the gods of the Amorites in whose land you dwell. But as for me and my house, we will serve the LORD"** (Joshua 24:15).

Four Reasons We Give for Not Establishing Priorities

Doesn't everyone have priorities? Sadly, no. Do you? Have you established the chain of importance in your life so you can decide on the spot that

"I will not do this because this comes first; this is more important"? Or do any of the following excuses describe you?

1: *I'm too busy surviving.*

"I don't know where you live, man, but I am too busy surviving. I don't spend a lot of time making choices about what's important, I just take it as it comes. My main goal is to make it through another day. I do what has to be done from the moment I get up until the moment I go to sleep."

So how is that working for you? Do you even buy that yourself? Can you see that life could be better lived with priorities?

2: *I've got too many important things going on.*

"My career is important. Financial security is important. The kids, their education, *my* education, my marriage, my church, my hobbies—they're all important. Sometimes I feel like my head is going to explode because *everything* is a priority."

Wow! You must be really tired. Does the phone ring on the loudest tone for everything? Is every wheel in your life squeaking a demand for grease? If you feel bewildered by demands, it's because you haven't decided for yourself and for your family what's going to be most important.

3: *I think priorities narrow my life.*

"I get the value of the 'priority' thing at work. I sure get it at church. But when I get to my house, I want to be a little more laid-back. I want to take it easy. I don't need someone banging on me all the time about what matters. I'll tell you what matters—nothing matters! I love days like, 'What are you going to do today?' 'I don't know.' I don't need all of that heavy-duty 'what's important' stuff. Get off my back."

That's your life, is it? You think it's too narrow or too restrictive to have priorities? Do you even find yourself saying, "My kids can

make up their own mind about their priorities. I mean, who am I
to judge? It's too narrow, man"?

4: *I just want to take it easy, buddy; you know, it's all good.*
Really? It's all good? You don't buy that any more than I do, do
you? Do you really think you can fashion a life philosophy out of
something guys say at a bar or on a ball diamond? Can you really
look in the mirror and say, "Life is perfect just as it is"?

Family Values

In every home that Kathy and I have lived in since we've been married,
we've framed or painted on the walls the five family values that we have
chosen to govern how we relate to each other. They've been our family's
rules, our priorities based completely on God's Word. We have intentionally and increasingly lived by these priorities God has given to us for
honoring relationships within the walls of our home:

1: *Love God.*
Well, that's no big surprise. What is the greatest commandment?
"Love the LORD your God with all your heart" (Deuteronomy
6:5). Our first priority is to get the vertical right.

2: *Put family first.*
We're gonna be loyal to each other. We're in these lifelong relationships together. Our family relationships come first. Jesus said that
closely tied to the first priority was the priority to love our neighbor—our family is our first circumference of neighbors.

3: *Work hard.*
My mother gave me her maiden name, Sherwood, as my middle
name. When I was a kid doing some job around the house, my
mom would pull me in close and whisper in my ear, "Sherwoods
know how to work hard. Don't you ever forget your family trait."

What a great vision to give to a kid! It's followed me my whole life. Now our family is working on it.

4: *Tell the truth.*

Yes, even when it's hard. Even when it's going to get you into more trouble. Just get the truth on the table. God can do a lot with any situation and with your heart when you tell the truth.

5: *Be kind.*

Think of someone else before yourself. Do the thoughtful thing. Speak the encouraging word. People matter to God.

Now these are *our* family values. You can have your own. But whatever you do, get some family priorities and put them up around your home. Honor them, even when it's hard. We have friends who have painted their family values in large letters across the wall in their garage so they see them every time they pull in their car.

Priorities are the driving force behind a life well lived. Your kids won't forget them when you frequently discuss what's important to you and make constant reference to them. Look at the biblical precedent for this in Deuteronomy 6:4–9. Point out examples of those who are blowing off their priorities. Talk about and celebrate people who are living by their priorities. Bring your priorities up and discuss them in various settings, showing your children how they apply.

Over the years people have asked us if we had a regular family Bible study. We never did at our house, but we made God and His Word priority in how we lived. We read God's Word together frequently, we prayed together often, and we talked constantly about God's priorities for this world and for our family and how they were being lived out on a day-to-day basis individually and as a family.

We made our share of bad decisions, but praise God, the pattern of our lives has been seeking God for wisdom to make good choices that come from established priorities.

I Cannot Fail at Family

So let's get on this priority. Our seventh of the ten choices that can change our lives is, "I choose to love my family first." Humanly speaking, after God, my family comes first. Nothing comes before that.

Marriage and family are completely God's idea. He loves it when life is working at your house and at mine according to His design. On the flip side, the Bible has nothing good to say about divorce. Malachi 2 says God hates it. At every point we need to fight and resist any effort to undermine the marriage structure God has blessed. We must protect, defend, and give our greatest effort for the success and the strength of our families.

Now, I know I'm walking a thin line here. I'm aware that many wonderful, godly people have experienced the heartache of divorce, and I don't want to cause you more pain by making you despair in this. I also want you to believe that by God's grace, going forward you can get it right.

At the same time, I don't want people who are looking for a way out of their struggling marriage to think, *Well, I'll just start over and everything will be fine.* It won't be fine.

I think it was Margaret Atwood who said, "A divorce is like an amputation. You survive it, but there is less of you after the operation." That is a very insightful metaphor, and, sadly, I know too many people who are examples of its truth. If you are in a hurting family today, you need to know that hardly any divorced person reading this would encourage you to go the way that he went. If his heart were right with God, every divorced person would plead with you to fight for your marriage and do everything you can to save it.

For those of you who have experienced marriage failure, I would tell you the greatest expression of your gratitude to God for the grace and forgiveness He has given is to begin again to dedicate everything you have to make sure that you never come back to that place of failure.

Two million people went through a divorce last year in the United States. Some people say the divorce rate is 50 percent. Actually, 69 percent of married men and 76 percent of married women were still in their first marriage in 1996. In 2007, only 58 percent of married women were on their first marriage.[1]

If you're not married yet and you think that God has marriage for you in the future, you must establish some priorities for choosing your spouse. If you're in a marriage and have made some vows to God, God's plan for you for the rest of your life is to make that marriage flourish.

Our church was filled with people who were at the end of their marriages. They thought they could never turn around, but they followed God's Word and obeyed His principles, and they've seen healing and restoration and love come back into their homes like they never dreamed could happen.

When it comes to family failure, we tend to think about marriage because that's what the courts require us to legally register. But what about the children? What about the severing and shattering and shredding of family relationships through family breakdown and failure? Family failure devastates everyone.

Family Failure Is Not Final

If you've experienced family failure—or if you're struggling and burdened in your family right now—you need to know that failure is not final. God's grace extends to you to go forward from wherever you are today and do everything you can to be the family member that God calls you to be.

Jesus' blood, like Noah's flood, can cover the failure of the past. But you can't use that grace as an excuse to keep on sinning. You can rise . . .

- Rise from the soot of selfish choices, and establish priorities for your future.

- Rise from the tattered shreds of torn dreams, and purpose to make better choices for your family.

- Rise from the shame of what your family has been and the disappointment that goes with that, and show God your sincerity by establishing priorities for your family in the future.

Get this in your heart: *I cannot fail at family. I have to give this everything I have every day for the rest of my life.* You can accomplish so much, but without this, nothing matters. You can build a big company, you can become wealthy, but when you get to the end, if you don't have your family, you have nothing.

You can have many disappointments in your career, but if you have your wife and your children around you when you come to the end of your life, you are a wealthy man. You've accomplished the greatest possible thing you can with your life. But this achievement will not happen unless your family has been established as your priority.

My Family Is My Treasure

The mistake that our rich guy building barns didn't learn is found in Matthew 6, **"Do not lay up for yourselves treasures on earth, where moth and rust destroy and where thieves break in and steal, but lay up for yourselves treasures in heaven"** (vv. 19–20a).

I don't understand—I thought you couldn't take your money to heaven. How do you lay up treasures in heaven? Only two things are going to heaven with you. Jesus said, **"Heaven and earth will pass away, but my words will not pass away"** (Luke 21:33). God's Word is going to heaven, and God's people (by God's grace) are going to heaven. Just those two things are going to last forever.

Do you want to lay up treasure in heaven? Invest in them. What you build here won't last. **"Lay up for yourselves treasure in heaven, where neither moth nor rust destroys and where thieves do not break in and steal. For where your treasure is, there your heart will be also"** (Matthew 6:20–21).

Your heart is with your treasure. Your treasure is with your heart. What you love most becomes treasure to you. What you treasure most becomes what you love. Those two are inseparable.

If your treasure is your career, your heart will be at work. Your treasure absorbs most of your time. If your treasure is your reputation, you come out of your seat when someone says something negative about you. Your reputation is your first love. Perhaps you treasure your possessions. You could see one of your kids run off into the world and might lose some sleep about it, but if a hundred dollars flew out the window of your car, you would cry about it for a year. Your priorities are wrong. If your treasure is your hidden pleasure—your private-whatever—your heart will be captive to that secret. Your treasure will be the focus of your imagination.

If any of the above pursuits are your treasure, they are receiving from you your best resources—time and energy.

When the chips are down, you're going to go with your treasure. Your treasure serves as your default mind-set. When the sun goes down and you've come to the end of another day and you lay your head on a pillow, you think, *I've got my treasure taken care of because it's got my heart.*

I wonder if any of this hits home. Are your greatest joys family joys? Are the things that delight your heart the successes of your family, the arrival of your children, and the key milestones in their lives? We all have different family makeups, but whatever your family is, aren't they your greatest joy?

> PRIORITY CHOICES COME RIGHT AFTER CAPACITY CHOICES BECAUSE PRIORITIES HELP US ASSIGN OUR LIMITED CAPACITIES TO WHOM AND WHAT IS BEST SERVED.

What are your greatest burdens? My greatest burdens are those of my family. Why? Because I treasure them. Everything is on the line when my family is hurting.

Most people would agree that their family is their treasure. So why the gap? Why aren't their hearts always there? Some might say, "I couldn't agree with you more, James. God forgive me, but I really do spend my time on stuff that is not my priority. I say I love my wife and kids but spend most of my time with them on cell-phone calls for work. I plan an evening home with the family and then sit for hours in front of a TV or computer screen, downloading useless entertainment or information. I just get sucked into it. How can I change? How can I make my family my treasure? I really want them to be my number one human priority."

Well, you've got the first step down: admitting it's true—they *are* the treasure, but you're not treating them that way. I'm not a super-smart guy, but here are two other things I know for sure will help.

The next step is to keep your nose out of others' stuff. Remember, you've only got so much time in a day. You just don't have room at the top of your priority list for things that don't immediately concern you and your family. Causes are fine, but your greatest efforts need to be serving the people under your own roof or who bear your name. You don't have the capacity to be involved in every good cause and driven by every worthy mission. If you try, you're just going to wear out your family! Priority choices come right after capacity choices because priorities help us assign our limited capacities to whom and what is best served.

What's more, you can't be everyone's savior. You can't solve everyone else's problems without neglecting your own. It's a perk to your ego to try, but it only hurts your family. Stick to the challenges at your own address. If the things on your mind just now do not carry the ball down your own family field or advance any important priorities in your family life, you're just spinning your wheels. Bluntly said, mind your own business. Stay on your own program, and take care of the things that matter most.

But here's the third part of making your family your treasure: it's not just what you stay out of, it's what you're really in to. You've got to be really into your family. Be passionate about them. Study them as the most fascinating people you know. Show them you are becoming an expert in all things concerning them. Make your time with them the subject of your greatest prayers and planning. Make your understanding of them your highest ambition and your greatest goal. When you do that, you will begin to experience your greatest joys being with your treasured family.

Express Your Commitment

A major way to communicate value to your family is to find creative ways to express your commitment to them. At the center of a family-first priority is commitment—a total, unswerving, unalterable, lifetime choice to do life together under God. Sure, you're going to have conflict and challenges. Some make the mistake of comparing themselves with other families and think strangers just naturally have it all together. "Wow—that couple has great chemistry. If we had their chemistry, we would have a marriage like them." Or, "Look at their upbringing—they've had a heritage of godly parents and grandparents. They don't have backgrounds like ours. Lucky heritage must be what makes a successful family."

But all of those observations are just perceptions—not reality. Those families have problems too. Every family has challenges, whether we see them or not.

Do you want to give your family first place? Then consider these four aspects to lasting, godly commitment that you need to make:

1: *Love your family first by having a total commitment to Christ.*
   It all begins with your vertical commitment to Christ. Anything less than a 100 percent radical devotion to Jesus is no commitment at all. Follow Christ first, above everything—above your spouse; above your children; above your family. Show them that you can actually love them better when you love Christ first than you could if you were ignoring Jesus and trying to love them in your own strength.

   In their honest moments, most people know the struggle not to love other people, especially their families, more than they love God. But Jesus said in Matthew 10:37, "**Whoever loves father or mother more than me is not worthy of me, and whoever loves son or daughter more than me is not worthy of me.**" Jesus must be first.

2: *Love your family first by calculating the cost.*
   Jesus said in Luke 14:28, "**For which of you, desiring to build a**

tower, does not first sit down and count the cost, whether he has enough to complete it?" If you want to build a tower, have a great lawn, lower your golf handicap, or have a marvelous, joy-filled family, it's going to cost you.

To be Christ's disciple demands careful analysis. It means you have to count the cost of that commitment ahead of time. *Can I finish the course? Can I give what success in this priority demands? Can I be a faithful husband for my whole life? Can I be the wife God has called me to be? Can I be the parent? Because if I can't keep my promises, I have no business making the commitment.* But to be standing beside your spouse ten, twenty, thirty, forty, fifty years later and to be able to say, "I *still* do" is powerful! And that power will flow down to your children and to your grandchildren.

3: *Love your family first by finishing the course.*
In a world of quitters, Jesus Christ is looking for finishers. It's not how your family started that matters most; it's where you all end up as a family and in eternity that really counts. Make no mistake, there are many eyes on you. People know what you profess, and they are watching to see if you can keep the commitment you've made to your family. The world is filled with starters—up like a rocket and down like a rock—but God's love in the heart of His children is what enables you to finish the course.

4: *Love your family first by paying the price.*
You need to know now that there is a price you will have to pay to have a God-honoring, successful family. Families that only stay together until hardship comes or conflict arises never experience the joy of all a family can be.

It's one thing to talk about commitment in a vague, generalizing way. But truly living the Christian life is hardest at home. Some of you are going to face something this year as a family that will call for a massive price to be paid! Get ready. When you want to pull back—that's the time to press in, push forward, and draw hard upon the Lord's strength to live a life of absolute total commitment to your family.

Express Your Love

We've done a lot of things through the years to try to cultivate the priority of family at our house. I don't think it's any secret that I adore my wife, Kathy. It seems that I get a chance to mention that fairly frequently. It's not only that I wouldn't say it if it weren't true, but it's also truer because I say it. Do you get that? By speaking or writing my appreciation, I remind her and myself that I choose not to take her for granted—I choose Kathy first.

Part of the family priority comes out in the way you show it—that includes expressing your love and not forgetting your parents, siblings, and those who live under your roof.

It starts with verbal confirmation. Confirmation means *to give assurance, to verify as worthwhile.* This happens when we affirm to our loved ones that *who they are* is what connects with us. A lot of the external things we compliment are going to fade over time. But our hearts desperately need to hear confirmation on this deeper level, especially in four critical times:

1: *When we fail*

You want to keep your marriage hot? Get beside your partner during failure. Maybe your husband had set some goals at work that he couldn't reach. Or maybe your wife worked hard on some dreams that fell flat. This is a critical moment. When we fail, we often try to connect the dots from what we didn't accomplish to who we are: "I'm a failure because I failed." That's when a loved one can snip that faulty line of thought by saying, "Yes, you may have failed, but you are not your performance. Who you are and who I love is the very same person whether or not you succeed." Many marriages break down in times of failure, partially, I'm sure, because this critical message is not sent.

2: *When others reject us*

When people in our world push us away, we desperately need to know that we won't be rejected by our loved ones. I believe Jesus Himself experienced this. In John 6, He had been teaching some pretty hard stuff and people were walking away. He said to the twelve closest to Him, *Do you also want to walk away?* In His deity, He knew some would reject Him; but in His humanity, He felt the pain. Peter came back with a phenomenal affirmation, *Where should we go?* (Notice the affirmation of who He is.) **"We have believed, and have come to know, that you are the Holy One of God"** (John 6:69). If Jesus Christ needed this confirmation in a time of rejection, don't you think we need it too?

3: *When circumstances send the wrong message*

How many times has the boss said, "Sorry, folks, we've got to work overtime (or weekends or whatever) until we get over this hump"? Of course you feel caught between your need to keep your job and provide for your family and the priority of time at home with them. What an important time to pull your lifetime partner close and say, "These circumstances are sending a message that I don't want to send. In my heart I want to be with you, but right now I can't." I really feel for young families. The husband says, "Everything was cool between me and my bride until these kids showed up. I come home and she's upstairs changing a million diapers. I don't even exist anymore." But the wise wife responds, "Here's my heart; here's how I'm really feeling as I'm trying to deal with the pressures of these little ones." Husbands and wives—communicate above your circumstances. Parents—don't let circumstances send the wrong message.

4: *When things are changing*

As our church has grown, I've felt again and again the necessity to get alongside some of the people who have been a part of the body from the beginning and say, "Although we can't spend as much personal time together as we used to, I want you to know my feelings for you are undiminished." Even as your family dynamic changes, it's easy to wonder if your loved one's commitment to you will also change. How vital it is for you to step toward your loved one and say, "No, no— times may change, but my commitment to you has only deepened."

Four Things Everyone Can Say

OK, *James,* you may be thinking, *but my problem is not knowing* when *but knowing* what *to say when it comes to expressing my commitment.* Let's get on that right now.

I Love You.

Men, the key is to say it deliberately. Don't mumble it into the phone and then hang up. "Whew. I said it, and it didn't get messy at all." Yeah, well, it needs to get a little messy. Get her in your arms, look in her eyes, and get it said: "I love you." Or pull your kids to you, no matter their age, and speak the words. They may fidget, but they'll remember and be altered by your genuine expressions of love.

I Need You.

I've been praying that the bedrooms of every married couple reading this will ring with these words. How about it, men? In your private moments, tell that woman who has stood by you how much you need her. Go ahead: "My actions may sometimes communicate the opposite, but I want you to know that I know I really need you."

There Is No One Like You.

OK, ladies. Every man is one among millions. At work, he's one among thousands. At church, he's one among hundreds. So when he walks through that door each night, he desperately needs to know he is your one and only. He is the first, highest, and best. Tell him.

And that leads to . . .

I Thank God for You.

Tell your beloved spouse, children, and parents that they are a gift from God to you. Better yet, pray aloud together. Let him or her overhear you tell the Lord how grateful you are that God gave him or her to you. Wives, tell your husband, "Honey, you've worked so hard lately, and I so appreciate the way you try to take care of our family and the energy and effort that you put into providing for us. Thanks for being a faithful man." Husbands, look for your opportunities to say, "Babe, thanks for one of the greatest meals I have ever had. What you made tonight was fit for a king." And after she picks herself up off the floor, she'll be like, "Uh, thanks."

Get the words said. Yes, it really matters. Expressing your love is a huge piece of making your spouse and your family the priority, lifelong relationship that God designed for you and that you all desperately want.

Lavish Love by Making It Exclusive

These words of affirmation are only for your family. Save the nicest, kindest, most thoughtful words for your family. Make them words you would never say to anyone else. Think of your family as a special culture made up of loving phrases and experiences that are unique to you and set you apart as people who share a deep commitment with each other. Think of your capacity to express love as rare coins that have immense value. You only get so many of them, so spend them lavishly on your own family.

We can bless other people, encourage those we meet, and appreciate the world, but nobody deserves to hear loving and affirming words like the people at our house. God forgive us for going out into the world and being so encouraging and complimentary yet starving our own families for the things that they need to hear. Express your love exclusively.

Lavish Love by Making It Creative

Find creative ways to communicate love within your family. One of the things that Kathy has done through the years is—in every house we've ever lived in, beginning with our little teeny apartment when we first got married—she has pictures everywhere. Just pictures, pictures, pictures everywhere throughout our house. We have sixty photo albums. Every one of them is filled with memory pages. The pictures are not just slapped in the books but are creatively and lovingly mounted alongside diagrams, notations, and added highlights. She has given a lot time to this, with not one minute of it wasted. Every single page communicates that our family is our treasure. Each of those pictures expresses a thousand words about what matters most. Family cannot be neglected. Some of the best uses of the talents and abilities God has given each of us involve creatively communicating love to our families.

Love Your Family

And lastly, I choose to love my family as my highest human priority. No other relationships will take precedence over these, not ever, not for a day.

Have you got some hurdles to overcome in your family relationships? You know, some things that need to change and improve at your house? All of us can at one time or another admit to having family problems or causing family pain. Every family is unique, and part of that uniqueness involves being a one-of-a-kind human system that requires the engagement of all its parts in order to function at its best!

I have just one word to offer you as you seek help and healing for your family: *love*. Love is relational dynamite that obliterates all obstacles in its path. Choosing this answer is the easiest part of the process; putting it into practice will require God's help and the best that you have to offer. Talking, as a single strategy, won't bring help and healing for your family (talking too often gets derailed into other negative verbal expressions). Pressuring won't; prodding, insisting, demanding, getting selfish—all these will only tear your life and family apart. So, how does the love answer work?

The concluding thought in the beautiful profile of love that is offered in 1 Corinthians 13 is the statement: **"Love never fails"** (1 Corinthians 13:8 NKJV). Love never fails to *what*? Let me point out three ways love can conquer what might be ailing your family.

Love Never Fails to Conquer Selfishness

I am selfish, and so are you. We never have to work at self; it's just right there barking for attention. Love conquers the biggest obstacle in me: selfishness. If you go back to the beginning of this love profile in 1 Corinthians 13, you can see why love must be lasting. Notice these characteristics of love:

- **"Love is patient"** (v. 4*a*). Selfishness isn't, but love is. Love is patient.

- **[Love is] kind"** (v. 4*a*). Selfishness is mean and demanding. But love overflows with random acts of kindness.

- **"Love does not envy or boast"** (v. 4*b*). Love does not get upset when one family member is doing well but is happy for each member's success. Love is not arrogant because it is not selfish.

- **"It is not . . . rude"** (v. 5*a*). Selfishness insists on the spotlight and will push others aside to get attention. Love would never be demanding or unreasonable.

- **"It does not insist on its own way"** (v. 5*b*) because it's not selfish.

- **"It is not irritable or resentful"** (v. 5*c*) because it's not selfish.

So love conquers the biggest obstacle in me, which is selfishness.

Love Never Fails to Conquer Skepticism

Over time, it's easy to doubt that anything is ever going to change. Your family disappoints you, and you want to bail, but love holds on. "I'm glad you brought that up," you might want to say, "because I'm not really sure that I'm the problem at my house." You've got a name in mind—it's your dad, sister, spouse, or your oldest son. "They're the problem at my house." Then we read God's Word, "[Love] **is not irritable or resentful**" (v. 5*c*).

Inside the safe haven of home, painful actions take place. Each of us sometimes takes advantage of that security by exercising shameful humanness. Like no one else, other family members disappoint you. They do something foolish, something wicked, something awful, or something hurtful. In those moments, you want to sell. *Sell everything now. Sell!*

But love does not sell out. Love does not bail in the crisis. And love is not skeptical. Love is not "You talk a good game, but you'll never be . . ." But love is believing the best in the person. Love is waiting for God's agenda to be accomplished in that person's life. Love holds on. Love is being used by God to transform that person.

When I choose not to love, I'm in God's way. When I choose to love, God is helping me, and I'm part of the solution. Love isn't skeptical.

Love Never Fails to Practice Flat-Out Persistence

Notice in verse 7 where it says, "**Love bears all things**"; because love is not skeptical, it keeps moving forward. It's not giving up. It's not keeping score. "**[Love] believes all things**" (v. 7*b*). Love tries again. Love trusts again. Love finds a way to give an opportunity for God to work.

"**[Love] hopes all things**" (v. 7*c*). Love can't wait for you to become the person God is making you—but amazingly, love does wait. Love is hopeful about it, believing it.

"**[Love] endures all things**" (v. 7*d*). In our wounded moments we think, *No one will ever do that to me again.* Those words are not a loving statement. When we say them, we've forgotten for a moment how desperately we hope others will give us another chance when we fail them. Love is part of the solution. Love is a tool in God's hands to work through you and transform your family.

But, James, we've got real problems over at our house! A pep talk on love is not going to fix it. You're right—that's why we need 1 Corinthians 13:6, "**[Love] does not rejoice at wrongdoing, but rejoices with the truth.**"

Love also doesn't settle for the status quo. Love doesn't sit back in some happy delusion that everything will be OK. Love doesn't deny problems but cooperates with God in making transformation happen. Love is an action before it's a feeling. Love works at seeing people change. This is why we've made "tell the truth" one of our five family priorities. We know that denial and dishonesty will lead to family failure.

How did you get together with your spouse in the first place? *Well, we just started hanging out, and I don't know what she saw in me, but she was working for me. In the end of it all, we just had a good thing going on.*

Well, just think. If you go back to doing for her what brought you together, you'll get back all those wonderful feelings again. Actions precede feelings, they don't follow them. You think you were hit by some bolt of lightning-love? No, you were not. You both did some things that led to your love developing into a commitment.

Hey, husband—or wife—return to the former things. Do those things again and see love rekindled in your family. If you and your spouse took a detour a long time ago, returning to the former things will take some time. Selfishness is when you say, "I'm not doing that anymore; I'm taking care of myself now." Recognize you are making a choice *not* to love, and your family will continue to fall apart from that moment on.

But when you start doing the loving things, the giving things, the selfless things again, you are choosing to love your family as your highest human priority. Making that choice will definitely change your life. Establish your family as your highest priority. I choose to love my family first. Nothing comes before them.

A Choice to Make

Acknowledge the Choice

- What other priorities in your life are demanding first place treatment?

- How does your family know where you place them on the list of priorities?

- Where have you been placing your family in the sequence of priorities?

Consider the Choice

- Read again the five MacDonald house rules early in this chapter. What would it take to develop a similar set of rules to live by in your family?

- What do you think would be the primary benefits to your family if you made the serious choice to treat them as your first human priority?

Make the Choice

- In love, serve your family even when they choose to be selfish.

- In love, challenge your family to come up with a list of four or five home rules to live by. Post them and let your family hold you accountable for them.

- In love, humble yourself before your family when conflict creates distance.

- In love, lavish your family with loving words and deeds of kindness and affirmation.

- In love, forgive your family by releasing them from the obligation that resulted when they hurt you. Don't hold it over them. They don't owe you anything. You don't even need to tell them that. Love gives God an opportunity to work. It's a tool in His hands to work through you in helping your family.

- And lastly, love them by speaking God's Word in any situation regardless of the cost. Speak the truth in your family; truth, delivered with love, is what sets us free.

A Choice Prayer

Thank You, God, for this clear, biblical reminder about what matters most. Lord, I know that I don't have the strength to love like this. I'm not under any pretention that my promised desire will really amount to very much. Lord, I know that You are the capacity to love. Jesus, You are the one who exemplifies selfless love. You are the one who demonstrates the power of giving Yourself.

So I pray, Lord, that Your power could be demonstrated in my life and through me. I ask you, Lord Jesus, to cause Your power to be my experience. Teach me to love. Help me to love. Strengthen my love, I pray.

In Jesus' name. Amen.

Beware of practicing your righteousness before other people in order to be seen by them, for then you will have no reward from your Father who is in heaven. Thus, when you give to the needy, sound no trumpet before you, as the hypocrites do in the synagogues and in the streets, that they may be praised by others. Truly, I say to you, they have received their reward. But when you give to the needy, do not let your left hand know what your right hand is doing, so that your giving may be in secret. And your Father who sees in secret will reward you.

—MATTHEW 6:1–4

Judge not, that you be not judged. For with the judgment you pronounce you will be judged, and with the measure you use it will be measured to you. Why do you see the speck that is in your brother's eye, but do not notice the log that is in your own eye?

—MATTHEW 7:1–3

I Choose to Be Authentic

I choose to be authentic, closing all the gaps between what I profess to be and who I actually am.

My wife is tricky sometimes. She puts out bowls of counterfeit fruit all around our kitchen, and I get so confused. I can't tell you how many times I've picked up a great looking pear and almost broken my tooth when I tried to bite into it! A cleverly painted wooden pear—how worthless is that? I think a bowl of fruit is a beautiful decorating idea—as long as I can eat the decorations!

I hate fake grass too. It reminds me of cheap shag carpeting. Football should be played on real turf. Where's the mud? Where are the grass stains?

My son Landon always tries to get me to watch the *Star Wars* movies. Ten minutes into it, and I'm like . . . *z-z-z-z*. Why? Because it's so fake! Darth Vader and the whole lot of them—phonies. State-of-the-art special effects are just another clever way of saying not-real! If that offends you . . . try to get over it.

Here's a fakeness I think we can all agree about: pro wrestling. They take fake to a whole new level! This crazy guy gets up in the corner of the ring, does a back flip and lands on the other guy's neck, and then moments later that guy's up pinning him. *I don't think so.*

I also hate fake laugh tracks on TV shows. What? Is the comedy so bad that it needs canned laughter?

I just hate fake stuff.

On Second Thought

I also know it's hard to avoid coming across as fake at times. We all have perceptions of one another that differ from reality. None of us is entirely what others perceive us to be. The problem is not in the unavoidable gap between others' perceptions and our reality. The problem is when we ignore the gap. The danger comes when we widen the gap by promoting it. The number one criticism leveled against people of faith is that we are hypocritical, that we knowingly nourish a substantive separation between the life we project and the life we practice.

> THE NUMBER ONE CRITICISM LEVELED AGAINST PEOPLE OF FAITH IS THAT WE ARE HYPOCRITICAL, THAT WE KNOWINGLY NOURISH A SUBSTANTIVE SEPARATION BETWEEN THE LIFE WE PROJECT AND THE LIFE WE PRACTICE.

Interestingly, the complaint against hypocrisy is something God Himself has in common with pagans (a very short list of similarities). He, too, despises duplicity. He, too, is incensed by insincerity. Not so much the superficial, silly things that bother me—God hates *soul* fakeness. He detests the gap in our lives between what we know to be true and how we're living it. The biblical term for this kind of living is *hypocrisy.* God hates hypocrisy.

For that reason, so must we. The opposite of hypocrisy is *authenticity,* a quality so illusive you don't get there by accident—you have to choose it.

That reality is what we are going for in this chapter. It's the next life-changing choice: authenticity. It's the decision to close the gap between who we appear to be and who we are. It's out with phoniness and in with more genuine, heartfelt realness. Change like this requires a choice on your part and mine. Vaguely wishing it will happen won't get it done.

There should be some kind of urgent alarm going off in your heart when you realize there's a substantive gap between what you say and what you do; between what you profess and how you actually live; between the appearances that you keep up at church in front of other people and what it's really like at your house. God *hates* counterfeit living. That's why Jesus says, **"Beware of practicing your righteousness before other people in order to be seen by them"** (Matthew 6:1).

Authenticity

Let me give you a fuller definition of this important word. Authentic means *genuine,* as in, *not forced.* I'm not going to church because my wife makes me. No one is forcing me to do or say anything. I want this for myself. My actions are not the result of coercion. Coercion is a subtle kind of pressure that manipulates another person. Coercion doesn't force directly but hints at a consequence if I don't conform. I don't want my faith to be the product of coercion in any way. I want to live for God because I love Him.

> AN AUTHENTIC LIFE HOLDS UP UNDER SCRUTINY. CERTAINLY NONE OF US CLAIM TO BE PERFECT, BUT WE WANT A LIFESTYLE OF GENUINE FAITH.

Authenticity is not contrived or calculating. I'm not saying and doing the right things because that's what is expected of me. I'm not acting. Don't you want to be doing the real thing? Take off the mask and live for Christ because you are passionate about Him. Authenticity flows from what is true. It's based in fact. An authentic person is sincere, without pretense, without performance—real.

That word *sincere* also explains a particular aspect of authenticity.

Centuries ago, when dishonest potters would try to pass off their cracked pots and jars as high quality, they would fill the fractures with wax and then smooth it all over so their customers couldn't see the defects. Gullible buyers wouldn't notice the cracks until they poured hot water into the jars; they would leak right away. Savvy buyers in the marketplace would examine a jar for cracks by lifting it to the sun, literally "sun-judging" it. *Sincere* is the transliteration of the Latin phrase *sine* (without) *cera* (wax). Honest sellers invited their wares to be sun-judged.

An authentic life holds up under scrutiny. Certainly none of us claim to be perfect, but we want a lifestyle of genuine faith—even in hot water. Those who know us best should be able to testify to how our private and public lives reflect the same deep love for God and sincere respect for His Word.

This discussion begs the question, *Why is hypocrisy such a hard thing to shake?* Why do we all nod our heads in agreement that we want authenticity yet identify in our own struggle with subtle forms of hypocrisy? I know why—because avoiding hypocrisy is flat-out hard to do.

It's hard to be authentic because . . .

I Cannot Please Everyone

I become like a circus juggler when I try to keep everyone's opinions of me high in the air. One person thinks I should be like this; another scrutinizes me for something else. And, oh, if you really want to be a Christian leader, you should give yourself to this other cause. Before long, all the expectations of other people come crashing down around my feet. Playing to the demands of others runs in opposition to authenticity.

Jesus lived with that kind of pressure. In His Sermon on the Mount, He focused primarily on the Pharisees, the Bible-thumpers of His day. On the positive side, the Pharisees took the Bible very seriously. They confronted error, they separated themselves from the world, and they were hypersensitive to the application of God's Word. *So what's wrong with that?* Nothing—that's all fine. But Jesus identified their acute internal problem in Matthew 15:8: **"This people honors me with their lips, but their heart is far from me."** Ouch! Furthermore, Jesus was simply quoting His Father, recorded back in Isaiah centuries before, when He gave the same spiritual diagnosis to the people of Isaiah's time.

The Pharisees put on a good show, but Jesus saw right through it. They wanted to look like they had it all together with God, but they hadn't privately done the heart business with Him. Looking the part was all they cared about. As Jesus said, **"Beware of practicing your righteousness before other people in order to be seen by them"** (Matthew 6:1). When Jesus used the term *righteousness* here, He was talking about practical righteousness, the things you do as a believer to outwardly express your heart before God—read your Bible, pray, share your faith, be in a small group, work for the Lord, give to the poor. *Don't do these to impress others*, He warns. *Pay attention, be on guard*, He cautions. *Play to an audience of One.*

Notice He didn't say you should hide your spiritual disciplines from people or enter a monastery. Some people have misunderstood His point. The issue isn't location. The issue is motive. People are going to see you live your life; that's not the problem. You don't have to keep secret the fact that you go to church, raise your hands in worship, and get on your knees to pray. You don't have to shield your Bible when you open it because you have written personal notes all through it. But when you do all those things *so that people will see you*—that's the problem. Doing spiritual things so other people notice goes right to motive. If you're acting godly with the desire to get attention, affirmation, or strokes from folks—you just got all the reward you deserve and lost God's approval in the process. When you get that pat on the back from your neighbor, then God is like, *If that's what you were going for, man, you got it! There's your reward, buddy.*

We are called to live for a higher reward—a reward from the Lord Himself.

Rewards

When the topic of rewards comes up, some people coo, *Oh, James, I don't need any rewards from Jesus. I just love Him so much. He doesn't have to give me anything.* Do you think that's the super-spiritual thing to say? Scripture is filled with the motivation of rewards. I'm going to go out on a limb and say that if God doesn't have a problem with giving rewards, then we shouldn't be shy about receiving them. If you're still uncomfortable with rewards, you can give me yours. I flat-out want them.

What the Bible Says about Rewards

Take some time to ponder for yourself what God's Word says about the perks in pursuing a godly life:

- Matthew 5:12 says, "**Rejoice and be glad, for your reward is great in heaven.**"

- Matthew 5:46 says, "**If you love those who love you, what reward do you have?**" (As in, there's no reward for loving people who are easy to love. It's the other people . . .)

- Luke 6:38 says, "**Give, and it will be given to you.**" You're going to be rewarded for sincere, unselfish generosity.

- First Corinthians 3:14 says, "**If the work that anyone has built on the foundation survives, he will receive a reward.**"

- Second Corinthians 5:10 says, "**For we must all appear before the judgment seat of Christ, so that each one may receive what is due for what he has done in the body, whether good or evil.**"

- Second Timothy 4:7–8 says, "**I have fought the good fight, I have finished the race, I have kept the faith. Henceforth there is laid up for me the crown of righteousness, which the Lord, the righteous judge, will award to me** [or reward me] **on that Day.**"

- First Peter 5:4 says, "**When the chief Shepherd appears, you will receive the unfading crown of glory.**"

- Revelation 2:10*b* states, Jesus said, "**Be faithful unto death, and I will give you the crown of life.**"

- Revelation 22:12 says, "**Behold, I am coming soon, bringing my recompense with me, to repay everyone for what he has done.**"

Just to be sure we understand God's heart in this, let's get very specific. Go back to Matthew 6:1 again. Jesus said, **"Beware of practicing your righteousness before other people in order to be seen by them, for then you will have no reward from your Father who is in heaven.** *Thus, when you give to the needy, sound no trumpet"* (v. 2, emphasis mine).

Jesus was making specific application to our motives in giving our tithes and offerings. He said if you're going to give, don't draw attention to it. That's what the Pharisees were doing. Just imagine that we're sitting in church and the offering plate is coming down the aisle. When it gets right in front of me, I pop a hundred-dollar bill and sound an alarm like some cheesy eat-a-five-pound-burger-and-ring-a-bell restaurant gimmick. *Look at me, everyone! Look at how much I'm giving. Aren't I a good Christian?* (Insert canned applause here.)

At our church, we've built a closed system so none of us are tempted to give in order to get noticed. We take the offering row by row rather than have a box in the back where people can watch you give. We pass a bag rather than an open plate so no one except a couple of people beside you even knows that you gave, and nobody sees how much you put in. A revolving team of church members count the offering each week, and only one or two staff even knows who gives what. It's all locked in a protected computer record. I have no idea what people give, nor do I want to know. That's an issue between them and God. God sees their gifts, and He's keeping track. He will reward them for their hidden generosity (or not). Why am I making a special case about giving? Because Jesus did in Matthew 6:2–3: **"Thus, when you give to the needy, sound no trumpet before you, as the hypocrites do in the synagogues and in the streets, that they may be praised by others."** He continued, **"Truly, I say to you, they have received their reward. But when you give to the needy, do not let your left hand know what your right hand is doing."**

How do I do that last part? My hands mostly work together, you know? Jesus is using hyperbole here, exaggerating the warning to be careful about not parading what you do. It's to be so secret that you don't even make a deal of it yourself.

By the way, some people have taken that to mean, "Well, I'm going to give what I want and not even tell my spouse." Incorrect. Jesus doesn't want you to divide your household; He just wants your heart undivided. Don't be doing anything for the praise of man.

The solution: don't do anything *to be seen*. Have a better and purer reason to do whatever it is you choose to do for God. Anything less than doing it for Him will get you nothing but canned applause.

Here is another reason why hypocrisy is so prevalent in the church and why it is hounding you and me. It's hard to be authentic because . . .

I Have These Torn, Divided Desires

There isn't a Christian alive or dead that hasn't battled divided desires. The apostle Paul admitted to this internal conflict in Romans 7:14–24. *I want what I want* (that's my old nature), *but I also want what God wants* (that's my new nature). And if that's not complicated enough, then there's *you* (each of us has a default audience we are tempted to play for—our *you*). *I want you to think that I want what God wants more than I sometimes want it.* (Stay with me, now.) *I don't want you to know how badly I want what I want sometimes.* If it isn't enough of a battle just between what *I* want and what *God* wants, we both want each other to want what God wants. But sometimes I settle for just *looking* like I want what God wants, which is really just a covering for the darkness that is in my own heart. We agonize in the process because we let people's opinions put weight on us, rather than feeling the weight of *God's* opinions. That's such a bad plan. I'm persuaded of better things concerning us.

Outward Appearances

I grew up in a good church with good people. But one issue I noticed even as a young person was a constant struggle with an outward focus. Folks were obsessive about appearances.

As a kid, I remember the day I found out that a man in our church smoked cigarettes. I was shocked. To be clear, I think smoking is an unhealthy, addictive habit. I wouldn't commend it to anyone. If it's something you have an addiction to, I hope the Lord sets you free. But somehow this external habit was blown way out of proportion and thought to be the most awful thing a Christian could do. In our twisted little grid, you could only be a good Christian if you didn't do "The Filthy Five": smoking, drinking, dancing, gambling, and going to movies.

Well, what about all the other things you're not supposed to do? Or the things you're supposed to do that you don't *do?*

We don't really talk about those. We just obsess about the ones people can see.

The external was put under the microscope. The outward appearances were scrutinized. You couldn't walk in the church foyer without everyone inspecting everyone else. It took me a long time to shake that in ministry.

I've felt the pressure of looking the part. Let me tell you a story of something that happened to me. At first you might think it's funny, but it paints a little portrait of something I've had to wrestle with my whole life.

Feeling the Pressure

In 1987, I went on the game show *The $25,000 Pyramid* (you can watch a clip of it at www.jamesmacdonald.com/classics_gameshow.aspx). You remember how the game goes; I partnered with a celebrity in getting through a list of words. In this specific case, I had to get the celebrity to say the word *revolution*.

If I had been brought up in the States, I would have given the clue, "In 1776 we fought a war called the American _____." But under pressure, all I could think to give as a clue was the Beatles' song, "Revolution" (*You say you want a rev-o-lution* . . .). My game partner didn't get my clue, and so we moved on. At the end of that round, Dick Clark looked at me, a young pastor, and said, "You must be a real Beatles fan, huh?"

First came the authentic response—I pumped my fist in the air, implying "Yes!" But then I remembered all the people in my church who would watch the show, and I quickly changed my expression and shook my head, "Nah."

To me this is such a portrait of a person struggling to be authentic but then giving in to the immense pressure to perform for people's expectations. What an awful way to live your life. If it's wrong, it's wrong. If it's not wrong, it's not wrong. It's one or the other. But it's crucial for you and me to recognize we feel the constant pressure to measure up to people's scrutiny based on the little list of things they've labeled appropriate. When that shows up in the body of Christ, it is *death* to authenticity. The pressure to conform and to look the part kills sincerity, and so much of it comes from the trap of trying to please other people.

> A LOT OF US HAVE LIVED OUR LIVES ON THE EXHAUSTIVE TREADMILL OF TRYING TO PLEASE OTHERS.

I preached a message a few years ago called, "Freedom from People-Pleasing." Every time it airs on *Walk in the Word*, the response is off the chart—a clear indication that a lot of us have lived our lives on the exhaustive treadmill of trying to please others. We need an exit ramp off this endless highway. The message is based on 1 Corinthians 4, in which Paul said, **"But with me it is a very small thing that I should be judged by you or by any human court. In fact, I do not even judge myself . . . It is the Lord who judges me. Therefore do not pronounce judgment before the time, before the Lord comes, who will bring to light the things now hidden in darkness and will disclose the purposes of the heart. Then each one will receive his commendation from God"** (vv. 3–5). Notice that Paul said, "I do not even judge myself": *I can't even trust myself to assess my own sincerity, let alone you who don't know what I'm thinking or feeling.*

I cannot please everyone. You can't either. The attempt on our part to keep trying leads first to a crease, then a crack, then a *canyon* of distance between who we are and who we try to appear to be. Let's be done right now with people-pleasing. I dream a better dream for us than allowing petty people, majoring on silly things about which the Bible does not even explicitly speak, to control our hearts and lives. Let's not allow even our brothers and sisters in Christ who have such strong opinions to pressure us into external conformity that doesn't reflect our hearts and doesn't please or satisfy God. No doubt about it, hypocrisy has to go. It's destructive to us and despised by God.

God Despises Hypocrisy

It would be hard to even frame language that could capture how much God hates hypocrisy. Most of the time we just don't get it—God isn't fooled by our cleverest act. How arrogant of us to think that God has forgotten what He told Samuel: **"For the LORD sees not as man sees: man looks on the outward appearance, but the LORD looks on the heart"** (1 Samuel 16:7*b*).

Keep in mind that the people in this world aren't guilty of hypocrisy. They don't profess to be anything other than what they are. That's why they can spot a fake when they see one. Fill in the blank: "I don't want to go to that church; they're such _____." You got it, *hypocrites*.

We see a good example of this in Matthew 6:16 when Jesus gives instructions on how to fast. Fasting is supposed to be a private spiritual discipline. It's when you willingly, voluntarily abstain from food for a period of time in order to heighten spiritual desire. Fasting involves letting the discomfort you feel when you're hungry remind you of the longing you have for God to show up in your life in some specific way. It's using the time you normally would be preoccupied with food to focus exclusively on God. Fasting is usually combined with intense prayer for a specified, special season. I hesitate to even tell you about the times we've done it as a church for fear it sounds boastful. But I report from experience how fasting points to private hours of discovering just how much I need God.

The Pharisees were into fasting big-time. They fasted as much as once a week and let everyone know about it. Jesus told them, **"And when you** fast, do not look gloomy like the hypocrites, for they disfigure their faces that their fasting may be seen by others" (Matthew 6:16).

The Pharisees acted sick with hunger and made everyone else sick with frustration. They might as well have hung placards around their necks that said, *Look how spiritual I am!* Their fasting was supposed to be for God, but they were trying to earn esteem in the eyes of others. They would come to their assembly looking pathetic with hunger. *Do you see me over here? Do you know why I'm in pain? Because I've been fasting, OK? That's how much I love God.*

God is so not into that playacting. "**When you fast, do not look gloomy like the hypocrites, for they disfigure their faces that their fasting may be seen by others**" (Matthew 6:16). He's like, *Is that what you're going for? You want people's attention rather than mine? You want others to say how spiritual you are? Great, you've got that now.* "**Truly, I say to you, they have received their reward**" (Matthew 6:16*b*).

In this case, fasting is an illustration of all spiritual activities. "**When you fast, anoint your head and wash your face, that your fasting may not be seen by others**" (Matthew 6:17–18). In other words, when you serve God in whatever capacity, look the best you can so that no one would guess your hard work or sacrifice. Do what you do for God without advertising! God knows the truth about the way that you've been seeking Him with your whole heart. If no one else knows, God does.

And notice the promise. "**When you fast, anoint your head and wash your face, that your fasting may not be seen by others but by your Father who is in secret. And your Father who sees in secret will reward you**" (Matthew 6:17–18). God will reward you. You don't need to be caught up in others' appreciation or approval. Perhaps no one else will ever know the effort or sacrifice or time you've invested in prayer, but God knows. A better plan is to hide your service from other people's eyes. God promises to see it and reward you.

I wonder if this gives you pause. Do you think, *James, I have a hard time believing that just because I struggle with not being appreciated by other people that God's going to withhold my reward from me. Maybe He'll be disappointed with me for drawing attention to myself, but is this little bit of hypocrisy really that big a deal?*

To answer that question, we need to go to a passage of scripture you may not have noticed before. Matthew 23 was written to Pharisees, the Bible-thumpers and the churchgoers of the first century. Jesus was speaking to people like you and me, who work hard at doing right things but can quickly fall into doing the right things outwardly while our heart is not where it needs to be.

Please don't skip over this striking section of Scripture. It dispenses with the illusion once and for all that somehow God is casual or indifferent about hypocrisy. In just a few hours, Jesus will be arrested and killed by these same Pharisees. So, for one last time in front of this stubborn and hardened audience, Jesus lets it be known *exactly* what He thinks about hypocrisy, then and now. To show us that there is nothing more detestable to God than hypocrisy and falsehood in religion, He expresses seven "Woes!" on the Pharisees. Jesus sadly but forcefully lets them know the judgment that they are bringing on themselves by their stubborn, prideful, religious pretense.

The Seven Woes and One Great Lament of Matthew 23

(Refer to these as you read through chapter 23 of Matthew's Gospel.)

- **"Woe to you . . ."** (v. 13). Jesus excoriates religious people for turning people away from God when they have no intention of obeying Him themselves.

- **"Woe to you . . ."** (v. 15). Jesus laments the way the Pharisees went to great lengths to create followers of their own misguided life.

- **"Woe to you . . ."** (vv. 16–22). The Lord gives three examples of meaningless religious hairsplitting that made Him want to pull out His hair!

- **"O Jerusalem, Jerusalem . . ."** (vv. 37–39). Jesus grieves over what will again happen to the city that has had so many opportunities to truthfully declare, "**Blessed is he who comes in the name of the Lord**" (v. 39).

Wow! Strong language. But in spite of the confrontations and dire warnings, Jesus didn't hate the Pharisees. He was angry at their hypocrisy and all that it cost in human suffering. But even when you imagine His stabbing tone of voice, you can't miss the tenderness of the last verses. He spoke tough love to these men and the whole of Jerusalem. He ached at their rebellion and what it would mean for their future. As always, even at Jesus' fiercest, He was a model of truth *and* grace. He went as far as He needed to go to give them indisputable evidence of their hypocrisy. It's apparent from the response of Nicodemus and other Pharisees that Jesus' words reached a few of the religious elites of His day. Sadly, though, most were only too eager to do away with this pesky man from Nazareth.

Now let's look closely at a couple of key themes that come out of Matthew 23.

1: Jesus' first target was the obvious gap between inside *and* outside.

In verses 25–26, Jesus said, "**You clean the outside of the cup and the plate, but inside they are full of greed and self-indulgence . . . First clean the inside of the cup and the plate, that the outside also may be clean.**" In verses 27 and 28, He compared the Pharisees to whitewashed tombs, "**which outwardly appear beautiful, but within are full of dead people's bones and all uncleanness. So you also outwardly appear righteous to others, but within you are full of hypocrisy and lawlessness.**"

Jesus was breaking down hypocrisy to its basic components. *Inside you're like this; outside you're like that.* The gap between what people see and what is really inside me needs to narrow over the course of my life. But as we noted previously, hypocrisy starts off as a crease between what I say and do and what I really am on the inside; then it becomes a crack, and if neglected, it becomes a canyon between me and God.

2: Jesus' second target was the chaos of spiritual sightlessness.

The Lord repeatedly declared, *You're blind!* (vv. 16–17, 19, 24, 26). Now, you'd never slap a blind person for not being able to see, right? Jesus' words indicate that the Pharisees don't have the capacity to discern their own desperate need. We can't see this about ourselves either. The sense of how much we need or don't need this challenge is completely lost on us.

The problem of spiritual blindness is a far greater issue for each one of us than we are capable of discovering on our own. That's why we go to church— we need a messenger to hold up the mirror of God's Word and say, "This is a problem, and here's how to fix it." Just because I don't sense a problem in my life doesn't mean I don't have one. At times, you and I desperately need someone else to speak truth into our lives. We need someone who knows us, loves us, and cares about us enough to say, "Hey, you might want to give some thought to the growing gap between what you profess and what you practice, what people see but who God knows you are."

I don't know how else to say it than to echo Jesus' warning that hypocrisy is very serious. God will help us leave it behind. If we don't give constant attention to it, the gap of duplicity only grows wider.

The Tragedy of a Double Life

Earlier in this chapter I described a little about the church where I grew up. Good people, sound doctrine, but, at times, an overemphasis on externals. There were several similar churches in our area. I'd like to tell you about one family, the Buxbaums, who happened to be members of one of these other churches. Helmuth and Hanna Buxbaum were widely known for their kindness to the Christian youth of our city. By the time I met them, they were rich—my goodness, they were rich.

In the mid-1980s, Helmuth Buxbaum owned a twenty-eight-million-dollar chain of nursing homes. He had come to Canada in the 1950s with just a few cents in his pocket and had worked hard to build this empire. He and his wife loved God and served the Christian community there in London, Ontario. They invited every youth group in our city over to their house on a regular basis.

One of my youthful highlights was an evening I spent in the Buxbaums' home. They had an indoor swimming pool and an incredible arcade. I had never seen anything like it in my life. To make it even better, the Buxbaums were generous with it all.

The summer after Kathy and I were married, before we went into full-time ministry, I worked at a Ford Motors assembly plant. I put car doors on Crown Victorias (so if you ever owned one of those and it was a little crooked . . . sorry about that!). It was not an easy job with ten-hour shifts through the night. People who do that for a living have my highest respect.

I'll never forget one particular night shift when I walked into the cafeteria for lunch. A couple of men sat at a table, reading the newspaper. On the front page was the heartbreaking news that on July 5, 1984, Helmuth Buxbaum's wife, Hanna, had been murdered on a highway near London. The couple was driving home from picking up their nephew at the airport and, just like they would, stopped by the side of the road to help some people with car trouble. One of the motorists decided to rob them, pulled Mrs. Buxbaum out of the car by her hair, and put three bullets into her head.

I said, "Oh, this is awful. I know these people. They're wonderful. I can't believe this has happened."

To my shock, one of my coworkers stared at me and said, "What are you talking about? That guy's a cokehead."

I said, "You don't know who you're talking about. These are the sweetest, kindest Christian people. You are wrong, man, and you need to stop saying that."

Within three or four days the truth came out. Witnesses revealed that despite his apparently wholesome life, Buxbaum was a cocaine addict with an appetite for young prostitutes. He was desperate to rid himself of his wife, Hanna, because he found her dull and unattractive. An eyewitness said that her last words to her husband were, "Oh, Helmuth, not like this."

The motivation for the murder also involved money. Nearly two million dollars had disappeared from Buxbaum's bank account, and he had recently taken out a one-million-dollar life insurance policy on his wife.

Buxbaum was as bent as my coworker had said—and a lot worse. He had paid his drug dealer ten thousand dollars to set up the horrible murder. Of course, Buxbaum went straight to prison and stayed there the rest of his life.

I can only tell you this story now because he died on November 7, 2007, and was buried right beside the wife he had arranged to have murdered.[1] Now they are both in eternity, and only God knows where they are.

Yes, God knows where *they* are, but let me remind you, eternity is racing toward you and me in this moment. Who are you in your heart of hearts? We may be able to fool one another here, but there will be no fooling God.

If you allow any creases and cracks in your life to go unattended, and if you nurse them and nourish them for a long period of time, a tragedy like this could happen to you.

I want you to know something about me. I am marked by the Buxbaums' tragedy. I'll never forget how sure I was about them and then how wrong I was. The pain of hypocrisy involves all those who are taken in and left betrayed when the truth comes out. A seismic event like this should cause each of us to take stock of ourselves.

I Want to Be Real

The passion is for authenticity. I want to be authentic. I don't want to pose for anyone. I don't want to position my life to match anyone's expectations. I don't want to appear to be something that I'm not. I am passionate for you in this area too. Just think of how many chances Buxbaum had to say to a trusted friend, "Can I tell you that I'm struggling? I'm not what you think I am. Please, I need help!" But he took a pass every time; he simply wanted what he wanted, and it put him on a collision course with disaster.

As I was thinking and praying about this for my own life, I wrote this little prayer. This is for me, but I'll share it with you in the hope that it will ignite a passion for authenticity in you.

I want to be real. I don't want to force it or fake it or fix it after the fact . . . I just want to be real.

I want to operate from truth, not from pressure to please or perform for people. I don't want to choose from fear of what others will think of me or of my motives. I want to choose what I know is right because it's good and because it pleases the Lord . . . Help me, God. I want to be real.

I have the information, mostly. I know I'm supposed to read and pray, and I know about worship too. I know I'm supposed to witness and work for the kingdom, and I know about loving others more than myself. Oh, yeah, I know all the stuff. I know nearly everything I'm supposed to know, and most of all, I know that knowing is not enough because it doesn't displace the denial in my heart . . . Help me, God. I want to be real.

By real, I mean ready, filled with anticipation when I arrive at Your house to worship You, heartfelt worship. Yeah, that's real.

By real, I mean ready with thanks for the cascade of blessings raining down on my head in this and every moment, genuine gratitude. Yeah, that's real.

By real, I mean an easy choice of obedience to silence my demanding flesh that calls me to choose what you lovingly forbid, obedient holiness. Yeah, that's real.

By real, I mean ready to be generous to people in need, not hoarding or hiding or helping out of guilt. Yeah, giving freely and continuously. That's real for sure . . . Help me God. I want to be real.

My choice is to be real, to be authentic down to the core of my soul, which will change me forever. I don't want to pose; I don't want to posture. I don't need a pat on the head or a slap on the back. I'm not looking for applause. I want to be real.

What a great body of Christ we would be if our generation chose to be authentic Christians! The world is dying for believers who are the real deal. God help us.

Here are three guidelines right from the mouth of our Lord that will help us with maintaining authenticity in our lives.

I Choose to Be Authentic—by Not Judging Others

*But doesn't Matthew 7:1 say that we should "**Judge not, that you be not judged**"?* Thanks for bringing that up. This is one of the most misquoted and misunderstood verses in the New Testament. People who don't even believe in God's Word quote that phrase as an infallible truth! It gets slapped onto everything: "No, no—remember, thou shalt not judge!"

But that's not what it means. Jesus didn't intend a categorical dismissal of all things evaluative. The context makes this abundantly clear. He was confronting the dual standard—expecting from others what we don't expect from ourselves. Picking at slivers in the eyes of others when there are logs protruding from our own! Jesus' answer isn't, "Ignore both the log and the slivers so you don't run the danger of judging." He gives the same counsel He gave the Pharisees in Matthew 23—haul away the logs in your own life, then you'll have a better chance to see and be sensitive to the stuff in your friends' lives. Remember Matthew 7:6, **"Do not give dogs what is holy, and do not throw your pearls before pigs."** By *pearls*, He's talking about precious teachings. Jesus is saying, *I'm not going to keep teaching people who don't want to hear it. I'm not going to keep sharing with people who just slap the truth away.* Don't you have to form a judgment to make that kind of decision?

A person's actions are among the few things that *can* be judged. But judgment, or discrimination, must be guarded wisely with the gift of discernment. In 2 Corinthians 5, Paul called a guy out for being a sexually immoral serial adulterer. On what basis? The man's actions.

Here's what Jesus said we shouldn't judge:

1: *Don't judge motives.*

You don't know why people do what they do. Don't ever let yourself say, "I know why she's like that" or "I know why he's doing that." No, you don't. Only God knows a person's heart. Nothing is more painful than someone incorrectly judging your motives.

God doesn't want us judging the territory that is His venue. God's job is judging the heart—let Him do it. We don't even fully know our own hearts, let alone someone else's. Judging motives is off-limits to us.

2: *Don't judge appearance.*

Don't judge a person by the color of his skin or the clothes he wears, or the car he drives, or the place he lives, or by the job he holds. Don't form judgments about people based on appearances. The adage is true—you really can't tell a book by its cover. And God hates it when we try.

3: *Don't judge harshly.*

When you do have to make a judgment call, don't judge harshly. Don't hold people to a standard that you're not even keeping. Don't be cruel and/or callous when you must expose another person's sinful actions.

Continuing on in Matthew 7, **"For with the judgment you pronounce you will be judged"** (v. 2). The standard of judgment that you pronounce on others is the same measuring stick God will use to measure you. So if you can't be satisfied with other people, and you're constantly judging, be warned. God could say, *Well, here's the script you were using, let me just read your standards back on you.* Yikes!

I Choose to Be Authentic—by Judging Myself

A genuine, real person evaluates himself honestly. Remember when Jesus cautioned us not to judge others by examining **"the speck that is in your brother's eye"** versus **"the log that is in your own eye"** (v. 3)? That's almost humorous. I'm sure when He described that picture the people snickered at its absurdity. The idea is that the serious thing in your life is so big that it keeps you from getting close enough to see the thing that the other person needs to work on. It also means that we are especially sensitive to problems in others' lives when there are problems in our lives!

When you've dealt with the big thing in your life and have really been honest about it before the Lord, your tone will be so different as you talk to someone else about how he needs to grow. When I'm dealing with my own stuff, I'll quickly admit that I don't have it all together. Part of being authentic is to admit we're all in process. Nobody has arrived. Humility can grow, thanks to authenticity and putting oneself under scrutiny before

God. Authenticity is looking in a mirror—a mirror that reflects your own soul. The followers of Christ know the standard. Instead of a basic outlook that judges everyone from our church to our workplace to our neighborhood, how about we open ourselves up before the Lord and say, *Search me, Lord. Show me my heart. Help me change what doesn't please You.* Start today.

I Choose to Be Authentic—by Pursuing Authentic Relationships

Nothing will help you become authentic more than spending time with authentic people. Try to steer clear of religious, fake, phony, surface-y, gossip-y, faultfinding people. Those who are determined to be like that don't want to change. If they are all about the gossip, and appearance, and the nonsense— get away from them. And make sure you're not just forming another group to talk about how bad the first group is! Love and care for them, help them grow, but don't make those people your closest friends. They're not going anywhere you want to go if your goal is authenticity. Instead, invest yourself in people who are sincere and genuine in their love for God. Get with people who are real. And the best way to find them is by being real yourself.

I long for you to be a part of an authentic Christian community. Don't you want to throw off the mask when you come to church? Aren't you relieved to know you don't have to act like you're better than you are because you are among people where you're known and loved, where you're growing and changing? This is where you and I have to be committed to growing. Authenticity will not happen unless we are serious about becoming more like Christ. Pursue authentic relationships. And instead of spending time with fakers, invest your life with genuine people who have a pure heart to honor God.

The decision to be authentic is definitely one of the ten choices that can change your life forever. I read a little book from time to time that really stirs my faith. *A Diary of Private Prayer* was written by John Baillie, a Scottish theologian from the early 1900s. He died five days before I was born. John Baillie really knew how to pray. Read this prayer carefully, thinking through all we've covered in this chapter about closing the gap between our private and public lives. Ask God to open your heart to His searchlight.

Oh Father, I have tried Your patience. Too often I have betrayed the sacred trust You have given me to keep. Yet You are still willing that I should come to You in lowliness of heart as I do now, begging You to drown my transgressions in the sea of Your infinite love.

Forgive me, Lord, for my failure to be true, even to my own accepted standards.

Forgive me, Lord, for my self-deception in the face of temptation.

Forgive me, Lord, for my choosing of the worse when I know the better.

Forgive me, Lord, for my failure to apply to myself the standards of conduct I demand in others.

Forgive me, Lord, for my blindness to the suffering of others and slowness to be taught by my own hardship.

Forgive me, God, for my complacence toward wrongs that do not touch my own case and my over-sensitiveness to those that do.

Forgive me for my slowness to see the good in others and my slowness to see the evil in myself.

Forgive me for my hardness of heart toward my neighbor's faults and my readiness to make allowance for my own.

Forgive me, Lord.

Create in me a clean heart. Renew a right spirit within me.[2]

A Choice to Make

Acknowledge the Choice

- Think of at least three areas of your life in which you strongly suspect there is some hypocrisy. If you can't come up with any, ask someone who knows you well to suggest some—but limit them to three!
- In what ways have you been injured by the hypocrisy of others?
- How have you been encouraged and influenced by the authenticity of others?

Consider the Choice

- Based on the last choice we made—to love family first—how is your authenticity, or lack thereof, affecting your family?
- What authentic people do you think you can identify who might provide honest feedback on your strides toward authenticity? How would you approach them?
- What changes are you asking God to bring about as a result of your choice to practice authenticity?

Make the Choice

- Identify one person you can tell about this choice you are making. Ask him to pray for you.
- Tell that person the three areas of hypocrisy you plan to give special attention to, and ask him for any counsel he might have for you.
- Give him permission not only to point out areas you may be missing, but also to ask you regularly about how you are doing.

A Choice Prayer

Lord, I choose to be authentic. Purify my heart. Create in me a clean heart, and renew a right spirit within me. Free me, Lord, from hypocrisy, and grant to me a fresh season of authenticity in my relationship with You and others. Purify me, I pray, in Jesus' name. Amen.

PART V

MY DESTINY CHOICES

Choice 9: I Choose to Serve

Choice 10: I Choose to Stand

Where is my life going? When it's all over, what will I have accomplished? To determine these answers for your life, you've got to pull the camera back to its widest angle and examine the big picture. What do you want for your life? What does *God* want for your life? If you are a follower of Jesus Christ, you were born for greatness. God made you to be great in His eyes as He fashioned you in your mother's womb.

But greatness in God's eyes looks very different than greatness in man's eyes. In these final two chapters of our ten choices, the focus is on your destiny. What do you want your life to be about?

Chapter 9 offers a surprising twist in your choices. If you want to be great in God's eyes, serve Him by serving others. Your Christian life will always be an obligation to you until you serve. It will always be a burden, just another responsibility, until you commit to serving. Do you want your life in Jesus to have all the joy you've heard about? Serve God with your whole heart—**"Whatever your hand finds to do, do it with all your might"** (Ecclesiastes 9:10 NASB). You'll be surprised how life begins to improve.

Our final chapter, "I Choose to Stand," deals with something deep inside you, something you may have forgotten about or neglected for a long time. When you think about your destiny, where you're going, and what you want to accomplish, this is the one thing every true follower of Christ must commit to. I choose to stand: I will not walk away from the Lord. I will live every day for Him. When I cross the finish line at the end of my life, I want Him to look me right in the eyes and say, "Well done. Welcome home." This is my destiny, and I'm going after it with everything I've got.

Then the mother of the sons of Zebedee came up to him with her sons, and kneeling before him she asked him for something. And he said to her, "What do you want?" She said to him, "Say that these two sons of mine are to sit, one at your right hand and one at your left, in your kingdom." Jesus answered, "You do not know what you are asking. Are you able to drink the cup that I am to drink?" They said to him, "We are able." He said to them, "You will drink my cup, but to sit at my right hand and at my left is not mine to grant, but it is for those for whom it has been prepared by my Father." And when the ten heard it, they were indignant at the two brothers. But Jesus called them to him and said, "You know that the rulers of the Gentiles lord it over them, and their great ones exercise authority over them. It shall not be so among you. But whoever would be great among you must be your servant, and whoever would be first among you must be your slave, even as the Son of Man came not to be served but to serve, and to give his life as a ransom for many."

—MATTHEW 20:20—28

I Choose to Serve

*I choose a life of serving God as the way to lasting
greatness in God's eyes.*

I believe with all my heart that you are destined for greatness. I believe God
has a plan for your life that includes fabulous blessings as you make choices
every day that can bring you favor with God and a life of great satisfaction.
Greatness is your God-given destiny. God's intended outcome as a result of
these ten choices we are discussing is nothing short of greatness!

*Well, it's finally happened, Martha. James MacDonald just crossed over to
the other side with all those slick televangelists. "Greatness is your destiny!"
What's next—should I name it and claim it? Should I demand my miracle?*

Those may be your thoughts right now—that I've joined the world in a
quest for greatness: power and control, health and wealth. Well, read on! I
think you'll find nothing of the sort.

I honestly believe you are destined for greatness, but God's path to greatness is way different than what most people might think. Destiny is the
course of events laid out for you by God Himself. It is the answer to your
question, "What will my life ultimately be about?" It is your opportunity to
choose your destiny. The alternative is to live at cross-purposes with God's
purpose for you.

God is working out a plan in your life that will make you great, but it
runs counterintuitive to the world's strategy.

Greatness Is Not Found in Position

In the world's estimation, greatness is achieved by being in charge of something or being the best at something. Be the president, be the pastor, be the prominent athlete, or be the successful entertainer. Certain positions are considered synonymous with greatness. And often, how you get there isn't as important as arriving.

But quite honestly, you could be the pastor of a church and not be great in any real way. You could be the president of a company and not be close to measuring up. You could be a politician in high office, the professor at a prestigious college, an Oscar-winning actor, or an NBA hotshot, and while the world might say you're great, you might not be in God's eyes. People might applaud you, line up to shake your hand or get your autograph or some other silly horizontal thing, but ultimately, eternally, in God's estimation, you could have all that status and not be great at all.

Greatness is not found in position. If you've ever lost a position or been fired, you understand the tenuous nature of position. You know how disappointing it can be to find yourself suddenly dismissed, downsized, and shown the door. I expect that more than one employee has gotten an encouraging message like "You're the greatest" scrawled on the back of the pink slip announcing his termination. Whatever greatness goes with position isn't lasting, and it isn't real greatness.

I've been fired before. (Not recently, thank goodness.) Back when I was in college, I took a semester off to pay down some school bills by working as a stock boy at a wholesale stationery store. A problem developed because I was so fired up about the Lord that I kept sharing my faith with people. The boss called me in and said, "You can't do that here. Just do your job, son." Well, I didn't stop, so on my next trip to the boss's office, I heard, "You're fired!" Back then I thought I was being persecuted for sharing my faith. Looking back, I realize I should have just done my job.

Another time in college, I worked as a security guard (that's funny all by itself). Kathy and I were seriously dating but separated by distance for a year as she attended a Bible college in another part of Canada. I worked the night shift at a factory, and one night we were having an argument on the phone. I was making hourly rounds in the cavernous building like I should, but in between I was talking to her on the phone.

Then the boss showed up. He approached my desk and said, "Hey, I need to talk to you for a second."

So I said, "Yeah, I'll be right with you, I'm on the phone with my girlfriend."

"No, I need to talk to you right now."

"Yeah, no problem," I whispered hoarsely with my hand on the phone. "Just a second, I'm talking with my girlfriend."

"No, no, I need to talk to you right now."

"Well, I'll be done in a minute. I'm on the phone with my girlfriend."

Instead, he got in his car and left. The next day I heard the Donald Trump slogan, "You're fired!"

So again: my fault. Both times I distinctly remember feeling a sense of loss. Those, however, were silly college jobs and not really very hard to talk about, but many of us know the pain of what it's like to work at a job for a long time and then lose it.

Maybe you lost your position in your family against your will. Maybe you lost your position in a company against your will. Maybe you lost your position in an organization or in a school against your will. The greater the injustice of the loss, the greater the wounding you feel.

Inevitably we've got to come to this reality: greatness is not found in a position. I am not my job. I am not my role. Mothers, especially, struggle with an empty nest when their kids grow up and fly. They may wonder, *I don't have my kids to care for anymore. Who am I now?* Life isn't going anywhere good when you define your life by your position. Men struggle with this when they lose a career from which they derived a lot of satisfaction. The disappointment leads not only to the thought, *I guess I wasn't all that great at what I was doing,* but also is often followed by the somewhat stunned realization, *I don't think I know how to do anything else!*

Pursuit of Greatness

Jesus had to deal with an overly zealous mother in search of greatness for her boys. In Matthew 20:20, **"the mother of the sons of Zebedee,"** who we know to be Salome, approached Jesus with a request. Before we get to what she wanted, you need to know that Salome and her boys were part of Jesus' inner circle of relationships. She eventually was at the crucifixion, standing right there at the base of the cross with Mary. She was with the women who hurriedly anointed Jesus' body for burial before His resurrection. She loved Jesus like a second mother.

Her sons were James and John. From Mark 3:17 and Luke 9:51, we know Jesus called them the sons of thunder. This nickname probably highlighted certain personality traits the brothers shared. On one occasion when some people were rejecting Jesus, they were the ones who suggested, *Hey, Jesus, why don't we just call down fire from heaven and wipe these guys out?* Jesus was like, *No, no, we're not going to do that.* These were seriously fired up guys.

James and John were on the inside track with Jesus, along with Peter. They were with Jesus on the Mount of Transfiguration, in the Garden of Gethsemane, and often with Jesus when He prayed. They were His closest friends.

A Mother's Request

So back to Matthew 20:20: **"Then the mother of the sons of Zebedee came up to him with her sons, and kneeling before him . . ."** In this case, His response was, **"What do you want?"** We can't be sure of Jesus' tonality, but we can guess it wasn't all sweet and patient because a bit later He says to her in verse 22, **"You do not know what you are asking."**

There may have been some tension in this exchange, but Salome sure had moxie. Kneeling in front of Jesus with her two "Sons of Thunder" hiding behind her skirt, she said in verse 21, **"Say that these two sons of mine are to sit, one at your right hand and one at your left, in your kingdom."**

Are you kidding me?

The invitation to sit at someone's right or left hand is not a big deal today. But in New Testament times, the person who sat the closest to the head of the table had the most honor. She was asking, first, *Hey, I don't want my sons standing in this kingdom of yours, Jesus, I want them sitting down.* Salome was assuming her sons were not going to serve, they were going to be served. *Pretty soon You're going to have Your kingdom, Jesus, and I don't want You to lose track of them. You know how much my sons love You, and if You could just, like, say it right now that they're going to be on Your right and left hand, that'd be great. You can be the CEO, Jesus, but they should be like the COO and CFO right there beside You. You're welcome to take the oval office, Lord, but my sons deserve to be right next door.*

Notice in verse 21 she begins with a request for Jesus to say it because she knows that if He pronounces it, it will happen.

You Don't Know What You Are Asking

Jesus heard her request but didn't give in to her. She wanted something good but was going about it all the wrong way. He said to her, **"You do not know what you are asking"** (v. 22). And isn't that the truth.

Salome's first mistake was in thinking Jesus' kingdom was coming in the next ten minutes. She was trying to get a jump on inauguration day the following week. But what she was anticipating hasn't arrived even today. Eventually, Jesus' kingdom will be on earth. But for now, He has been exalted to the right hand of God after His resurrection. In Christ, we, like Salome and her sons, are citizens of Jesus' kingdom, but He hasn't assigned eternal offices yet. The only kingdom He rules right now is our hearts.

When Jesus said, *You don't know what you're asking,* He could also have added, *Do you know that I'm going to suffer? Do you know that I'm going to be beaten and mocked and spat upon and ridiculed? Do you know that I'm going to be scourged and tortured and paraded through the streets and spat upon and crucified? Do you really want your sons to have some of that? You don't even know what you're asking.*

Instead, he asks a question that should have given them pause: **"Are you able to drink the cup that I am to drink?"** (v. 22). The cup, of course, is symbolic of all the suffering of the Cross. Remember when Jesus prayed in the Garden of Gethsemane, He said, **"My Father, if it be possible, let this cup pass from me"** (Matthew 26:39). He knew He must drink it right to the bottom. He prayed this even though He knew He was going to take all of the punishment for your sin. Think of your life and my life, and all the sins of the world. All of our punishment for all of our sin was placed upon Christ, and it was in that cup. In His humanity, Jesus didn't relish the cup any more than we would, but He chose to serve by saying, **"Not My will, but Yours be done"** (Luke 22:42 NASB).

Jesus asked them, **"'Are you able to drink the cup that I am to drink?' They said to him, 'We are able'"** (Matthew 20:22). *Sure, can do, Jesus. No problem.* So apparently at this point they peeked out from behind their mother's apron and answered. There's actually another account in Mark 10 that has them asking for the special seat assignment, too, so I wouldn't be surprised if they came back to this theme again, or perhaps they were all saying, *You bet; we're able.* What an outrageous assertion.

Not only did they not know what they were asking; they had no idea what they were claiming! When Jesus was arrested in Matthew 26:56, we learn that **"all the disciples left him and fled."** Humanly speaking, they were not able to stand. They were full of promises but not very much follow-through. One glimpse of the cup and they were out of there! But in Acts 2, after the Holy Spirit came to indwell them, they were used by God and **"turned the world upside down"** (Acts 17:6). Before we become judgmental, remember how much we're like the disciples in the Gospels. Would we have reacted any better? Only through the Spirit of God can we live our destiny of selfless service.

What the disciples James and John should have said was, *On our own, Lord, we are not able.* That's why Jesus responds to their "we are able" with, **"You will drink my cup"** (Matthew 20:23).

Jesus knew they would know suffering for His sake. James, standing there in front of Him, would be one of the first martyred disciples, beheaded for the gospel in Acts 12. John, his brother, suffered much for the gospel too. He would see every other disciple martyred and would be the last one to die in exile on the Isle of Patmos. Jesus looked not to their immediate failure leading up to the Cross, but to their ultimate victory in obedience to Him.

It's interesting to note Jesus' statement that positional greatness was not His to grant, **"But it is for those for whom it has been prepared by my Father"** (Matthew 20:23). He doesn't deny or grant their request, but says, *God, the Father, is in charge of that; I don't make that call by myself.*

What James and John were seeking (through their mom) was a position. They were seeking a status on Jesus' right hand and His left. Jesus does not condemn that desire for greatness, but He does restructure for them an understanding of what greatness really is. He turned their self-centered request into a teachable moment for the ages.

This woman wanted greatness for her sons, but she couldn't have been more wrong in how she pursued it. What Jesus was looking for in those two disciples had nothing to do with where they sat at the table. Do you get it? Greatness is not found in position—but it *can* be found.

Greatness Is Not Found in Power

When God looks at you, He's not impressed with your power. He's got the power market cornered, if you know what I mean. So He's not looking at you and thinking, *Wow! You're a powerful man! And you are an amazingly impactful woman!* He is flat-out unimpressed with power. Now, this doesn't mean all that much to us until we face up to the craving for power that resides in us.

"And when the ten heard it," (v. 24)—that's right, there were ten other disciples, and they weren't too happy with James and John's mom making an end-run like this. If you've ever played on a basketball team, just imagine if you walked by the coach's office and overheard a teammate talking to the coach, saying about you, "I don't think he should be the captain anymore. I want to be the captain." Can you imagine how that would make you feel?

The text says, **"And when the ten heard it, they were indignant at the** two brothers," or as the New King James Version translates it, "**they were greatly displeased**" (v. 24). Those are the best words to use that are still edifying. I'm going to guess they probably had some other words that got closer to their feelings that I'll leave to your imagination, beginning with *Who do you think you are?* and *Where do you get off?*

But notice Jesus' response to the men. He's so tender, calling them to Himself. He cut off their offended reaction with an intimate moment of truth. *First of all, James, John, you and your mom don't get it. The rest of you—it's OK. You need to just drop it. Everybody huddle up here.* And then He went on to do some pretty spectacular teaching.

Once Jesus had their attention, He said, "**You know that the rulers of the Gentiles lord it over them**" (v. 25a). Meaning, the secular crowd throws their weight around. *You know how it goes in the marketplace, don't you? You know how the pecking order works at corporate headquarters. You know how the system operates over at the local university. You know how the authority thing works anywhere out there. You've observed how people schmooze the boss and kiss up to the coach so their kid will get more playing time, or cut the corners to get a deal, or work something sly on the side. You know how it works when people use and abuse authority.*

Jesus said, "**You know the rulers of the Gentiles lord it over them and their great ones exercise authority**" (v. 25). The word *authority* implies *tyranny.* Is that not true in our world today? A little authority is dangerous; a little power is intoxicating. I'm not talking about people who really have authority and struggle to use it properly. Often, the people who are out of control with their power are those with the least real authority. Like the security guard at the library—watch out for that guy—or the president of the condo association. Many times they're the ones who are authority-tripping big-time.

Kathy and I and our kids went on vacation several years ago with some other families from our church. We rented a condo in Florida. We should have gotten a day's rent just for how much time it took to read the rules of this condo association. The written rules went on and on—and then there were the unwritten ones, such as you can't go to the beach through the parking lot;

you have to go through the gate by the pool; every dog needs a collar—not a license or a leash, mind you, but a collar. We found ourselves stuck in the Twilight Zone of rules.

While we were there, my parents came down to visit us. I went into the association office to get my dad a parking pass for one night. The sign said it was a hundred dollars a week.

"How much for one night?"

The attendant said, "One hundred dollars."

"That's for a week; how much for a night?"

"A hundred dollars."

"Well, one hundred divided by seven should be . . ."

"Well, whatever it should be, one hundred dollars is what it is."

"Well, I'm not paying that."

"Well, then, we'll fine you!"

"Fine me? When did you get the authority to impose fines? Can anybody just impose fines? Well, I fine you a hundred dollars for a dumb rule."

The whole week was like this.

Then on the last day of our vacation, I returned to the condo from the pool and got on the elevator. One of the condo association guys also got on, pushing a grocery cart. He said, "You can't be on the elevator with bare feet."

I sarcastically said, "Oh, but I'm sure you can bring shopping carts on the elevator!"

"You have to get off the elevator right now," he said

I just couldn't take it anymore. I said, "Call the police!"

People on an authority trip get out of control, don't they! It seems like anybody who gets a little bit of power can't wait to read the riot act. It's foolishness.

Jesus said that's just way it is with the world. We have to deal with it every day, but it's not supposed to be like that in God's family.

It's easy to poke fun at other people who don't exercise their authority well. What's harder is to look in the mirror and see how *we* are handling the authority that God has given to us where we work, in our home, and in our church. Sometimes we need help to see our own power-trips. Here are a few clues:

- *I know I'm abusing my authority when I keep reminding people of my title and my position.*

  Watch out if you hear yourself say, "Don't you know who I am? I'm your boss." If you have to keep telling people you're the boss, you might not have that role much longer. Be careful if you always want people to call you by your title or if you get offended when someone addresses you without your title. "I'm Dr. So-and-So." "I'm This-and-That."

  I absolutely refuse for people to call me *Reverend.* I'll never forget what an elder in our church told me years ago. He said, "Only Jesus is reverend. Only Jesus is to be revered; the rest of us are just regular people trying to serve God." It's not wrong to call someone by a title, and I never correct someone if that's meaningful to them. But if you insist on titles, you might be getting too attached to your authority.

- *I know I'm abusing my authority when I expect or demand privilege.*

  I'm losing my sense of position when I have to have a designated parking place or a special seat in the worship center or if I expect to be served first or have to be treated special because of my position. When you expect—or worse, *demand*—special treatment, that's a big fat clue you've got a problem.

- *I know I'm abusing my authority when I become comfortable with personal praise.*

  It's not wrong for people to thank you or appreciate you. The problem is when someone is doing that and you're thinking to yourself, *Wow, they finally figured out that I'm amazing.* Yeah— that's not great in God's eyes.

  There should always be something that makes you a little uncomfortable when people want to put the focus on you. I didn't see this coming, but when I started to write books, I discovered people often ask you to sign their copies for them. I've never really been comfortable with autograph requests, but then I haven't wanted to make a bigger scene by refusing because then they get the impression you think you're too good to sign their book. That's just a hallway with no exit doors, so I've decided every time I sign a book to include, along with my name, 2 Corinthians 4:7, **"But we have this treasure in jars of clay, to show that the surpassing power belongs to God and not to us."**

If you have authority or position or are in any situation where you're going to be singled out for your work, always deflect the praise. Thank the person, then thank the Lord because all that we have is from Him. First Corinthians 4:7 says, **"What do you have that you did not receive? If then you received it, why do you boast as if you did not receive it?"** If you have gifts and abilities, thank God for them. If you have opportunities God has given you, thank Him for them and use them for Him. To do otherwise is a mishandling of authority that can escalate into authority abuse.

- *I know I'm abusing my authority when I resent, react, or am threatened by challenges to my authority.*
  If you're put off when people ask, "Why is this like this?" or "Why can't this be different?" and you respond, "Because I'm your boss and I say so," you might have a problem with your authority.

  If you use your position as persuasion, then you are powering up over people. "And the answer is, I'm your pastor and I say so." If you resent having to explain your decisions because of your position, you may have a problem with authority. I understand the rules are different when we deal with smaller children. But be careful you're not powering over people. God hates that kind of abuse.

- *I know I'm abusing my authority when I'm unmoved by an individual.*
  It breaks my heart to hear politicians talk about the loss of human life in war as if it were collateral damage, necessary to the effort. It's sad they're not more deeply touched in their heart by the reality of families who are losing their loved ones in the cause of freedom. Similarly, it's wrong if you're a professor and you say (or think), "I'm

very educated; I don't really have time for the students." Or if you're a pastor and don't love the people. If you're in spiritual leadership, family leadership, educational leadership, or political leadership and you're not moved by the individual, that's wrong. Every person matters to God, and they need to matter to you in your position of authority. If they don't matter to you, either humble yourself and change or remove yourself from being their authority.

Greatness is not found in position or power—but it can be found.

True Greatness Is Found in Serving

True greatness is what we've been working toward in this whole chapter. Jesus said this kind of position or power play **"shall not be so among you"** (Matthew 20:26). *It might be that way in the world, but it's not going to be that way in My kingdom, in My family, and in My church*, Jesus would say, even to us today. **"It shall not be so among you. But whoever would be great among you must be your servant, and whoever would be first among you must be your slave, even as the Son of Man came not to be served but to serve, and to give his life as a ransom for many"** (Matthew 20:26–28).

Let's go back through Jesus' words a little at a time. Notice the hope found in verse 26: **"It shall not be so among you."** I find that really moving. Jesus has a heart for me to be better than I am. He has a heart for me to use my authority better than I do. He has a heart for me to pursue true greatness. Even though the world constantly teaches me to do it a certain way, He's persuaded of better things concerning me. He says to me constantly, *You can do this better than this. You're not going to assert your rights. You're not going to demand your way. You're not going to hold the failures of other people over them and abuse your authority.*

"But whoever would be great among you . . ." (v. 26). Notice the strong contrast that Jesus lays down. Be reminded that Jesus has not condemned the desire for greatness. He's not saying, *Don't desire to be great*. Another passage, Jeremiah 45:5, says it's all about motives: **"Do you seek great**

things for yourself? Seek them not." Deep inside your heart God put the desire to do something great with your life, to want to make a difference in this world, to have a purpose, to live for something that will last. The desire for greatness is a God-given and awesome thing.

The pursuit of greatness is not wrong, but it does cause some people to desire wrongly—to desire the wrong thing in the wrong way and the wrong amount. That's why Jesus said, **"But whoever would be great among you must be your servant"** (v. 26). That's greatness in God's eyes: the greatest person is the greatest servant.

Who is the greatest person in your family? In your church? In God's eyes, it's the greatest servant. Matthew 20:16 says, **"So the last will be first, and the first last."** What a radical flip from what the world expects. All the while we're patting people on the back and applauding the ones who are in the spotlights, God's saying, *Yeah, they're OK. But it's the servant that I'm fired up about.* True greatness in God's eyes is found in serving.

So let's bring Jesus' teaching to bear upon the five most massive problems in the world. Do you want to be a resource for good in the world system but doubt whether your effort makes any difference in light of the immensity of the problem?

1: *Poverty*

   Nearly half of the population of the planet (2.8 billion people) lives on less than two dollars a day. Over one-quarter of those live on less than one dollar a day.[1]

2: *Child labor*

   An estimated 211 million children (from five to fourteen years of age) work in order to support their families. More than half of these work under hazardous conditions.[2]

3: *Health*

   In 2000 there were thirty-four million cases of HIV/AIDS around the world, and five million of them were newly infected with HIV in 1999. All of those people will likely die prematurely.[3]

4: *Education*

Do you know there are more than one billion adults worldwide who are illiterate? They couldn't read a Bible if you gave it to them.[4]

5: *Genocide*

The twentieth century was one of the bloodiest in history. World leaders killed their own citizens—Mao in China killed 72 million; Stalin in Russia killed 50 million; Hitler in Germany killed 21 million—to say nothing of the genocide in Nanking (300,000), Cambodia (2 million), Bosnia–Herzegovina (200,000), Rwanda (800,000), Uganda (500,000), and Nigeria (1 million).[5] Millions of people were murdered by their own governments and leaders. What a colossal, staggering abuse of authority!

Those are horrible problems, but I don't see how I could influence any of those overwhelming needs. Yes, I would agree. It's tempting to feel helpless. But I think you can make a very good choice in light of these overwhelming circumstances if you can get beyond four bad choices that sidetrack many people who care. Seeing the world's massive problems, many people sadly choose only to . . .

1: *Cry*

They get in a corner and mourn the cost of shocking injustice. They grieve over conditions and wring their hands in agony over their helplessness.

2: *Complain*

This stinking, sinful, twisted, dark world is going to hell in a handbasket. At the religious end of the spectrum, complainers hold God responsible for the mess.

3: *Criticize*

All the poor people wouldn't be in poverty if they just worked a little bit. And those with AIDS, well, they're suffering because of their own immorality. Yes, thank you for those easy answers. God forgive us for judgmentally dismissing things because we think we have a position of moral superiority.

4: *Get cynical*

Nothing's going to change. Nothing will ever get better. The world is going over the falls. I can't stop it. I don't care. I can't give the time to it. Don't tell me about those things. I've got nothing to do with any of it. Cynicism is the destination of those who begin with crying, complaining, and criticizing.

In light of the world's massive problems, here's the only impactful choice I can make: I choose to serve. This is a life-altering choice that will take you to a lot of incredible places. Crying, complaining, criticizing, and becoming cynical are all ways to react to the crises in the world; only service offers an authentic, hands-on, effective, God-honoring response.

I Choose to Serve

This is a choice that will change your life. *My life is not going to be about myself. I'm going to be part of the solution, not part of the problem. I can't change the world, but I can change my own destiny. I know what God wants. I know what God's looking for. I'm going to be a servant.* Jesus said, **"It shall not be so among you. But whoever would be great among you must be your servant"** (Matthew 20:26).

Your Christian life will never make sense to you until you learn how to serve, commit to serve, and then actually roll up your sleeves and jump in. At our church we call it *shouldering weekly kingdom responsibilities.*

Until you serve, your Christian life will always be an obligation. You will feel burdened by just another responsibility until you get off the bench and into the game. Spiritually speaking, you'll never get the wind in your sails until you commit to imitating Christ in regular, humble, faithful service. You'll only know the duty and never the delight of the Christian life until you serve God with your whole heart, whatever that specifically means for you. Ecclesiastes 9:10 says, **"Whatever your hand finds to do, do it with your might."** What's more, you'll never experience long-term growth in your Christian life until you serve in some kind of personal ministry. Look at the two simple charts that follow.

I've seen the truths of these graphs bear themselves out over decades of ministry. The first chart is the potential of your walk with Christ. On the vertical axis is your spiritual maturity—your growth and fulfillment in the Christian life. That's our goal. If we plot it from one to ten, we can go from zero (baby Christian) to ten (the apostle Paul). You're somewhere in between those extremes, and so am I. Across the bottom, plot the number of years that you've been in the Lord. The longer you've known the Lord, the more mature you should be. So the graph of a healthy Christian should look like this:

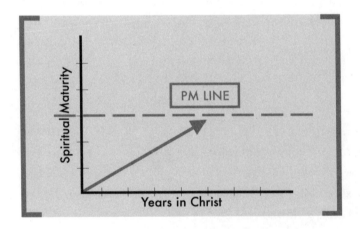

The fact is, however, that a lot of people's spiritual life reaches a ceiling. You grow to a point and then you plateau. You say to yourself, *Man, when I first came to Christ, I was so fired up about Him. I grew like crazy in my spiritual life. I couldn't learn enough in the Word. I was going on for God. All of a sudden I hit this ceiling, and it feels like I'm stalled and I can't grow anymore. What's holding me back?* That horizontal line is what we call the personal ministry (PM) line.

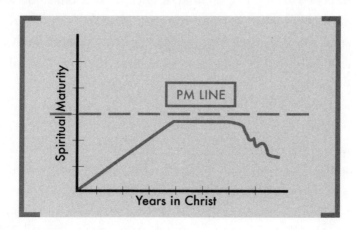

The early years of following Christ involved a lot of taking in and not so much giving out. You grew largely because of the loving efforts of others who came alongside and ministered to you. Unless you come to the place where you begin to start using what you've been given and teaching it to others, you're going to plateau and then spiral down. Until you come to the place where you realize, "I've had too much receiving and not enough giving going on in my life; I need to roll up my sleeves and work for the Master," you won't break the PM ceiling. Until you make that choice, you're going to be spiritually frustrated. Eventually your spiritual life will weaken and wither. It's the folks in spiritual decline that make pastors crazy. They've got all the information: they sit in church every week and could finish your next sentence in most sermons, but they aren't doing anything with all they have learned. Unless you break through the personal ministry line, your spiritual life will inevitably drift from dynamic to decline. The breakthrough comes when you choose to serve.

Full-Time Service

People frequently ask my advice about going into full-time ministry. "I'm praying about it," they say.

To which I answer, "Don't pray about it; just go for it." For sure God has called every one of us into a lifetime of service: **"It is God who works in you, both to will and to work for his good pleasure"** (Philippians 2:13). We don't have to ask Him if He wants us to serve! If your desire is to work for Him vocationally, just go for it! Let God close the door. Don't shut your heart to your destiny. God wants to do something great with you—and it begins with you serving Him however you can, in a regular job or, if He desires, full-time vocational work. Whatever God's calling you to do, do it with your whole heart.

Above all, serve Him every week. Serve in the kingdom, serve in the family, and serve at church. We're on the bull's-eye right now—true greatness is discovered in serving. Others may never assign greatness to your life, but in serving Christ you will know you have lived a great life—and better than that, God knows!

Christ loves the church and gave Himself for it. **"On this rock I will build my church, and the gates of hell shall not prevail against it"** (Matthew 16:18). I can't change every church in the world, but I'm going to account to God for the church I attend. If you're hanging out on the fringes, man, what are you waiting for, an invitation? Get into the center and serve. If you always come in late and sit in the back, try something really radical—show up early and sit down front! Your perspective will instantly change. If you really don't know where to start serving, locate someone in the lobby who looks a little frazzled and approach him, saying, "How can I help?"

Jesus Models Exemplary Service

Do you want to be like Jesus? Do you express a desire to follow Him? If you're not serving, no matter how loving and kind and truthful you are, you're not like Him. Jesus models service. He's our example. He issued our service orders: **"But whoever would be great among you must be your servant, and whoever would be first among you must be your slave, even as the Son of Man came not to be served but to serve, and to give his life as a ransom for many"** (Matthew 20:26–28).

You will have to develop a new mind-set—the mind-set of service. The apostle Paul outlined that way of thinking and living in these words: **"Do nothing from rivalry or conceit, but in humility count others more significant than yourselves. Let each of you look not only to his own interests, but also to the interests of others. Have this mind among yourselves, which is yours in Christ Jesus, who, though he was in the form of God, did not count equality with God a thing to be grasped, but made himself nothing, taking the form of a servant"** (Philippians 2:3–7).

Some of the greatest servants of Jesus Christ on the face of the earth are filling the pews in our churches—tireless people who work for God. They are often unnoticed, often underappreciated except by God, and unpaid. There wouldn't be churches without them. Join their ranks, not only for their sakes but also for the experience of your life-changing choice to serve.

Don't aspire to top-row service either. Don't be like, "When you've got a seat open at the head of the table, call me, and I'll show up." Start lower down. You won't have to look far to find something that urgently needs doing. Begin there and serve humbly and faithfully. God will send for you when He needs more of what you're already doing.

Of course, Jesus modeled humility. Notice, **"even as the Son of Man came not to be served"** (Matthew 20:28). Now, if anybody could have come into the world expecting to be served, it would have been Jesus. He should have had a royal robe and crown. He should have stayed in five-star hotels and eaten gourmet meals. But instead, He pitched His fleshly tent on straw in a stable under a star and began the greatest demonstration of humility and servanthood that the world has ever seen. Jesus set the bar high. He was truly a servant. **"[He] came not to be served but to serve, and to give his life as a ransom for many"** (v. 28).

Not only did His life prove His selfless service, but His death also paid the ransom for your sin and mine. He bought our tickets to heaven, forgiveness, and a life here and now of joy and satisfaction. If Jesus chose to serve, how can I choose anything less?

After my decision to follow Jesus Christ, the choice to serve Him has been more formative in my spiritual life than any other decision. My commitment to serve keeps me in God's Word. I can't afford to wander away for days or weeks. Serving Christ tethers my heart to the Cross. People are counting on me—and you have to know people are counting on you too. You have an awe-inspiring opportunity to serve in Christ's kingdom. If you just open your heart to this, you will begin to see an incredible banquet of service choices set before you each day.

> **IF JESUS CHOSE TO SERVE, HOW CAN I CHOOSE ANYTHING LESS?**

You may wonder: *How do I keep serving when I get discouraged?* Yes, I'm so glad you brought it up. Humbling yourself and serving is tough, and it's easy to want to throw in the towel. Colossians 3:23 has been the key clarifier for me, **"Whatever you do, work heartily,"** and then verse 24 says, **"You are serving the Lord Christ."**

Motivation Upgrade

Honestly, some people are difficult to serve. I must keep in mind that I'm not serving my spouse or my kids; I'm not serving my pastor or elders; I'm not serving that cranky church member; I'm not serving that troublesome person at work. It really helps me to be reminded that I'm serving *Him.*

Even as you serve your children, you're serving Christ.

Even as you serve your husband, you're serving Christ.

Even as you serve at church, you're serving Christ. He's the center of your attention. (I find that to be a motivation upgrade.) When the people are dirty or difficult or discouraging in some way, just tell yourself, *I'm serving Jesus.* Wouldn't you do whatever you could for the Lord?

Appreciation Upgrade

You have probably figured out that Jesus doesn't send a lot of thank-you notes—at least not in this life. What Jesus thinks about my service is a message that is yet to get to me. If other people don't appreciate me or pat me on the back or applaud me, that's OK because I'm serving Christ. He is keeping track of everything that I do. He'll sort it all out some day, and He promises me a commensurate reward.

Significance Upgrade

"So what did you do this weekend?" That casual, water cooler question really begs for a thought-provoking answer!

Just think, if your mind-set was focused on serving Christ, you could answer, *Well, I was just helping the God of the universe with a couple of things He's working on.* Service is a big deal! You're plugged into eternal purposes! You're making a difference that will last forever! Even when your service is humble and unseen, your life is taking on a significance upgrade.

Faithfulness Upgrade

Serving Christ helps you to stay faithful. When you want to tell the director of children's ministry that you're going to quit teaching the fourth grade class, he might say, "Well, it's Christ that you're serving, so you might want to check with Him, but I'm guessing that He might want you to keep doing it until we find a replacement." Remembering who it is you serve helps you to be faithful. It helps *me* be faithful. If I get a little frustrated with something in my service for the Lord, I remember it's not about anybody but the Lord. Jesus models exemplary servanthood. I choose to serve Him.

I need to ask you, what is the manner of your life in regard to these things? After the choice to follow Christ, the choice to serve Him is the most important choice you will ever make. All of life comes into perspective when you see yourself as a servant. Priorities come in line when you recognize "I'm here to serve Him." The Christian life is not about Jesus serving me; it's about me serving Him.

So here come the practical questions: In what ways are you serving Jesus Christ? In what ways are you personally shouldering weekly kingdom responsibility? You don't get that many weeks in a lifetime. What will you do for Christ *this* week? I realize that much is required of you in your home and at work, but what have you volunteered for? In what situations have you willingly offered, "Add this to my responsibilities. I want to serve Christ"?

Do you want to change your life? Make the choice to serve. If you do, your life will be eternally altered by it. Sadly, others will read this and do nothing. They will feel that tug of possibility, that longing that leads to greatness, but they will think, *Nah, that sounds too much like work.* What a tragic waste of opportunity.

Do you want a life of fabulous blessing, favor with God, and great satisfaction? Choose to serve (just ask anyone fully engaged in his ministry for his testimony, and you'll find out it is true). Jesus' life proves it. **"If you want to be great,"** He said, **"you must be the servant of all"** (Matthew 20:26 CEV). Greatness is your God-given destiny, and it all begins with the decision only you can make: I choose to serve Jesus Christ.

A Choice to Make

Acknowledge the Choice

- In what ways has your life been significantly affected by the selfless service of others?

- How have you experienced the satisfaction that comes from performing a service for someone else?

- What were your specific answers to the earlier questions in the chapter about your present service for Christ?

Consider the Choice

- Describe one attitude, association, or arrangement that would have to change if you chose to make your life about service?

- Why would you say that service for Christ is the most effective way of responding to all He has done in service for you?

Make the Choice

Humble yourself before God, and enlarge on these three sentence prayers:

- "Lord, I choose to continue serving You (but more intentionally and enthusiastically) in the following places where you have already placed me . . ."
- "Lord, I choose to serve You in the following places that will require me to find a specific place or role of service . . ."
- "Lord, I choose to serve You beyond the two areas I've already brought before You, simply placing myself at Your disposal for service . . ."

A Choice Prayer

Lord Jesus Christ, You are worthy of my service. Forgive my selfishness. Forgive my distractions. Forgive my consumer mentality. Call me forth to serve in Your kingdom today. Grant me the joy that You reserve for those who belong completely to You. Grow me as a disciple because of this, and please hear my prayer.

My eyes are on You, Lord, for You see and know what I'm seeking to do for You. For some who are in a season of fruitlessness, might Your Spirit pursue them until they step into an opportunity of work for the Master. Help us, God. For some who do not want You to reign over them, might they feel the weight of submission to You until they find the joy and the release of humble submission to Your Word and Your ways.

Lord, teach us afresh what it means to serve You. Not to work for any man, but to serve the Lord Christ.

In Jesus' name. Amen.

You are the salt of the earth, but if salt has lost its taste, how shall its saltiness be restored? It is no longer good for anything except to be thrown out and trampled under people's feet. You are the light of the world. A city set on a hill cannot be hidden. Nor do people light a lamp and put it under a basket, but on a stand, and it gives light to all in the house. In the same way, let your light shine before others, so that they may see your good works and give glory to your Father who is in heaven.

—MATTHEW 5:13–16

[Choice 10]

I Choose to Stand

*I will not walk away from the Lord when things get
hard. I choose to stand for Him.*

The weirdest thing happened the other day. I was walking out of a local
restaurant called Jimmy's Charhouse when I noticed a round table filled
with (I'm sorry) obviously Italian men. Now, that is not an unusual thing
in Chicago and, of course, Chicago is famous for its history of organized
crime and so on. I'm not trying to stereotype, but these gentlemen had the
whole "look" thing going on: leather jackets, pinky rings, and the total wise-
guy persona to the max.

So I kinda slowed down when I walked past their table, my ears tuned
into eavesdrop mode. And I hear the obvious main guy, the boss as it were,
say these words: "It must be done!"

One of the guys near him just nods his head and says in a perfect Chicago accent, "It will be done!"

Now I guess the response was not quick enough or certain enough
because the first guy says in a much louder voice (all this while I am walking past in slow motion), "It must be done!"

This time, the biggest of the guys nods and agrees with a slap on the
table that rattled the silverware, "It will be done!"

Well, maybe it's just my imagination, but it all felt strangely like a scene
from a gangster movie. I half expected to see Elliot Ness appear at any
moment. Of course, I have absolutely no idea of the context of that exchange,

and I truly hope no one ended up in a trunk that day, but what I do know is this—they had set a course of action together, and nothing would deter them. *Nothing!*

The Tenth Choice

We have set a course of action for our lives through the choices in this book. We have made some life-changing decisions together. But here's the thing: without this last choice, everything that we have gained could just as easily be lost. The final choice is the choice that seals our future and keeps us going forward into all the blessing that these incredible choices can bring. It's the choice to stand. I'm not going back; I'm not caving in; and I'm not going to regress or retreat or regret the choices I've made. I'm going to stand.

Jesus made the issue pretty clear: **"But whoever denies me before men, I also will deny before my Father who is in heaven"** (Matthew 10:33). What exactly is *denying?* When any kind of pressure comes, if you back down, falter, become skeptical or suspicious—that's denying. If you turn to unbelief or uncertainty, if you vacillate or waver, if you refuse to take a stand for Christ, if you don't fly the flag at the top of the pole, you're going nowhere good.

Now, take a breath. I'm not talking about one time. Jesus wasn't referring to stumbles and slips along the way. He had twelve stumblers constantly around Him during His time here. Jesus is saying, *If the pattern of your life is denying Me, then what you can expect in eternity is to be denied.* Of course, I think you know this is as serious as serious gets. Jesus says, *If you don't stand up for Me, then someday when you stand up in heaven, the Father will look at Me and ask, "What about him?" And I'll say, "Yeah, I don't know him."* He will flat-out deny you! You'll be like, "Jesus! Jesus! I did all these things for you . . ." *No, I don't know you.*

I suspect that Matthew 10:32–33 was still ringing in Peter's ears when he was sitting at the Last Supper. Jesus had looked at the disciples and said, *If you deny Me, I'm going to deny you before My Father.* I doubt Peter had forgotten Jesus' words.

No wonder as they left the Upper Room headed for the Garden of Geth-semane, Jesus turned to the disciples and said, **"You will all fall away because of me this night. For it is written, 'I will strike the shepherd, and the sheep of the flock will be scattered'"** (Matthew 26:31). Can you imagine how that hurt their hearts? *Fall away from You, Lord? We love You! We've followed You for three years. We left everything for You.*

Yeah, well, you're going to fall away from me.

And who spoke up? It was Peter. *Not me, Lord.*

And Jesus said, *Yes, you will.*

Peter said, with force, *No way!*

And Jesus said, *Way!*

I will not fall away. Even if everyone falls away, I won't fall away. If there is one man standing—it'll be me! Peter was certain.

Jesus was like, *Actually, before a rooster crows, you're going to deny Me three times.*

Peter replied, *I will not!*

And Jesus nodded, *Yeah, we'll see. We'll see.* (Matthew 26:33–35).

Peter must have been stunned by how quickly his resolve melted.

I think you know what followed in Matthew 26:69–70, one of the saddest sections of Scripture. **"Now Peter was sitting outside in the courtyard. And a servant girl came up to him and said, 'You also were with Jesus the Galilean.' But he denied it before them all, saying, 'I do not know what you mean.'"** Don't know what she means, Peter? She's asking you if you belong to Jesus. How hard is that to understand? Are you afraid of a servant girl? *How pathetic!* **"And when he went out to the entrance, another servant girl saw him, and she said to the bystanders, 'This man was with Jesus of Nazareth.' And again he denied it with an oath"** (vv. 71–72). This time he swears and says, **"I do not know the man"** (v. 72).

Don't know Him, Peter? Don't know how He loved you and called you? You weren't there when He healed the sick? Raised the dead? You weren't there when He fed the five thousand, Peter? What about the miraculous catch of fish, remember that, Peter? Walking to Him on the water? *You don't know Him?*

That wasn't you there with Him on the Mount of Transfiguration? You were blown away to see Him in all His glory on the Mount—so much so that you didn't even want to leave the mountain, Peter. Didn't you call Him the Christ, the Son of the living God? You've had some amazing high points with Jesus.

He was like, No (*expletive deleted*), I *don't know Him*.

"After a little while the bystanders came up and said to Peter, 'Certainly you too are one of them, for your accent betrays you.' Then he began to invoke a curse on himself and to swear, 'I do not know the man.' And immediately the rooster crowed" (vv. 73–74). Notice *immediately*—not ten minutes later. God was watching. It was all choreographed to the second. **"And Peter remembered the saying of Jesus, 'Before the rooster crows, you will deny me three times.' And he went out and wept bitterly"** (v. 75). Can't you see his bent form convulsing in sorrow at the shame and regret he felt? *Why am I so weak? Why am I so ashamed of the Lord? What is wrong with me that I can't stand up for Him? He's done so much for me, and I can't stand for Him?* He denied the Lord that he claimed to love.

Let us take to heart Peter's example. As we think about our future, we cannot deny the Lord. I'm not saying that there won't be moments in your life that you will regret. Perhaps you had the chance to get the flag to the top of the pole and you blew it. You had that moment when you could have declared what Jesus means to you, but you froze or mumbled something to change the subject. Those responses may be what we sometimes do; but they aren't who we want to be! Examine the increasing pattern of your life. Are you becoming more loyal to and standing for Jesus Christ? The flag of loyalty needs to be going up the pole, not down.

How often have you heard the rooster crow? At the office? With your extended family? When was the last time something was said that you knew should prompt you to speak, and you sat there *silent*, afraid of the consequences your allegiance to Jesus would bring? How often has the rooster crowed in your family where you've chosen peace over loyalty and fidelity to Jesus Christ? How often have you heard the rooster crow in the face of opposition? How often has the rooster crowed where you work as the name of Jesus Christ is blasphemed or ridiculed or misappropriated?

I guarantee that on the day you stand before Christ, you're not going to be excusing yourself with, "Well, my faith was just a personal, private thing no one else had the right or need to know about." Christianity is not a secret society. The people who know you best should be absolutely certain that you love Jesus Christ as your highest priority. Something is desperately wrong if they don't know Whom you serve. You may need to go to work this week and say, "Hey, there's something I've never told you about myself before. Let me tell you what matters to me most."

Matthew 10:33 says, "**but whoever denies me before men . . .**" If this is the pattern of your life, expect to hear the rest of the statement, "**I also will deny before my Father who is in heaven.**" The word *acknowledge* in this text (v. 32) is also translated *confess* in the NASB and NKJV, meaning *a public declaration of belief.* The flip side of this concept is in verse 32 where Jesus is saying, *If you stand for Me, if you persevere with Me, if you remain loyal to Me, if you confess Me, I will confess you.* The negative is in verse 33: *If you don't stand for Me, if you don't persevere for Me, if you don't remain loyal to Me, if you do not confess Me as the pattern of your life, I will not confess you.*

> CHRISTIANITY IS NOT A SECRET SOCIETY. THE PEOPLE WHO KNOW YOU BEST SHOULD BE ABSOLUTELY CERTAIN THAT YOU LOVE JESUS CHRIST AS YOUR HIGHEST PRIORITY.

There will be a day (unless the Lord returns first) that you will have a tombstone. Written on it will be the summary of your life. Wouldn't it be wonderful if the phrase *He confessed Jesus Christ* were chiseled into the granite? Will those at your funeral be able to say without hesitation, "He had a growing loyalty and an allegiance to Jesus, a consistent pattern of standing with and for Jesus Christ," when they talk about your life? What would be more important to your eternity than this?

A hundred years from today, all that will matter to you is your life pattern of loyalty to Jesus Christ. Nothing else will concern you, and we're not on a small subject here. Do you regularly confess your loyalty to Jesus Christ? Not just at church, but everywhere you go? Is there a growing pattern of fidelity to Him? Do your love and allegiance to Him continue to move your heart? Can you say with conviction, "I cannot deny the Lord! Whatever else I get done in this world, God help me, I will not deny Him. I will not lower the flag, I will not back up or shut up or hide the reality of my allegiance to Jesus Christ. I will not do that. I cannot do that."

> **A HUNDRED YEARS FROM TODAY, ALL THAT WILL MATTER TO YOU IS YOUR LIFE PATTERN OF LOYALTY TO JESUS CHRIST.**

You ask, "Well, how do I avoid denying Christ?" Here it is: I choose to stand. By standing, I mean a state of mind from which you refuse to choose doubt. Standing means developing a life increasingly bursting with these qualities: allegiance, assurance, backbone, certainty, certitude, commitment, confidence, decisiveness, fidelity, firmness, fortitude, grit, loyalty, persistence, steadfast resolve, tenacity, and trust, to name a few.

Its opposite would be a life marked by qualities such as: backing down, doubting, faltering, hesitating, indecision, skepticism, suspicion, unbelief, uncertainty, vacillation, and wavering. In short, a life that stands for nothing and falls for everything.

Several years ago I was struck by the slogan of an African-American church in Kansas City. I think you'd have to have big stationery to fit this on your letterhead, but it certainly makes a statement about where this church wants to take its stand. This is its posted purpose:

Wake up, sing up, pray up, and pay up, but never give up or let up or shut up 'til the cause of Christ is built up in this world.

Is that great? That's their slogan. And you know what? That should be true for all of us. Never give up or back up or shut up until the cause of Christ is built up.

Our tenth and final life-changing choice is *I choose to stand.* I commend this choice to you for the rest of your life. This is your destiny. Wherever life takes you, whatever happens to you, whatever you have to face or deal with that you couldn't possibly know of right now, I ask you to seal this choice to your own heart as your deepest passion and commitment. *I cannot deny the Lord. I'm going to stand for Jesus Christ. Every chance I get. Every place I go. This is what my life is going to be about. God helping me, I'm going to stand for Jesus Christ.*

Do you know what a powerful commitment that is? God can do awesome things with a person who is totally yielded to Him.

A Choice to Stand Has Changed History

Powerful events have changed the course of history when people made the choice to take a stand for something. Let's review some of them.

German reformer Martin Luther was called on the carpet in 1521 at the Diet of Worms for his criticisms of the corrupt Catholic Church. When ordered by Emperor Charles V to recant, Luther replied, "Here I stand. I can do no other. God help me." He said, *I cannot back down on this. Whatever happens, happens.*

Luther's stand against corrupt doctrine ignited a widespread return to *sola fide* (by faith alone) and *sola scriptura* (Scripture alone) within Christianity. Those two priorities continue to this day—to this moment. What's going on right now, here in this study, is because of Martin Luther and the stand that he took five hundred years ago.

In 1775, Patrick Henry urged the American people to take up arms as the armies of the oppressive British government were marching on Richmond, Virginia. He understood that a fight was on its way. He ended his speech before the legislature with this famous rally cry, "Give me liberty or give me death." He said, *I will die for this cause. Nothing is more important.* His fortitude and action rallied the American people. The British forces turned back, people gave their lives, and we enjoy the freedoms for which they stood.

William Wilberforce rose before Britain's parliament and forcibly argued for the abolition of slavery in 1789. He proclaimed, "God Almighty has set before me two great objects: the suppression of the slave trade and the reformation of morality." He stood against an evil that people could not and would not see. His courageous stand broke the back of the slave trade in England, but it would take over one hundred years for the power of that stand to reach our shores.

Martin Luther King Jr. received a call during the Montgomery bus boycott in 1955 from a white supremacist who promised to blow King's brains out and then blow up his house. After King committed the matter to prayer, he heard an inner voice saying, *Stand up for righteousness! Stand up for justice! Stand up for truth! And I will be with you to the end of the world.* It was the Lord speaking to him, of course. And the stand he took ended the evil of racial segregation and moved racial prejudice from toleration to something that thinking people everywhere resist and despise.

Why? He took a stand. *I don't know where this is going, I don't know what this is going to cost, but if it costs me everything, I'm standing here on this point.* There's awesome power in that.

In 1989, more than a hundred thousand pro-democracy Chinese students in Tiananmen Square stood against the Communist government in spite of a military crackdown. Do you remember the famous image of an unknown Chinese student who halted a row of tanks and said, "Why are you here? You have caused nothing but misery." The students took a stand, and many died because of it. The report of the number killed in this conflict ranges from three hundred to ten thousand—no one knows for certain, but the courage the students showed emboldened freedom-loving people around the world.

Henry Hyde persistently opposed abortion through his long distinguished career in Congress. In 1976 he introduced a piece of legislation later known as the Hyde Amendment that severely limited the use of tax dollars to fund abortion. He said, "*Roe v. Wade* should be reversed, and I live for the day that it is."

We could go on all day with these stories and examples, but in summary, when you're living in the moment of choice, when you're in that crucible, when loyalty is on the line and fidelity is the issue, you have an opportunity to choose. The most powerful choice you will ever make is: I cannot, I will not, I must not deny the Lord; I choose to stand!

I Choose to Stand—by Salting the Earth

There's so much power in this choice to stand. One of my favorite passages in Scripture is Matthew 5 because it lists some of the things that standing people do and the amazing benefits that flow from those choices.

One of the things that people who are standing for Jesus Christ do is they salt the earth (v. 13). Sometimes I think people want to make that into some sweet little statement, but we dare not fail to hear the intensity behind it as we imagine Jesus speaking with authority (Matthew 7:29).

Bible teachers have frequently told us that salt is a preservative and a purifier. So when Jesus said, **"You are the salt of the earth"** (Matthew 5:13), some have drawn the conclusion that He was telling us that we're a preservative and a purifier in the world. That may be true, but I'm a little more basic in the way that I look at things.

What does salt taste like to you? Yeah, salty. There isn't another word that you could use to describe it. Nothing is really quite like salt. While other things look like it and have the same texture, nothing else really tastes like salt or does what salt can do. As a follower of Jesus Christ with the Spirit of God living in you, you have something that nobody else has on this earth. What we understand about life and eternity and the forgiveness of sins and soul-satisfaction found in Christ positions us for great impact.

By calling us *salt*, I think Jesus was referencing the impact we can make when we stand up in His Name. The *you* is emphatic. "*You* are the salt of the earth." You, the genuine God-fearing people—not the military zealots, not the political power-hungry, not the religious hypocrites, but you, God's family—are the salt of the earth. Jesus was saying, *When you're around, people should taste the difference!*

> **WHAT WE UNDERSTAND ABOUT LIFE AND ETERNITY AND THE FORGIVENESS OF SINS AND SOUL-SATISFACTION FOUND IN CHRIST POSITIONS US FOR GREAT IMPACT.**

We are the salt of the earth. No one else can do in the world what God has called us to do. We are to impact every single person we come in contact with. Standing for Jesus Christ means salting the earth.

This mandate prevents us from just going along, minding our own business and leaving everything alone. You were made to impact people. You may say, "James, I find that overwhelming. I don't think that I'm a very influential person." That's OK! You impact the world within the framework of your own personality, within the context of how God made you. It is not just what you're doing individually; it's what we're doing together. Aren't you glad this whole kingdom of God thing isn't just on your shoulders? Together we are to salt the earth.

A more technical analogy probably would be that we're the salt shaker. The salt itself is the Word of God. But together, we can take the salt to the world. Let's recommit ourselves to that work.

I Choose to Stand—by Shining the Light

Here's another analogy Jesus made that overlaps salt a bit but expands the illustration. Jesus continued in Matthew 5:14, **"You are the light of the world."** Salt has the capacity to impact, and light has the ability to illuminate. The world is a dark place, but you can bring it light.

Notice that both times Jesus said, "You are." *You are the salt; you are the light.* He doesn't say, *Just try to be,* or *Make yourself into.* He emphasized that *you are* salt and *you are* light. It's the very nature of who you are as a follower of Jesus Christ.

Imagine for a moment that you have been sitting in pitch blackness for the last hour. I'd be your best friend if I showed up with a flashlight. We have the Light of Life, but the world is in so much darkness that they *love* the darkness (John 3:19); they don't even understand or comprehend the light.

We have the Light of Life, Jesus Christ, who said, **"I am the light of the world"** (John 9:5*b*). When He says we are the light, He means we reflect Him. We are the lamp, He is the Light, just as the Word of God is the salt and we are the salt shaker.

Notice Matthew 5:14 says, **"A city set on a hill cannot be hidden."** Having a light but not shining it is ridiculous. **"Nor do people light a lamp and put it under a basket"** (v. 15). If God went to the trouble to put the Light of Christ in your heart, does He want that hidden? Who would light a lamp and then hide it? The answer is, no one would—or at least not a real Christian.

You're the light of the world. Stop hiding the light in the office where you work! Stop hiding the light in the school where you teach! Stop hiding the light on the sales route that you follow every week! Get off your horizontal agenda and be what God has created you in Christ to be: you're the light of the world.

Notice Matthew 5:16 goes on to say, **"In the same way, let your light shine."** *Let* it shine. Don't hide it, don't cover it, and don't bury it. Let it shine! You may wonder, *James, I want to let it shine—tell me what would hide it?*

Three things hide your light:

1: *Unconfessed sin in my life hides the light.*
"I could be shining on my family and my loved ones more if it weren't for the sin in my life that I haven't dealt with." The enemy uses guilt and shame to convince Christians they have no right to share their faith with others.

2: *Suffering hides the light.*
"I was doing good for a while, but then things got hard for me, and I didn't know how to deal with it. I should have gone to God, but

I didn't. I tried to carry the burdens myself, and I lost my light." We certainly understand the burden there, but we also know that it doesn't have to be that way.

3: *Silence hides the light.*

"I kept having these little opportunities to answer questions or join a conversation that was lacking the perspective of a follower of Jesus. But I passed those up, and now I rarely notice those chances anymore." Silence easily becomes habitual silence.

A couple of years ago, Kathy and I went to a party to celebrate a friend's fiftieth birthday. When we got there, we immediately felt tension in the air. *What was wrong?* Turns out everyone was holding their breath. One of the couples at the party had just received news that their son Mitch, who had gone up to northern Wisconsin on a rafting trip, had been reported missing. We had known Mitch Swaback since he was a little boy. Kathy used to carpool with his family, dropping our kids off at school every day. Mitch had struggled with his faith in high school but had recently come back to the Lord in an amazing way. He was an influential participant in our college ministry, a dynamic force for God in our church, and an enthusiastic worker on mission trips.

I immediately thought of the day I had met him for breakfast, and he'd said, "James, I have so many friends that I didn't tell about Christ in high school." We sat in this little restaurant while he made out a list of people he needed to follow up with. He felt so ashamed that he hadn't shined the light. He said, "I'm going back to every one of them." And he did, one by one, visiting every one of those young men and women, telling them what Christ meant to Him. It was an awesome thing. Mitch's light was bright!

So you can imagine how disturbing it was to get over to this party and find out that Mitch was missing. The rafting party had stopped along the river to go swimming, and he had dived into the water and hadn't come up.

One guy in our group was an official in the local police department. He got on the phone and made some connections that broke through the red tape. I was there in the room along with Bob and Gaye Swaback, Mitch's parents, when we got the news that Mitch had drowned. He was gone.

In that moment, I saw two parents' hearts break in very different ways. Gaye cried out in her pain; Bob turned white and silent. Mitch was gone. All of us grieved. We couldn't believe it.

Mitch's funeral was one of the most difficult things I've ever been through. We were devastated. How do you comfort parents who have lost children? With his casket front and center in the church and the auditorium filled with people, I had to stand up and preach. We were all suffering and grieving such a great loss. How wonderful to be able to assure the room packed with mourners that Mitch's light was shining bright when he left this world.

Now what about your light, Christian? Now what about your salt? Everything's great when everything's great, but what about when things are awful? What then? When the world, anxious to avoid any searching questions about life's meaning, starts talking about closure even while the reality of a loss is sinking in, how do we as believers in Jesus Christ grieve as those who have hope?

Within a couple of months, Bob and Gaye, heartbroken and sleepless, started the Mitchell Swaback Foundation. They determined that Mitch's influence would continue. They decided to channel their grief into something productive.

In the years since Mitch's death, they've focused their energies to bring relief to people's suffering and to walk in the footprints that their son left with his brief life. They've built an orphanage in Pachacamac, Peru, and a daycare center in Manchay, Peru, where Mitch went on mission trips. They've completely renovated Tabitha House, a home for battered women and their children in downtown Chicago. And very close to home, they built a spectacular 26,000-square-foot athletic center at our church's Elgin, Illinois, campus. They have channeled their grief into productive service for the kingdom of God to make a difference in this world. (Learn more about their wonderful ministry at www.mitchellswabackfoundation.com.)

When we dedicated the Mitchell Swaback Athletic Complex, I said, "Suffering is not going to derail us." We all have disappointments, and we all have hurt and sorrow—but not like people who don't have hope (1 Thessalonians

4:13). We don't despair. We don't curl up into ourselves and wait to die. We channel our grief into something productive. We're the salt of the earth. We're the light of the world. We are made to impact. We are made to illumine.

When difficult things happen, God gives us the grace to direct our energies and efforts, our disappointments and grief into something very productive for His glory. This is part of what it means to stand.

I Choose to Stand—by a *Single* Focus

Sometimes the thing that derails us from standing for God is distraction. Think about Peter. He denied the Lord three times. What was Jesus' response to him? Was it, *Forget you, man, you blew it! You denied me. It's all over for you now.* Is that what Jesus did?

No. He met His disciples in His resurrected body. Jesus Christ stood on the shore while they were out fishing (John 21). In despair, the disciples had gone back to their old gig. They were out all night trying to catch fish but came in empty. *Yeah, business as usual.* But Jesus waited for them. Obviously He didn't have any trouble fishing because He had breakfast waiting for them on the fire.

He called out to them, *Have you caught any fish, lads?* They were like, *No.* Then He gave them a miraculous catch of fish (someone stopped to count—158 fish!), and immediately Peter knew it was the Lord.

As they were finishing breakfast, Jesus turned to Peter so lovingly and said, *Let's take a walk.* Remember the last time Jesus looked at Peter? It was in the midnight courtyard after Peter so vehemently denied Him (Luke 22:61). A few horrible days later, Jesus asked Peter:

> "Simon, son of John, do you love me more than these?" . . .
> "Yes, Lord; you know that I love you." . . .
> "Feed my lambs." He said to him a second time, "Simon, son of John, do you love me?" . . .
> "Yes, Lord; you know that I love you." . . .

"Tend my sheep." He said to him the third time, "Simon, son of John,
  do you love me?" . . .
"Lord, you know everything; you know that I love you."
"Feed my sheep."

—John 21:15–17

Interesting, that was the first time they'd talked since the cock-a-doodle-
do thing. How many times did Peter deny Him? Surely it was no coincidence
that the Lord asked him to confirm his love three times? Lovingly, Jesus said,
*Peter, I'm not done with you yet. I see what's in your heart. You don't want to
deny me. You want to be faithful to me.* In fact, Jesus said to him, *Peter, you're
going to be faithful to Me. You're going to give your life for Me.*

However, moments after that amazing restoration in John 21, Peter was
back to his impulsive self: *What about him?* (He was referring to John.) *Is
he going to have to give his life?* Then Jesus' tone changed. He said, **"If it
is my will that he remain until I come, what is that to you?"** (John
21:23). Jesus basically said, *Get your eyes off of other people, Peter, and back
on Me.*

Nothing has so destructively derailed my faith as having my eyes on
other people. *What about how she's following you, Lord? Is he really faithful?* I've wasted so much time looking around at others until God rocked
my world with Romans 14:4: **"Who are you to pass judgment on the
servant of another? It is before his own master that he stands or falls.
And he will be upheld, for the Lord is able to make him stand."**

I wish I could be a perfect example of this verse, and I'm very aware that
I am not. But God continues to change me through its truth. *I will not keep
my eyes on other people, other churches, or other families. I only will account
for my life, my family, my church. That's it.*

How about you? Have you lost your saltiness and hidden your light
because your focus is on other Christians? Do you think, *He's not following
You right, Lord. I don't think she really gets it, God. Why should I give my
life a second thought when theirs is so messed up!*

Hear this from the Lord. "**Who are you to pass judgment on the servant of another? It is before his own master that he stands or falls. And he will be upheld, for the Lord is able to make him stand**" (Romans 14:4). Get your eyes back on the Lord. The moment we take our eyes off Him, we get distracted and divided. Stand by a single focus.

I Choose to Stand—by a *Surrendered* Will

The closing thought in our study of *10 Choices: A Proven Plan to Change Your Life Forever* is this—you choose to stand with a surrendered will. You make all of these choices with your will. You don't choose with your mind, although you have to understand. You don't choose with your emotions, though ultimately it helps to *want* to make the choices. Ultimately, you choose with your will. You must have a surrendered will. Every one of these choices has been presented from God's Word to your will. Without the surrender of your will, I can predict you have not made any of these choices. The choices you have made have come about, whether you fully realize it or not, by the surrender of your will. Each of these choices has presented a decision between God's will and your own way. The surrender of our will always comes down to saying, "Not my will, Lord, but Yours be done."

First Corinthians 16:13 breaks down into four great challenges to help us in our choices: "**Be watchful, stand firm in the faith, act like men, be strong.**"

1: *Be watchful.*
   Pay attention. Take a stand. Don't compromise. Engage. Participate. The apostle Paul was wrapping up his first letter to the Corinthian church with summary words about the long-term aspects of following Jesus when he alerted them to be watchful.

2: *Stand firm in the faith.*
   Be determined. Certain. Resolute in your commitment. There are many ways to fall but one way to stand. Root yourself in Christ.

3: *Act like men.*

The equivalent today might be something like, "Don't waver and wallow with excessive emotion. Choose your course and stick to it. Don't let your feelings rule your actions."

4: *Be strong.*

Don't be weak. Don't be passive. Engage your will. Step up. Don't be indifferent. There's a lot on the line here. Life is short. Take a stand. Fly the flag. Live for Jesus. Make the choice: *I don't know where this whole life is taking me exactly, but I want to stand for Him.*

Want some practical applications of that compound challenge? Here they come:

- *Down with passive parents!*
  Man, step up and lead your kids. Enough of, *Well, I don't really want to know what's going on over there.* Pay attention, engage, and get involved in their lives. Take a stand on what is good and not good for them. Parents, put down the remote and get off the couch. This is your season of opportunity to make a difference in your child's life.

- *Down with distracted spouses!*
  When you walked to the front of a church and said, "I do," you committed to make your spouse the most important human relationship of your life. All else pales by comparison. Today, give yourself to that person with your whole heart! Don't let anything derail you from your passionate pursuit of your mate. Act like a man! Be strong! Do what you promised.

- *Down with wandering children!*
  Let's have an end to kids who don't want to live for God today. *Yeah, I'll wait to commit when I'm further down the road. Let me do*

my own things for a while. Listen, you don't know what tomorrow
will bring. Engage your will now! (James 4:13 and Hebrews 3:15)

As a memorable example of a surrendered will, let me introduce you to
Tony Groves, one of the greatest guys in our church. Tony grew up in
Cabrini-Green, a public housing development on Chicago's North Side,
fraught with gang violence and neglect. Before he was twenty, Tony had
been robbed and then shot three times in the chest. By age twenty-five, he
was a Golden Gloves boxer but had become addicted to drugs and alcohol.
Ten years ago a coworker invited him to our church. He began attending a
small group dedicated to freedom from addictions through Christ. He
turned from his former life and gave his heart to Christ. Soon after, he
started serving in our parking lot ministry. He constantly witnessed to others about life change. Remember that "got milk?" slogan? He used to tell
people, "I got Jesus." This guy was salt and light for sure.

Then Tony got cancer. It was first discovered in his leg, then after some
chemotherapy, it looked like it had gone into remission. The cancer came
back in his hip several months later, and it seemed like the doctors were
able to stop it again. He had a three-month breather, but then the cancer
came back with a vengeance and spread through his whole body.

So how's it going now, Tony—Mr. Joy? And his answer: *It's going awesome.* I wish that every person reading this could have spent ten minutes
with Tony. He was so full of the Lord and so filled with joy. He said to our
elder board chairman, "Hey, if I live, I win; if I die, I win." Philippians 1:21:
"For to me to live is Christ, and to die is gain."

Well, Tony Groves left the planet a winner not long ago. He's with his
Lord and Savior. Before he died, Tony left these parting words for our
church family:

*Trust the Lord with all your might. You've got to give everything to Him. Don't
play with this life. I'm going all the way with Jesus. I look in the book of Job,
and I don't know how Job stood up to that. Like when I was going through all*

those tests and all the chemo stuff—the only thing that kept me going was the Cross. It's what Jesus took for me. How could I complain?

I want everyone who hears me right now to know that God is in control. I know right now that I'm going to be with my Father. Whatever happens to me, I'll be with my Father. He has me in His hands, and I ain't worried about nothing right now.

Amen! Let me tell you, Tony's life has been a good example of what the Christian life looks like. When the sun is not shining, when the valley is deep, when the going gets tough, you let your light shine right there in that moment. How awesome when a Christian lives his life out in such a public way so that you and I can see what salt and light looks like during tribulation or persecution. His example speaks volumes to the world. Some will hear or see the message and will walk away from the Lord, shaking their heads. Others will openly deny a God who allows suffering. But some, by God's grace, will make the choices they need to make to experience all that God has in store for them. I pray you are in this last group.

As you think about your life and about your destiny, choose this: I will not deny the Lord. Whatever comes my way, I choose to stand for Jesus Christ.

A Choice to Make

Acknowledge the Choice

- How many of these ten life-changing choices would you describe as settled, permanent choices in your life?

- What are the three longest-held commitments of any kind that you've kept to this point?

- What, if anything, is holding you back from seeing all these choices as representing where you will stand from now on?

Consider the Choice

- The choice to stand for Jesus Christ involves infiltration (salting), illumination (lighting), intentionality (single focus), and surrendered will. Which of these have been or will be a challenge for you to do over the long haul?

- How would you explain the difference between standing in your own strength and standing by the strength God gives you day by day?

Make the Choice

- Review each of the other nine choices you have considered in this book. Make sure you have made each choice. Now give them permanence by adding "for the rest of my life" to each choice:
  - I choose God's love . . . for the rest of my life.
  - I choose God's forgiveness . . . for the rest of my life.
  - I choose Jesus Christ as Lord . . . for the rest of my life.
  - I choose the Bible as God's Word . . . for the rest of my life.
  - I choose to forgive . . . for the rest of my life.
  - I choose to trust God with my future . . . for the rest of my life.

- I choose to love my family first . . . for the rest of my life.
- I choose to be authentic . . . for the rest of my life.
- I choose to serve Christ . . . for the rest of my life.
- I choose to stand for Jesus Christ in all these choices . . . for the rest of my life.

A Choice Prayer

Father, thank You for the privilege of calling upon Your name. Thank You that in Your mercy, You didn't create us just with minds to think. We don't just have emotions to feel. We have a will. We can choose. We do it every moment of every day. We choose the right and the wrong. We choose the good and the bad.

By Your grace and by Your Spirit, I'm going to make better choices. Your Word has renewed my mind and moved my spirit. But I pray most of all, Lord, that it has engaged my will.

Forgive me for being passive about my life and for letting things just happen to me. Cause me to be deeply, personally engaged in choosing what matters most. I know what I'm asking is consistent with Your will, so I believe that You will do it.

I choose to stand for Jesus Christ. God helping me, I cannot, I will not, I must not deny the Lord. Help me, Lord. Help us all to choose to stand. Amen.

[Epilogue]

*I call heaven and earth to witness against
you today, that I have set before you life and death,
blessing and curse.*

*Therefore choose life, that you and
your offspring may live.*

—DEUTERONOMY 30:19

This verse is where we started, and it's a good place to end. Life is about choosing—each day, all day, every step of the way. You chose to read this book, and I'm grateful for your investment of time. But even more important than reading this book has been your responses to the choices presented.

Every choice is a fork in the road. To choose to go one way means you're also choosing *not* to go the other way. It's the power of an alternative. Throughout our study, we have not only embraced the good in our choices, we have also pushed the wrong ones away. Let's run back through our choices again and survey not only what we're choosing to wrap our arms around but also what we're turning away from. As you will recall, we have seen these as couplets of related choices.

The First Couplet: My Identity Choices

I choose to believe there is a God who loves me. This choice also means I choose to believe that I'm not alone in this world. I was created with a purpose by the God who loves me. At the same time I have rejected the choice of meaninglessness the world offers me as an alternative. When life raises issues about my identity, I turn to the God who loves me.

As part of the foundation of my identity, I also choose to believe God can, will, and does forgive me. This choice involves my decision to accept the fact that I'm not perfect and I need to get on a new page with God. Because I need the kind of forgiveness that establishes my relationship with God as well as the ongoing kind of forgiveness that repairs my relationship with God, I choose to receive from Him what I could never earn or create on my own—God's forgiveness.

I choose God's love. I choose God's forgiveness.

The Second Couplet: My Authority Choices

I have come to believe that my life is not my own—I belong to the God who made me. I'm not the boss, and I don't run my own life. I have discovered that what I want is not always the best for me. So I'm not in charge. Jesus is the ruler of my life. I choose Jesus as Lord.

I need a plan; a blueprint that I cannot create on my own. I can't make it up as I'm going along. I am not the ultimate authority in my life; I am not even the practical authority in my life. God is the architect and builder. His Word keeps me on schedule and on target. God's Word is my blueprint. God expresses His ownership and direction over my life in His Word— God's written authority. When His Word tells me to do something, I do it—for it is God's Word.

I choose Jesus as Lord. I choose God's Word.

The Third Couplet: My Capacity Choices

I don't have the capacity to carry the past anymore. I see how unforgiveness destroys me and those I love. I choose, with God's help, not to hold an offense against anyone else ever again. God didn't make me to bear the weight of everything awful that's ever happened to me. Forgiveness off-loads the past—so I choose to forgive.

I am incapable of carrying the past, and I can't control the future either. Wondering what's up ahead may be a natural human tendency, but it easily slides into worry. Fear and anxiety about the unknown would consume me if I didn't know Someone does know and control the future. I choose to trust the future to God. In making this choice I also have let go of my attempt to control the future, choosing instead to live in today.

I choose to forgive. I choose to trust.

The Fourth Couplet: My Priority Choices

Even when my opportunities and responsibilities are reduced to the "most important" category, there's always more to be done than there is time to do it. The demands of all that is good can overwhelm me. If I don't have a prearranged sequence of action, the urgency of the moment will destroy my best intentions. I choose my family as my first, human-level priority. They are the most immediate recipients of the love for my neighbor that God requires as part of the great commandment. This choice also means I choose to lose at anything else before I fail in my family relationships.

I face daily invitations to be false and fake as an easier way to life. I see people succeed at being someone other than who they are. I also see people gain the world at the cost of their own soul. That I will not do. I choose to be authentic as a guiding priority. The negative side of this decision means I also choose not to pose or posture in order to impress or measure up to people's expectations. I cannot please everyone, but I know I can please God if I am true to who He made me to be.

I choose my family as my first relational priority. I choose to be authentic.

The Fifth Couplet: My Destiny Choices

I know that life can easily boil down to being about me. I recognize a deep temptation to be served rather than to serve. I can easily expect God to go out of His way for me as an underlying assumption behind decisions. But I also have come to realize that if I'm going to follow Jesus as Lord and example, then I must serve. He set service as the standard operating procedure of those who belong to Him. So I choose to serve—my family, my church, my Lord. I recognize that God's loving purpose behind my life is to pursue the greatness of service to others. In choosing to serve, I also choose to accept the fact that I cannot change the world, and I focus instead on what I can do. I choose to serve.

And lastly, I have a history of short-lived decisions. My choices don't mean much if they don't last. The journey of living for God starts with a choice, but it doesn't end there. It ends with my last breath. All the best choices in life involve a point in time as well as a lifetime of follow-through. Therefore, I choose to stand for Jesus Christ. I want to finish with the Lord. I don't want to get offtrack. I want to fight the good fight. I want to run the whole race and keep the faith. I want to break the tape accelerating. I want to go with the Lord till the very end. I choose to stand. In making that continuing choice, I am also determining a choice to never deny the Lord.

We all know about people who have walked off the track. They were good for a while in the beginning, and then, for whatever reason, they just stopped. They were up like a rocket and down like a rock. *Bam!*—and that's the end of them. I just don't want to be one of those people. I don't want that for you either. Spiritual longevity and endurance doesn't happen by accident; it happens by choice. You and I need to choose to stand.

I choose to serve. I choose to stand.

Choose Life!

Remember, you have made a choice regarding each of the decisions presented in *10 Choices: A Proven Plan to Change Your Life Forever.* These are not choices you can put on hold until you get around to them. The sober truth is that when we consider any of these choices, we do so from a previous decision in place. Notice, in Moses' classic summation of the purpose of his message to Israel, he says, **"Therefore choose life"** (Deuteronomy 30:19). He doesn't have to say, *Therefore, choose life or death.* Israel, as people like us, needed to realize that as things stood, they had already chosen death and curses. The choice was between staying with their current choice or taking the alternative God was offering.

The same offer is true today. As you review the ten choices, have you settled and clarified each of them in your life? If you haven't made those choices, then you have made alternate choices that will lead to undesirable consequences. That destination is not what I have prayed and wished for you in writing this book. I have much higher hopes for you, and I know God's hopes for you are even greater!

So I say, along with Moses, "Choose life!" Making the choices that change your life means choosing life! God has set before you His way, and there is no better way to live your life. There is no better life in which to take your stand.

Throughout these pages I have consistently tried to remind you that every choice has a momentary side and a lifetime side. We make a choice and then live out a choice. My prayer for you is that you will live out your choices in such a way and with such a stand that you will be able to say, as life on this side of eternity comes to a close, echoing the apostle Paul . . .

I have fought the good fight,
I have finished the race,
I have kept the faith.
Henceforth there is laid up for me the crown of righteousness,
which the Lord, the righteous judge, will award to me on that Day,
and not only to me but also to all who have loved his appearing.

—2 TIMOTHY 4:7–8

[Appendix A]

That's My King

Dr. S. M. Lockridge

Do You Know Him?

The Bible says that my King is the seven way King.

He is the King of the Jews. That's a racial king.

He is a King of Israel. That's a national king.

He is the King of righteousness.

He is the King of the ages.

He is the King of heaven.

He is the King of glory.

He is the King of kings

He is the Lord of lords.

That's my king.

Do You Know Him?

David said, "the heavens declare the glory of God and the firmament shows His handiwork."

My king is a sovereign king.

No means of measure can define His limitlessness.

No far-seeing telescope can bring in the visibility of the coastline that His shoulders supplies.

No barrier can hinder Him from pouring out His blessings.

He is enduringly strong.

He is entirely sincere.

He is eternally steadfast.

He is immortally graceful.

He is empirically powerful.

He is impartially merciful.

Do You Know Him?

He is the greatest phenomenon that has ever crossed the horizon of this world.

He is God's Son.

He is a sinner's Savior.

He is the centerpiece of civilization.

He stands in the solitude of Himself.

He is august and He is unique.

He is unparalleled and He is unprecedented.

He is the loftiest idea in literature.

He is the highest personality in philosophy.

He is the supreme problem in high criticism.

He is the fundamental doctrine of true theology.

He is the corner and necessity for spiritual religion.

He is the miracle of the age. Yes! He is.

He is the superlative of everything good that you choose to call Him.

He is the only one qualified to be an all-sufficient Savior.

I Wonder If You Know
Him Today?

He supplies strength for the weak.
He is available for the tempted and the
tried.
He sympathizes and He saves.
He strengthens and sustains.
He guards and He guides.
He heals the sick.
He cleanses the lepers.
He forgives sinners.
He discharges debtors.
He delivers the captives.
He defends the feeble.
He blesses the young.
He serves the unfortunate.
He regards the aged.
He rewards the diligent.
And He beautifies the meager.

I Wonder If You Know Him?

Well, this is my King.
He is the key to knowledge.
He is the wellspring of wisdom.
He is the doorway of deliverance.
He is the pathway of peace.
He is the roadway of righteousness.
He is the highway of holiness.
He is the gateway of glory.

Do You Know Him?

Well, His office is manifold.
His promise is sure.
His life is matchless.
His goodness is limitless.
His mercy is everlasting.
His love never changes.
His Word is enough.
His grace is sufficient.
His reign is righteous.
His yoke is easy.
His burden is light.

I Wish I Could Describe
Him to You,

but He is indescribable.
He is incomprehensible.
He is invincible.
He is irresistible.
You can't get Him out of your mind.
You can't get Him off your hand.
You cannot outlive Him and you can't live
without Him.
The Pharisees couldn't stand Him, but
they found out they couldn't stop Him.
Pilate couldn't find any faults in Him.
The witnesses couldn't get their
testimonies to agree.
Herod couldn't kill him.
Death couldn't handle Him. And the
grave couldn't hold Him.

That's My King! [1]

[Appendix B]

Scriptures to Pray

Heartache:

Psalm 147:3
Proverbs 16:9, 33
Psalm 34:18-19
Matthew 11:28-29
Isaiah 33:10
Psalm 9:9-10
Psalm 138:3
Isaiah 58:11

Disappointment:

Psalm 141:1-2
1 Timothy 6:12
Hebrews 5:8
2 Timothy 4:7-8
Ecclesiastes 3:14
James 3:17
1 Peter 2:19-20
1 Corinthians 13:7

Failures:

John 12:25
Colossians 3:2
1 Timothy 6:17-19
Proverbs 19:20
Ecclesiastes 9:1
1 Peter 2:9
Psalm 103:10-12
Psalm 55:22

Rest in His protection:

Psalm 27:1-5
Proverbs 1:33
Psalm 142:1-2
Psalm 121:5-8
Psalm 20:2
Psalm 4:8
Isaiah 54:17
Psalm 4:8
Isaiah 43:2
2 Thessalonians 3:3

Trust in His power:

Psalm 11:1-7
Psalm 62:8
Psalm 125:1-5
Psalm 18:28-30
Psalm 56:3-4
Psalm 56:11-12
Psalm 91:4
Psalm 22:3-4
Psalm 3:1-8

Dealing with illness:

James 5:14-15
Isaiah 26:3-4
1 Peter 2:24
Jeremiah 17:14
Psalm 77:6
Psalm 77:10-14
Psalm 48:14
Psalm 49:15
Psalm 23:4
2 Corinthians 5:1
Psalm 146:2
Psalm 119:67-68

Handling financial problems:

Luke 12:42-44
Psalm 122:6
Matthew 4:2-4
Philippians 4:19
James 2:5
Proverbs 11:28
Luke 12:22-24
Proverbs 13:18

Worrying about the future:

1 Corinthians 13:12
Psalm 92:12-15
Romans 14:7-8
Proverbs 10:27
Psalm 90:10, 12, 14
Titus 2:2-4
Psalm 31:14-15
Job 19:25-26

Contentment:

Isaiah 54:10, 13, 17
Philippians 4:11-12
Romans 8:1-2, 5-6
1 Timothy 6:6-8
Psalm 23:1
2 Corinthians 3:5
Isaiah 58:11
Psalm 121:5, 8
1 Corinthians 2:9
Colossians 2:10

Hope for eternal life:

Psalm 147:7-13
Colossians 3:1-4
1 Thessalonians 5:8-11
Ephesians 2:4-7
Galatians 2:20, 26
Romans 8:14-18, 24-25
2 Timothy 4:7-8
1 Peter 1:3-9
Colossians 1:5-6

Power to defeat fear:

Romans 8:37-39
Psalm 18:28-30
Psalm 27:1-7
Proverbs 3:25-26
Deuteronomy 31:3, 8
Isaiah 30:21
John 8:12
Psalm 37:4-6
Psalm 18:1-3

Courage to be a person of integrity:

Psalm 1:1-6
Psalm 7:8
Proverbs 20:7
Proverbs 12:17-19
Psalm 112:5-7
Psalm 101:2-8
Psalm 7:8
Job 31:5-6
Job 27:5-6
Psalm 119:1-8

Handling stress:

John 14:27
Philippians 4:6-8
Isaiah 41:10
Psalm 23:2-4
1 Peter 5:7-10
Psalm 46:1-3
Ephesians 4:26-27
Mark 4:38-40
Psalm 91:3-7
Psalm 56:3-4

Facing old age:

Psalm 92:12-15
Proverbs 9:11
Psalm 103:5
Ecclesiastes 11:10
Psalm 90:10, 12, 14
Romans 14:7-8
Job 19:25-27
Titus 2:2-4
Psalm 48:14
Proverbs 10:27

Dealing with monotony:

Hebrews 6:11-12
Proverbs 26:14
Ecclesiastes 2:23
Galatians 6:9
Nehemiah 8:10
Ephesians 5:1-2
Philippians 2:4

[Notes]

Choice 1: I Choose God's Love

1. Hugh Ross, "Fine-Tuning for Life on Earth," www.reasons.org/resources/apologetics/design_evidences/2001_fine_tuning_for_life_on_earth.shtml.
2. Ibid.

Choice 2: I Choose God's Forgiveness

1. *Ol' Blue Eyes: A Frank Sinatra Encyclopedia* (Westport, CT: Greenwood Pub. Group, 1998).

Choice 3: I Choose Jesus Christ as Lord

1. David Gates, "Bob Dylan Opens Up," *Newsweek*, Oct. 4, 2004.
2. Singles Konnexion, www.skfriends.com, www.k4a4.com//mcveigh-final-statement.htm.
3. D. Lee Chesnut, *The Atom Speaks* (Grand Rapids: Eerdmans, 1951), 38.

Choice 4: I Choose the Bible as God's Word

1. Josh McDowell, *Evidence That Demands a Verdict* (Orlando: Campus Crusade for Christ, 1972).
2. Kevin D. Miller, "Did the Exodus Never Happen?" *Christianity Today*, Sept. 7, 1998, www.ctlibrary.com/ct/1998/september7/8ta044.html.
3. McDowell, *Evidence That Demands a Verdict*.
4. Used with permission.

Choice 5: I Choose to Forgive

1. "Forgiveness is an emotion-focused coping strategy that can reduce health risks and promote health resilience: Theory, review, and hypotheses," *Psychology and Health* 19 (2004): 385–405.

2. "Forgiveness as a secondary prevention strategy for victims of interpersonal crime," *Australasian Psychology* 12 (2004): 261–63.

3. Carol Buckley Frazier, "Giving Up the Grudge for Health's Sake," www.invocaremedallion.com/wellness.

Choice 6: I Choose to Trust

1. Paul Davis, *Inspirational Hymn & Song Stories of the Twentieth Century*, Marijohn Wilkin's story (Worcester, MA: Ambassador Books, 2001).

Choice 7: I Choose to Love My Family First

1. Madeline Chambers, "If You've Been Married 25 Years, You're in the Minority," *Houston Chronicle*, Sept. 19, 2007.

Choice 8: I Choose to Be Authentic

1. CBC News Canada, "Helmuth Buxbaum, convicted in 1980s murder, dies in jail," Nov. 2, 2007, http://www.cbc.ca/canada/story/2007/11/02/helmuth-dies.html?ref=rss.

2. John Baillie, *A Diary of Private Prayer: A Devotional Classic*, "Day Two Evening" (New York: Simon & Schuster, 1996).

Choice 9: I Choose to Serve

1. www.guardian.co.uk/politics/2002/oct/30/uk.eu.

2. www.hrw.org/children/labor.htm.

3. State of the World Forum Simulconference, Sept. 4–10, 2000, "State of the World Index," www.simulconference.com/clients/sowf/dispatches/dispatch2.html.

4. Ibid.

5. The History Place, "Genocide in the 20th Century," www.historyplace. com/worldhistory/genocide/index.html; United Human Rights Council, "20th Century Genocides," www.unitedhumanrights.org/Genocide/ bosnia_genocide.htm; "Source List and Detailed Death Tolls for the Twentieth Century Hemoclysm," http://users.erols.com/mwhite28/ warstat1.htm.

Appendix A

1. S. M. Lockridge, "That's My King." Dr. Shadrach Meshach (S. M.) Lockridge (March 7, 1913–April 4, 2000) was the pastor of Calvary Baptist Church, a prominent African-American congregation, located in San Diego, California, from 1953–1993. A graduate of Bishop College in Marshall, Texas, Lockridge is best known for "That's My King"—a six-minute description of the Lord Jesus Christ.

[About the Author]

Dr. James MacDonald has committed his whole life to proclaiming the truth of God's transforming power. As a pastor, author, radio Bible teacher, speaker, friend, and family man, James ignites a bold passion for God in every avenue of influence. He's most at home in the pulpit at Harvest Bible Chapel in the northwest Chicago suburbs, ministering to a growing flock of God's people on multiple campuses, now eleven thousand strong. The founding and senior pastor of this church, James has launched twenty-three thriving new churches in the US and abroad.

James's teaching, which emphasizes the precise exposition of God's Word and its practical life application, can be heard on *Walk in the Word*, a daily thirty-minute radio program heard on more than eight hundred outlets across North America.

James also regularly speaks at Bible and pastors' conferences throughout the world and hosts a ministry leadership conference called, STRAIGHT UP: ENGAGING IN MINISTRY GOD ENERGIZES. His personal revival conferences, DOWNPOUR: HE WILL COME TO US LIKE THE RAIN, call people back to a fresh relationship with God through repentance and grace. For more information, please visit www.downpour.org.

The author of several books, James also has contributed to the following publications: *Preaching Today, Worship Leader,* and *Leadership Journal,* as well as *Our Journey,* the daily devotional from *Walk in the Word.*

Born in London, Ontario, James received a D. Min from Phoenix Seminary. He and his wife, Kathy, have been married twenty-five years and have three children.

For more information about James's life and ministry, please visit

www.JamesMacDonald.com.